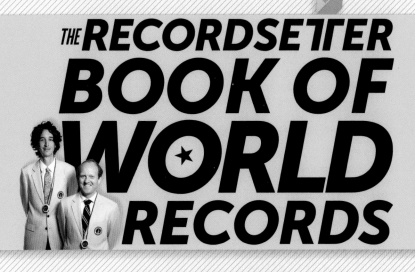

THE RECORDSETTER BOOK OF WORLD RECORDS

BY FOUNDERS
COREY HENDERSON
AND **DAN ROLLMAN**

★ ★ ★

EDITED BY **ELLA MORTON,**
LINDSEY WEBER,
AND **ROGER BENNETT**

WORKMAN PUBLISHING

DEDICATION

THIS BOOK IS DEDICATED TO THREE RECORDSETTER WORLD RECORD HOLDERS WHO ARE
NO LONGER WITH US: JACK BUTLER, WHO HOLDS THE RECORD FOR SHORTEST TIME TO MAKE
AN AMPUTATION JOKE AFTER HAVING A CANCER-RELATED AMPUTATION; DONNA KRAMPF,
RECORD SETTER FOR MOST BLUEBERRIES FIT INSIDE A BELLY BUTTON; AND HONEY,
WHO ONCE HELPED HER OWNER CAITLIN PEARL SET A RECORD FOR MOST HANDSHAKES
ELICITED FROM A DOG IN 30 SECONDS.

Copyright © 2011 by Universal Record Database, LLC

All rights reserved. No portion of this book may be reproduced—mechanically, electronically, or by any other means, including photocopying—without written permission of the publisher. Published simultaneously in Canada by Thomas Allen & Son Limited.

Library of Congress Cataloging-in-Publication Data is available.

ISBN 978-0-7611-6577-4

Cover design by Raquel Jaramillo
Design by Sara Edward-Corbett
Author photo by Jenna Bascom
For additional photo credits, see page 290.
Illustrations by Jason Schneider and Sara Edward-Corbett; see page 290.

RecordSetter and the RecordSetter logo are trademarks of Universal Record Database, LLC.

Workman books are available at special discounts when purchased in bulk for premiums and sales promotions as well as for fund-raising or educational use. Special editions or book excerpts also can be created to specification. For details, contact the Special Sales Director at the address below, or send an e-mail to specialmarkets@workman.com.

Workman Publishing Company, Inc.
225 Varick Street
New York, NY 10014-4381

www.workman.com

Printed in the United States of America
First printing November 2011

10 9 8 7 6 5 4 3 2 1

DISCLAIMER

The RecordSetter Book of World Records encourages the breaking of records, not bones. The pursuit of any record that may cause physical injury or harm is highly discouraged. Always take care to use caution and sound judgment when inventing or attempting to beat any world records. If you are uncertain about your ability to safely perform a record, don't even try it.

Contents

CHAPTER 2

Food and Drink

Sports and Games

CHAPTER 4

Science and Technology

CHAPTER 5

Money and Style

CHAPTER 6

Groups

Visionaries

Earth and Environment

CHAPTER 9

The Human Body

Introduction

Ever since I was 10 years old and got my first *Guinness Book of World Records,* I've been a world record junkie. Awed by the many ways people were pushing the limits of human achievement, I spent countless hours reading the book, always thinking about how I could someday become a record setter myself.

While I was in college, I researched setting a Guinness record, but quickly got scared away by the fees, paperwork, and, most importantly, the limited range of categories, none of which aligned with my areas of talent. Sadly, I concluded that setting a world record was well beyond my reach.

In 2002, I began attending the Burning Man festival. The event, held annually in the Nevada desert, is built around participation and creativity. It proved to be the perfect testing ground for developing what RecordSetter has become today: a world record organization built on a belief that everyone can be world's best at something.

Every day of the festival for 5 years straight, our Burning Man camp donned yellow blazers and invited people to dream up and set whatever world records they wanted. No fees, no judgments, and no rules beyond keeping their achievements quantifiable (so we could measure them) and breakable (so others could raise the bar). Creativity was highly encouraged.

The camp grew and competition flourished. Wanting to extend the project globally, bringing it online was the next natural step. I met technology guru and fellow world record fanatic Corey Henderson in 2006. We quit our jobs and spent the next 2 years building RecordSetter.com. Our vision was (and is) to empower people worldwide to document and upload world records themselves.

Today, over 25,000 people in fifty-plus countries have set RecordSetter world records, with hundreds of new records submitted weekly. Our site is used by summer camps, church groups, juggling clubs, professional skateboarders, ex-Olympians, and heck, even the folks who run National High Five Day. Led by a team of moderators, our community plays an active role in approving records, much like Wikipedia does with encyclopedic knowledge.

This book represents just a fraction of the thousands of extraordinary feats in our database. Visit RecordSetter.com to see the rest. I hope this book inspires you to not just see world records in a new light, but to use your imagination and go set some yourself. Take it from someone who used to hold the record for Most Bananas Fit in a Pair of Pants While Wearing Them—it feels great to be a world champ.

Dan Rollman
President / Cofounder
RecordSetter

Acknowledgments

First and foremost, thanks to Ella Morton, Lindsey Weber, and Roger Bennett. This trio edited the entire book, pouring hundreds of hours into writing, research, phone calls, and interviews. We would've been lost without them.

Thanks to superstar project manager Marc Haeringer, RecordSetter interns Caitlin Walsh, Alaine Vescovo, Laura Yan, Audrey Chow, David Elmaleh, and Barak Falkovitz, plus punch-up master Jon Friedman. This team worked their butts off day in and day out. (Bonus thanks to Wiredrive for behind-the-scenes magic. We heart Wiredrive!)

Special thanks to our agent Kate Lee at ICM, who not only got us our book deal, but provided emotional support throughout. Thanks to Colin Graham, too.

Heaps of love to everyone at Workman Publishing for believing in the book, especially Suzie Bolotin for her wisdom and patience, Mary Ellen O'Neill for her editing, and Sara Edward-Corbett for designing the heck out of the book. Thanks also to Selina Meere, Page Edmunds, and David Matt.

The book would be nothing without the people that make RecordSetter HQ the best place to work in NYC, most notably Marc Covitz, Rob Birdsong, Simon Kirk, Benjamin White, Schuyler Van Horn, Alastair Coote, Cliff Gray, Peter Craig, Dan Leatherman, Emily Miethner, Evan Altshuler, Lucie Kim, and Team P. We're honored to work with all of you.

Gargantuan thanks to investors Corbin Day and Chris Sacca, advisors Craig Kanarick, Cindy Gallop, Uncle Marvin, and Jake Bronstein, and legal gurus Michelle Francis, Deirdre Sullivan, Robert Strent, and Ward Breeze. The guidance you've all provided along the way has been of immeasurable assistance.

Special shouts to Jim Juvonen, Jimmy Fallon, and the entire team at *Late Night with Jimmy Fallon* for inviting us into your magical world and giving us a chance to shine. We're beyond grateful for the many opportunities you've provided.

Dan would like to thank his parents Gary and Barbara and his brother and sister-in-law Eli and Dina for their love and encouragement, plus the Playa Book of Records (and everyone at Burning Man!) for helping to birth this project.

Corey would like to thank his wife Emily and his parents Gordon and Vonn for their unwavering support.

Finally, hugs and love to the thousands of RecordSetters around the world. You're the people who inspire us daily and continue to make this entire project worthwhile.

Dan Rollman and
Corey Henderson
Cofounders, RecordSetter

CHAPTER 1

THE Creative Arts

No less a talent than Pablo Picasso once said, "Every child is an artist. The problem is how to remain an artist once we grow up." While the master cubist did not live long enough to hold one of our records (although perhaps he could posthumously qualify for Most Expensive Painting Sold at an Auction with Out-of-Place Facial Features—*Dora Maar au Chat*—brought $95.2 million in 2006), we like to think he would approve of this chapter. From Most Strangers Marker-Mustached in 30 Seconds to The Slowest Keyboard Rendition of "The Imperial March (Darth Vader's Theme)," each achievement is a testament to the record setter's creativity and artistry.

Most Polaroid Shakes in 1 Minute

RECORD: 207

NAME: Matt Spangler

LOCATION: Brooklyn, New York

DATE: March 31, 2009

TOOLS: Polaroid camera, Polaroid film, powerful wrist

Brooklyn's Matt Spangler takes his music literally. He heard the catchy "Shake it like a Polaroid picture" line from Outkast's 2003 hit "Hey Ya!" and felt compelled to shake a Polaroid image 207 times in 1 minute before a stunned audience at a warehouse party. "Given my impressive arm strength, I had to worry about not ripping the photo in half during the shaking," Spangler recalls. Contrary to popular belief, shaking has no practical benefits. According to company experts at Polaroid, flicking their film might cause unsightly blobs in the photo. For best results, "the picture should be laid on a flat surface and protected from the wind."

CRITERIA

- [ ] Each up-and-down wrist flick counts as a "shake."
- [ ] Must start shaking immediately after photo emerges from camera.

Tips for Beating This Record

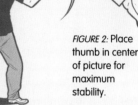

FIGURE 2: Place thumb in center of picture for maximum stability.

FIGURE 1: For best results, brace yourself, with legs spread and knees bent. Relax and loosen your shaking arm, as tense muscles will cause pain and fatigue.

FIGURE 3: Spread fingers to ensure a firm grip.

RELATED RECORDS

- ▶ Most Booty Shakes in 1 Minute: 92
- ▶ Longest Comment Thread on a Facebook Photo: 49,681 comments

RECORD BEGGING TO BE SET

- [ ] Most Polaroids Taken While Riding on a Roller Coaster

SPANGLER SHAKING.

3

Most Photographs Taken of People Jumping

RECORD: 777

NAME: Mike Hedge

LOCATION: Multiple locations

DATE: Began in 2006 (ongoing)

TOOLS: Camera, photogenic participants, precision timing

Mike Hedge is a man who has learned that timing is everything. As a photographer who shoots his subjects mid-air in the act of jumping, he has become the master of freezing the image at just the right moment. "The trick with jump shots is to catch the person at the height of their jump," he says.

Hedge's photographic passion is an outgrowth of his interest in Parkour, the athletic pursuit of leaping around urban settings and overcoming obstacles in near-superhuman fashion. "My passion for taking photos of people jumping was inspired by my passion for jumping over things back in the mid-'90s when I did lots of 'freestyle walking,'" he explains. But when he saw the results, amassing a collection of jumping photos became an obsession. "I realized that when people are in the air, for one split second, they are totally free," he says now.

"When I photograph people jumping, I feel I am capturing the true *them.*"

CRITERIA

☐ All photos must be taken by the same person.

☐ Jumpers' feet must be completely off the ground.

☐ Faces of jumpers must be visible.

Yellow Jacket Comment

COREY: Hedge's inspiration was *Life* magazine photographer Philippe Halsman's famous "jumpology" pictures from the 1950s, in which he captured dozens of celebrities—Marilyn Monroe, Richard Nixon, Groucho Marx—in mid-air. Hedge visited Halsman's family in New York and photographed his daughter Irene. A jump shot, naturally.

Tip for Beating This Record

"Human beings are almost incapable of launching at the same time," says Hedge. "That's why group jumps can be a disaster. The trick is to make everyone count down together rather than jump at your command. People have different reaction times, but let them count for themselves, and they will leap like clockwork."

RELATED RECORDS

▶ Most Jumping Jacks in 10 Seconds: 21

▶ Largest Group to Jump in Unison: 87 people

RECORD BEGGING TO BE SET

☐ Most People Leapfrogged over in 1 Minute

Most Googly Eyes Attached to Body

RECORD: 100

NAME: Reverend Matthew Nunnery

LOCATION: Shreveport, Louisiana

DATE: August 20, 2009

TOOLS: Googly eyes, glue or similar adhesive, positive body image

Tip for Beating This Record

Double-sided fashion tape is an effective and nonmessy way to stick on googly eyes. It's also much less painful to remove than superglue.

CRITERIA

- ☐ All eyes must stick to body for at least 1 minute.
- ☐ Eyes may be attached anywhere on body.
- ☐ Use of adhesives permitted.

RELATED RECORDS

- ▶ Most Pairs of Glasses Worn at Once: 20
- ▶ Most Single Eyelid Flips in 30 Seconds: 30

RECORDS BEGGING TO BE SET

- ☐ Fastest Time to Apply Googly Eyes to a Dozen Eggs
- ☐ Most Googly Eyes Attached to a Grapefruit
- ☐ Longest Staring Contest

Attaching one hundred googly eyes to his chest and claiming a world record was a brave endeavor, but, as Reverend Matthew Nunnery discovered, reversing the operation proved to be a greater challenge. "I had attached them with superglue," he recalls, "and I had to use tweezers to rip them off, pulling patches of body hair along with them." Borrowing the mantra of a world-class athlete, Nunnery says the glory was worth the suffering: "I'm a big believer in 'No pain, no gain.'"

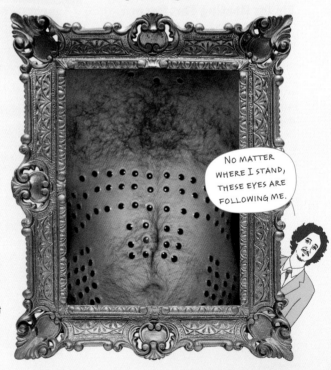

NO MATTER WHERE I STAND, THESE EYES ARE FOLLOWING ME.

Most Strangers Marker-Mustached in 30 Seconds

RECORD: 23

NAME: Brian Brushwood

LOCATION: Austin, Texas

DATE: March 13, 2010

TOOLS: Nonpermanent marker, crowd of willing strangers, artistic flair

Magician Brian Brushwood's motivation was simple yet pure: to crush late-night talk show host Jimmy Fallon. Fallon created this record on his show, setting the mark to beat at thirteen. Says Brushwood: "If you're going to steal a title, it might as well be from the highest-profile target you can find." The twenty-three people who assisted Brushwood in his record-setting performance left his SXSW event in Austin with a semipermanent souvenir of the feat: a brand-new marker mustache. Brushwood's upper lip remained clean—barring a light sheen of sweat—as he departed triumphant, hailing it as "easily one of the greatest nights of my life."

=ATTENTION=
DO NOT MUSTACHE STRANGERS WITHOUT THEIR PERMISSION.

CRITERIA

☐ Must use black marker.
☐ People receiving mustaches must be previously unknown to record setter.

RELATED RECORDS

▶ Most Images of Justin Bieber Mustached in 10 Seconds: 21
▶ Fastest Time for a Baby to Crawl 10 Feet While Wearing a Fake Mustache: 1 minute, 31.5 seconds
▶ Fastest Time to Shave off One's Own Mustache: 36.65 seconds

RECORD BEGGING TO BE SET

☐ Most Times Twirling a Mustache in 30 Seconds

IF THERE'S ANYONE YOU SHOULD TRUST TO GIVE YOU A NEW FACIAL HAIRSTYLE, IT'S ME.

Most Stick Figures Drawn in 5 Minutes

RECORD: 167

NAME: Edmond Petres

LOCATION: Miercurea-Ciuc, Romania

DATE: June 9, 2010

TOOLS: Pen, paper, ability to draw circles and lines

Romania has a population of over 22 million, but criminally, Edmond Petres is the only RecordSetter record holder from that country. If you are a resident of—or visitor to—the so-called land of Dracula, please put down this book immediately and rally the locals to participate in as many locally flavored records as possible. (Most People Dressed as Vampires in a Transylvanian Castle would be brilliant.)

CRITERIA
☐ Each stick figure must have a head, torso, two arms, and two legs.

RELATED RECORD
▶ Most Cats Drawn on a Hand: 56

RECORD BEGGING TO BE SET
☐ Most Games of Hangman Played in 1 Hour

Fastest Time to Draw Ten Homer Simpson Heads

RECORD: 1 minute, 58.04 seconds

NAME: Jordan Miller

LOCATION: Lansing, Michigan

DATE: December 14, 2009

TOOLS: Pen, paper, appreciation of Homer Simpson

CRITERIA

☐ Images must clearly resemble Homer.

☐ Tracing not permitted.

Yellow Jacket Comment

DAN: Hey, Matt Groening, if you're working on a deadline and need help on an upcoming episode, we'll happily put you in touch with Jordan.

RELATED RECORD

▶ Fastest Time to Draw Fred Flintstone: 5.5 seconds

RECORDS BEGGING TO BE SET

☐ Fastest Time to Draw Ten Dora the Explorer Heads

☐ Most Characters on *The Simpsons* Named in 30 Seconds

D'oh! A great admirer of *The Simpsons*, Jordan Miller showed off both his Springfieldian fandom and artistic flair with this Homer drawing feat. Miller carved nearly 10 seconds off the original record set by category creator Ryan Loecker. Now all we need is for Mayor Quimby to declare December 14 "Jordan Miller Day."

D'OH!

BIRDS OF A FEATHER

Photography

Forget the clunky old "a picture says a thousand words" adage; these photos raise a million questions. For example, is a photo of a car really a photo of a car if said automobile is barely visible behind twenty-nine horses? What inspired Art Hoffman's decades-long quest to photograph every state capitol in the country? Each of these snapshots has not only secured a record, but created a sense of intrigue.

Most Curly-Haired People in a Photograph

RECORD: 16 people

NAME: Reboot Summit Attendees

LOCATION: Park City, Utah

DATE: June 7, 2009

Fastest Time to Take a Photo of One's Son with an iPhone and Digitally Apply a Mustache to It

RECORD: 31.05 seconds

NAME: Cheryl Altshuler

LOCATION: New York, New York

DATE: May 25, 2010

Most Dog Photos Glued to a Nightstand

RECORD: 123 photos

NAME: Kirsten Buchanan

LOCATION: Columbia, Missouri

DATE: June 23, 2009

JACK'S CAR

I WONDER IF SOMEONE WILL SET A RECORD FOR MOST HORSES VISIBLE IN A PHOTOGRAPH OF THIS BOOK?

FINGERS CROSSED.

Most Photos Taken at a Party

RECORD: 3,987 photos

NAME: PHTHRD III Attendees. PHTHRD stands for "Photo Hard." This photography-themed party encouraged shutterbug attendees to take as many snapshots as possible.

LOCATION: Brooklyn, New York

DATE: March 31, 2009

Most Horses Visible in a Photograph of a Car

RECORD: 29 horses

NAME: Jack Raleigh

LOCATION: Orlando, Florida

DATE: December 13, 2009

Most U.S. State Capitols Photographed

RECORD: 42

NAME: Art Hoffman

LOCATION: Multiple U.S. states

DATE: Began in 1968 (ongoing)

Slowest Time to Dance the Macarena

RECORD: 1 minute, 46.90 seconds

NAME: Mick Cullen

LOCATION: Round Lake Heights, Illinois

DATE: August 12, 2010

TOOLS: Knowledge of the macarena, patience

The macarena is the fast-paced giant of group dancing fun, but radio host Mick Cullen transformed the giddy tune into a funereal ballet by boldly executing the slowest macarena of all time. Cullen shattered record creator Opus Moreschi's feat on his first attempt: "I watched the video of the original record and decided I could do the dance twice as slowly, stripping it down to one single movement for each full cycle of the song, instead of two." While the macarena isn't exactly the hardest dance to master (hand-hand palm-palm elbow-elbow head-head butt-butt shimmy), the feat was a test of mental endurance. Cullen had to simultaneously monitor the number of verses sung while maintaining the super-slow-motion at a steady pace. "I discovered there's a real danger. You can hypnotize yourself with the macarena," claims Cullen. "It's a one-hit wonder that could become a useful interrogation technique for the CIA."

"When I dance they call me Macarena and the boys they say 'que estoy buena' . . . "

CRITERIA

☐ Must sing chorus tune for entirety of dance, ending each chorus with "Hey, macarena!"

☐ Must complete every move of the dance.

RELATED RECORDS

► Most Dancers Wearing Fake Mustaches in a Conga Line: 48

► Most People Dancing to a Song Playing from a Car Stereo: 208

RECORDS BEGGING TO BE SET

☐ Fastest Performance of the Electric Slide

☐ Most People Dancing in an Elevator

Highest Tap Dance

RECORD: 17,598 feet

NAME: Heather O'Neal

LOCATION: Mount Everest's South Base Camp in Khumbu, Nepal

DATE: April 15, 2009

TOOLS: Tap dance shoes, strong lung capacity, knowledgeable sherpa

Travel guide Heather O'Neal went to great lengths to set her record: 17,598 feet up Mount Everest to be exact. By the time she arrived at Everest's South Base Camp, the air was so thin and the sherpas so glum, dancing was the last thing on her mind. But then, amidst the slippery ice and jagged rock of her surroundings, she spied a boulder so perfectly flat it was as if the gods had placed it there. Swiftly swapping her boots for tap shoes, O'Neal ascended this natural stage and thrashed out her routine as jauntily as Fred Astaire. Now an exhilarated record holder, she already has plans in the works to shatter her own mark. A return trip to Nepal is scheduled, and the dainty-footed climber has vowed to tap at 18,300 feet.

CRITERIA

☐ Must perform at least five tap dancing steps.

☐ Must wear tap shoes.

RELATED RECORDS

▶ Highest Concert Performed in the United States: 14,111 feet

▶ Most Clogging Dance Steps Performed in 30 Seconds: 42

RECORD BEGGING TO BE SET

☐ Most People Tap Dancing in a Sauna

TOP OF MT. EVEREST
29,029 feet

THAT'S 23 EMPIRE STATE BUILDINGS!

25,000 FEET

20,000 FEET

MT. EVEREST BASE CAMP
17,598 feet

THAT'S 14 EMPIRE STATE BUILDINGS!

15,000 FEET

TECHNICALLY THE ELEVATION WAS 17,598.2 FEET, IF YOU ADD THE HEEL HEIGHT OF HEATHER'S TAP SHOES.

10,000 FEET

5,000 FEET

TOP OF EMPIRE STATE BUILDING
1,250 feet

Most Ballroom Dancing Dips in 1 Minute

RECORD: 85

NAME: Joey Lawton and Mollie Herman

LOCATION: San Francisco, California

DATE: October 18, 2009

TOOLS: Ballroom dancing chops, willing partner

CRITERIA

☐ Must dip partner at least 45 degrees.

☐ Dips must be done consecutively on one side.

☐ Must return partner to vertical position between each dip.

Tip for Beating This Record

A strength-training program will increase stamina for both participants. The dipper should concentrate on upper body workouts—try three sets of twelve bicep curls using a docile human or rolled-up carpet.

RELATED RECORD

▶ Most Girls Simultaneously Danced with on a Dance Floor While on Crutches: 2

RECORD BEGGING TO BE SET

☐ Most Times Dipping Cookie in Milk in 30 Seconds

Joey Lawton and his girlfriend, Mollie Herman, were on their way to work when they first attempted this feat at San Francisco's Treasure Island Music Festival. After spying a RecordSetter booth, the duo stepped up and perfectly executed a dizzying fifty-two ballroom dancing dips in a 1-minute period.

Returning the next day, they were stunned to discover their record had already been bested by a single dip. Not easily discouraged, the pair resolved to reclaim their crown. Whipped on by a frenzied crowd, they performed feverishly. "I don't know how Mollie didn't get sick," admits Lawson with admiration, "but we somehow kept going."

Despite their achievement, another work shift lay ahead. "Our arms were so sore we were nearly useless," Lawson recalls, "but our coworkers rallied round our victory."

Most *The Big Lebowski* Catchphrases Recited in 1 Minute

RECORD: 31

NAME: Matt Reynolds

LOCATION: New York, New York

DATE: June 29, 2010

TOOLS: Appreciation of The Dude, bathrobe (optional)

Channeling The Dude, the über-slacker at the heart of the 1998 comedy classic, *The Big Lebowski,* Matt Reynolds donned the character's signature bathrobe to break this record. Brandon Martinez had originally set the catchphrase record at ten. Considering the achievement "an embarrassment to Lebowski fans around the world," Reynolds became hell-bent on trumping it. The movie's creators, the inimitable Coen Brothers, stuffed the script with zingers, making it purpose-built for speed-quoting. He approached the challenge with both a sharp memory and a sense of moral responsibility: "I decided choosing the shortest catchphrases would violate the spirit of the record. The honorable thing to do was recite a variety of phrases, mixing up the short/long, common/obscure, vagina-related/Johnson-related." The Dude abides.

CRITERIA

☐ Quotes must be recited from memory.

Tip for Beating This Record

Lebowski Fest cocreator Will Russell suggests a sneaky work-around: turning a curse into a quote. "The F-word is said 287 times in the film, so technically if someone could string together some F bombs they could exceed 287." The Fest, a celebration of all things *Big Lebowski*, is held every year in multiple locations. Fans of the film unite to drink White Russians (The Dude's drink of choice) and bowl. Visit lebowskifest.com.

Fastest Time to Name All James Bond Movies in Chronological Order

RECORD: 9.93 seconds

NAME: Rob Wilkinson

LOCATION: Litchfield Park, Arizona

DATE: May 26, 2010

TOOLS: James Bond expertise, strong memory

In this age of 3-D movies and super-special effects, it may seem to some that the James Bond movie franchise has seen better days. But don't whisper a word of that to 18-year-old student Rob Wilkinson. At the age of 10, the Arizonan saw *Die Another Day* and his life was changed forever. "I love the way Bond's career spans four decades, yet he is always able to keep up with the times." Wilkinson soon had Bond on the brain, renting each of the twenty-two movies on DVD and using his 20-minute daily bus ride to school as a chance to practice listing every film in chronological order—a remarkable skill that was criminally underappreciated until he became a world record holder. "Only one of my friends likes James Bond, so no one was particularly impressed by my ability," he explains with understandable sadness. Undeterred, Wilkinson clings to Bond as a role model: "If I were offered the chance to be anyone, it would be him. The way he is always saving the world is unbelievably appealing."

CRITERIA

☐ Must recite films from memory.

Yellow Jacket Comment

COREY: This record involves twenty-two movies, not twenty-three. Many consider *Never Say Never Again,* the 1983 Bond flick with Sean Connery and Kim Basinger, as part of the James Bond canon. But purists recognize it as a rogue remake of *Thunderball*—which was written by Fleming and others as an original screenplay before it was a novel.

RELATED RECORD

▸ Fastest Reenactment of "I'm Gonna Bash Your Brains In" Scene from *The Shining*: 39.10 seconds

RECORD BEGGING TO BE SET

☐ Fastest Time to Prepare a Martini*

*(SHAKEN, NOT STIRRED.)

16

Fastest Time to Recite Ezekiel 25:17 Verse from *Pulp Fiction*

RECORD: 17.40 seconds

NAME: John Mulhern

LOCATION: North Richards Hills, Texas

DATE: March 27, 2010

TOOLS: *Pulp Fiction* fanaticism, strong memory

CRITERIA

☐ All words must be completely understandable.

☐ Reading the verse is permitted.

RELATED RECORD

▶ Most *Ferris Bueller's Day Off* Quotes Recited in 1 Minute: 25

RECORDS BEGGING TO BE SET

☐ Most Kangol Caps Worn at Once

☐ Fastest Reenactment of John Travolta's *Saturday Night Fever* Dance Solo

As hit man Jules Winnfield in Quentin Tarantino's *Pulp Fiction,* Samuel L. Jackson ritually quotes a version of the biblical passage from Ezekiel 25:17 before murdering each of his victims. To John Mulhern, that meant Jackson held the record for the fastest time to recite the verse, albeit unwittingly. This was all the motivation necessary for a challenge to be mounted. "I felt Jackson needed to be dethroned," the Texan explains. "I mean, even if that guy lost just a little of his awesomeness, he's still the coolest man around."

"THE PATH OF THE RIGHTEOUS MAN IS BESET ON ALL SIDES BY THE INEQUITIES OF THE SELFISH AND THE TYRANNY OF EVIL MEN. BLESSED IS HE, WHO IN THE NAME OF CHARITY AND GOOD WILL, SHEPHERDS THE WEAK THROUGH THE VALLEY OF DARKNESS, FOR HE IS TRULY HIS BROTHER'S KEEPER AND THE FINDER OF LOST CHILDREN. AND I WILL STRIKE DOWN UPON THEE WITH GREAT VENGEANCE AND FURIOUS ANGER THOSE WHO WOULD ATTEMPT TO POISON AND DESTROY MY BROTHERS. AND YOU WILL KNOW MY NAME IS THE LORD WHEN I LAY MY VENGEANCE UPON THEE."

Most Consecutive Viewings of *Dirty Dancing*

RECORD: 3

NAME: Lindsay Gagnon

LOCATION: Hudson, Massachusetts

DATE: March 18, 2009

TOOLS: Copy of *Dirty Dancing*, viewing device, tolerant friends and family

CRITERIA

☐ Ten-minute break permitted between each screening.

☐ Film may not be paused at any time.

☐ Talking during screenings is permitted.

RELATED RECORDS

▶ Most Disney Movies Named in 10 Seconds: 12

▶ Most Consecutive Bounces of a Table Tennis Ball on Alternating Sides of a DVD: 588 bounces

"My friends kept telling me I had a Johnny Castle addiction and it was becoming a problem," Lindsay Gagnon confesses, referring to Patrick Swayze's well-toned dance teacher character in the epic summer movie *Dirty Dancing*. Eschewing their feeble efforts at an intervention, Lindsay took her "problem" and turned it into a world record. Gagnon watched Johnny Castle and the rest of the ensemble three times over before retiring. "There was more in me," she boasts, "but I figured someone would try to break my record and it's more fun to try and out-watch somebody else." Gagnon's achievement was not without its challenges. After experiencing the treacly movie twice, her parents kicked her out of the family home rather than be exposed to another screening. Lindsay rose to the challenge: "I ran to my best friend's home and forced her to watch with me."

STEP ONE: Assemble provisions.

STEP TWO: Make yourself comfortable.

STEP THREE: Keep your eyes on the screen by whatever means necessary.

Fastest Rendition of Backwards Alphabet While Balancing Egg on Head and Spoon on Nose

RECORD: 2.4 seconds

NAME: Adriana Yugovich

LOCATION: New York, New York

DATE: August 12, 2009

TOOLS: Egg, spoon, reverse knowledge of alphabet

CRITERIA

☐ Spoon and egg must remain on head and nose until alphabet is finished.

☐ May sit or stand while attempting feat.

Tip for Beating This Record

Give the spoon a quick lick before placing it on your nose. Saliva adds friction, which prevents silverware from sliding down your face. Experiment with different cutlery sizes—soup spoons are good for large snouts, while a teaspoon will suit a dainty sniffer.

RELATED RECORDS

▶ Fastest Time to Knock Seventeen Spoons off Counter Using Nose: 4.75 seconds

▶ Largest Group Egg Toss: 72 people

▶ Most Sporks Fit in Open Mouth: 27

RECORD BEGGING TO BE SET

☐ Most Eggs Held Under Armpit at Once

A raw egg wobbled on top of Adriana Yugovich's head. A silver spoon hung off her nose. Perfect conditions for a speed recitation of the alphabet backwards. Before spoon or egg had a chance to plummet, Yugovich raced from Z to A in under 3 seconds. Giddy with success, the noted illustrator was soon plotting her next victory: "My dream is to be pulled over by a cop, be asked to say the alphabet backwards, and then ruin his world."

Fastest Time to Spell "BACKWARDS" Backwards Ten Times in a Row

RECORD: 10.97 seconds

NAME: Mick Cullen

LOCATION: Lindenhurst, Illinois

DATE: March 8, 2010

TOOLS: Reverse thinking ability

Mick Cullen calls himself a "fluent speaker of backwards-ese"; when bored, he finds nearby signs and pronounces them backwards. "Undoubtedly nerdy, yes. But this record was right up my alley," says Cullen, who was inspired to start S-D-R-A-W-K-C-A-B G-N-I-L-L-E-P-S after RecordSetter challenged its community to attempt this very feat. Mick's other hobbies include reversing his car, rewinding old VHS tapes, and forcing toothpaste back into its tube.

LOOC!

REPUS LOOC!

CRITERIA

☐ Must spell out each letter: S-D-R-A-W-K-C-A-B.

☐ Eyes must be closed or blindfolded.

RELATED RECORDS

▶ Fastest Backwards Recitation of the English Alphabet: 3.5 seconds

▶ Fastest Time to Spell "Supercalifragilistic-expialidocious": 3.75 seconds

RECORD BEGGING TO BE SET

☐ Most Palindromes Recited in 10 Seconds

Fastest Time to Burp the English Alphabet

RECORD: 17.56 seconds

NAME: Giovanni Mann

LOCATION: Kansas City, Missouri

DATE: August 26, 2010

TOOLS: Burping ability, knowledge of English alphabet

"Burping on command is harder than it looks," says Giovanni Mann. Therein lies the paradox of the burped alphabet: Belching, a behavior most often associated with slovenliness, requires diligent practice and discipline. "It takes so much air out of you," Mann adds, confessing that breaking his previous record of 39.93 seconds required multiple attempts. In one try, he managed to get through the letters even faster than his current time of 17.56 seconds, but, after watching the video replay, disqualified himself for not saying the letters clearly. This noble act is a lesson for aspiring burpers: Enunciate through each belch.

CRITERIA

☐ Each letter must be audibly burped.

☐ Multiple breaths per burp permitted.

Tip for Beating This Record

Mann has detailed instructions for aspiring burpers: "Take air into your stomach by loosening the 'pipe' in your throat. Then force the air out with your muscles. As for speaking while burping, all you have to do is move your mouth as you would normally if you were talking, only instead of using your voice box, use the air in your stomach to speak." This technique allowed Mann to go from A to Z in three burps.

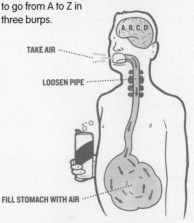

TAKE AIR

A, B, C, D

LOOSEN PIPE

FILL STOMACH WITH AIR

Yellow Jacket Comment

DAN: Note: "Elemenopee" is not a letter.

COREY: Neither is "queueressteeuvee."

RELATED RECORDS

▶ Most Burps in 10 Seconds While Holding a Dog: 43

▶ Fastest Recital of the Alphabet: 2.3 seconds

RECORDS BEGGING TO BE SET

☐ Largest Group to Burp at Once

☐ Fastest Time to Spell out the English Alphabet Using French Fries

Most Native Languages Represented in a Group "Cheers!"

RECORD: 14

NAME: David Ross's students

LOCATION: New York, New York

DATE: August 16, 2010

TOOLS: International group of friends, beverages

CRITERIA

- ☐ Each participant must raise a beverage while toasting.
- ☐ Each participant must use a phrase from his or her native country.
- ☐ No duplicate countries permitted, but repeat phrase is okay as long as participants are from different countries.

Yellow Jacket Comment

DAN: It's the General Assembly of the United Libations!

RELATED RECORD

▶ Most Glasses Clinked in 1 Minute: 102

RECORD BEGGING TO BE SET

- ☐ Fastest Time to Whistle Theme Song from *Cheers*

Following one of his English as a second language classes, New York City instructor David Ross led his students in the world's most diverse group "Cheers!" All participants made the toast in their native languages. The "Cheers!" used in their record were:

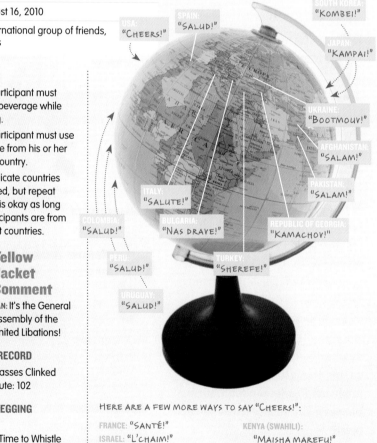

USA: "CHEERS!"

SPAIN: "SALUD!"

SOUTH KOREA: "KOMBEI!"

JAPAN: "KAMPAI!"

UKRAINE: "BOOTMOUY!"

AFGHANISTAN: "SALAM!"

PAKISTAN: "SALAM!"

ITALY: "SALUTE!"

COLOMBIA: "SALUD!"

BULGARIA: "NAS DRAVE!"

REPUBLIC OF GEORGIA: "KAMACHOV!"

PERU: "SALUD!"

TURKEY: "SHEREFE!"

URUGUAY: "SALUD!"

HERE ARE A FEW MORE WAYS TO SAY "CHEERS!":

FRANCE: "SANTÉ!"

ISRAEL: "L'CHAIM!"

PORTUGAL: "A SIA SAIDE!"

KENYA (SWAHILI): "MAISHA MAREFU!"

CANADA: "CHEERS, EH!"

Slowest Keyboard Rendition of "The Imperial March (Darth Vader's Theme)"

RECORD: 4 minutes, 16.18 seconds

NAME: Taylor Michael Pope

LOCATION: Loomis, California

DATE: August 16, 2009

TOOLS: Keyboard, sheet music

In the humblest of settings, greatness can reside. Wrapped in the gloom descending upon the bottom level of his bunk bed, with an electronic keyboard at his knees, Taylor Michael Pope used heavy fingers to pound out all sixty-six notes of John Williams's "The Imperial March" at a Yoda-like pace. The look of concentration on his face never wavered. The Force was with him. At a rate of one note per 3.88 seconds, Pope's rendition set a new world record. A message to all those who thought he'd never be able to do it: He finds your lack of faith disturbing.

CRITERIA
☐ Must play entire song.
☐ No audible pauses permitted.

RELATED RECORDS
▸ Most Led Zeppelin Guitar Riffs Played in 1 Minute: 14
▸ Longest Star Wars Quote Burped: 5 words

RECORDS BEGGING TO BE SET
☐ Most Star Wars Characters Named in 1 Minute
☐ Longest Light Saber Battle
☐ Most Greedo Tattoos on a Shoulder

Longest Vocal Note

RECORD: 19 minutes, 18.76 seconds

NAME: Michael Kennedy

LOCATION: Blackburn, U.K.

DATE: May 27, 2011

TOOLS: Circular breathing ability

Operatic Tenor Michael Kennedy sang one note for over 11 minutes, using the circular breathing technique along with his own secret "microbreathing system." Circular breathing is a vocal technique that involves drawing breath through the nose while simultaneously expelling it through the mouth and storing extra air in your cheeks. It's a difficult trick to learn but once mastered, the world becomes your stage. As Kennedy says, "I was practicing my 1-hour cadenza in the car with the window open at a traffic light when I heard applause!"

CRITERIA

- ☐ Circular breathing permitted.
- ☐ No audible pauses allowed.
- ☐ Must stay on one note.

RELATED RECORD

- ▶ Fastest Vocal Rendition of "Sixteen Going on Seventeen": 38.58 seconds
- ▶ Longest Pronunciation of "Fresh": 1 minute, 4.75 seconds

RECORDS BEGGING TO BE SET

- ☐ Longest Yodel
- ☐ Longest Time Playing Guitar While Jumping on a Trampoline

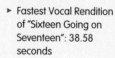

Fastest Accordion Player

RECORD: 20.3 notes per second

NAME: Peter Grigorov

LOCATION: Billerica, Massachusetts

DATE: November 25, 2007

TOOLS: Accordion, nimble fingers

To prepare for this record, computer engineer Peter Grigorov trained rigorously. "I played every day, and each time I got faster and faster," he remembers. But even months of practice could not prevent unforeseen hiccups the nimble-fingered maestro faced: "The day I attempted the record, my wife was doing the laundry and I had to stop repeatedly because of the noise coming from the washer-dryer." Once the clothes were whiter than white, there was no stopping him. Grigorov tore through Nikolai Rimsky-Korsakov's "Flight of the Bumblebee" on his accordion at an extraordinary twenty notes per second. That's 300 BPM (beats per minute). At that rate the titular bumblebee likely succumbed to a heart attack. Hail and farewell, speed-bee.

CRITERIA

☐ Must play "Flight of the Bumblebee."

☐ BPM based on average speed of entire song.

RELATED RECORD

▸ Fastest Accordion Rendition of "The Devil Went Down to Georgia": 1 minute, 20 seconds

RECORD BEGGING TO BE SET

☐ Fastest Time to Play Every Note on a Piano

P-p-p-polka face, p-p-polka face.

MATT STECK

Largest Boom Box Collection

RECORD: 170

NAME: B. Box Original Crew

LOCATION: São Paulo, Brazil

DATE: Ongoing

TOOLS: Boom boxes, boom boxes, and more boom boxes

Record creator Matt Steck of University Park, Pennsylvania, got the boom box ball rolling, building an admirable collection of nineteen ghetto blasters rescued from flea markets, yard sales, and passersby. "Sometimes people would see me carrying a box and say, 'I have one of those in my basement!' To which I would reply, "How much do you want for it?" Most people were happy to take whatever I offered." But his accomplishment is positively puny compared to that of the current world record holders—the B. Box Original Crew from São Paulo, Brazil, who have amassed a giant treasure trove over the past 4 years. The Brazilians have built a Smithsonian-worthy collection, marking their sprawling megalopolis as the place where boom boxes go to die. "We go looking for boom boxes like archaeologists search for relics," explains the Crew. Fans of '80's hip-hop culture, the group says their mission is "to rescue the rarest boom boxes out there." Bring the noise, yo.

CRITERIA

☐ Boom boxes do not have to be functional.
☐ No duplicate models permitted.

B. BOX ORIGINAL CREW

RELATED RECORD

▶ Most Metallica Songs Named in 30 Seconds: 25

RECORD BEGGING TO BE SET

☐ Most Clocks Worn Around Neck

Largest Group Rendition of "Don't Stop Believin'"

RECORD: 122 people

NAME: Treasure Island Music Festival Attendees

LOCATION: San Francisco, California

DATE: October 17, 2009

TOOLS: Lyric sheets, large group of Journey fans

At the Treasure Island Music Festival outside of San Francisco, John Cabral led 121 singers in the largest group rendition of the song many connoisseurs consider to be the pinnacle of prog rock: Journey's "Don't Stop Believin'." A perfect musical moment, right? Not according to an anonymous commenter, who posted below the video: "Estos yankies son unos putos frikies!" translating himself from the Spanish for extra effect: "America is the capital of freak show!"

CRITERIA

- ☐ All singers must sing in unison.
- ☐ May sing with backup music or a cappella.
- ☐ Must sing entire song.
- ☐ May not occur at a concert where song is played on stage.

RELATED RECORD

- ▶ Fastest Vocal Rendition of "Can't Touch This": 59 seconds

RECORD BEGGING TO BE SET

- ☐ Largest Group of Cher Impersonators to Sing "Believe"

TO HEAR DAN AND COREY SING A SONG ABOUT THIS RECORD, CALL 646-543-1732.

27

Longest Flute Trill

RECORD: 22.28 seconds

NAME: Alexandra Young

LOCATION: New York, New York

DATE: March 25, 2009

TOOLS: Flute, nimble fingers, breath

A lexandra Young started playing the flute in third grade, but her life changed when she discovered RecordSetter at a New York City event and realized her instrumental abilities could help land her a world record. I thought, 'What talents do I have, and how can I make them quantifiable?'" Young practiced her flute trill, a technique that consists of quickly alternating two adjacent notes, diligently. She stepped onstage at RecordSetter's next event and turned a lifetime of practice into a heroic trill that clocked in at just over 22 seconds in length. Young hopes her record will inspire other flautists to step it up: "I feel like someone can do that for a little longer."

Alexandra flaunting her flautist flair.

CRITERIA

☐ No audible pauses permitted.

☐ Circular breathing not permitted.

RELATED RECORDS

▶ Fastest Time to Assemble Bagpipes and Play a Note: 2 minutes, 20.05 seconds

▶ Fastest Time to Play "When the Saints Go Marching In" Melody in Five Octaves on an Electric Organ: 45.34 seconds

RECORD BEGGING TO BE SET

☐ Fastest Time to Play the Overture from *The Magic Flute* on a Flute

Most KISS Songs Named in 1 Minute

RECORD: 45

NAME: Tyler Hampton

LOCATION: San Francisco, California

DATE: September 24, 2009

TOOLS: KISS fanaticism, forked tongue (optional)

If you want to break this record, it will help to be a real music fan from back when vinyl rocked the world. Just thinking about it causes record-setter Tyler Hampton to wax nostalgic. "Back then, the visuals of the album art were an essential part of the music experience," he explains. "You'd put on your headphones and pore over every inch of the

cover for half an hour, and the song titles would just rub off on you." So when it came to preparing for the record, Hampton merely summoned up his youth, "consulting the Rolodex in my head." In a testament to muscle memory, he named most of the material in chronological order, "focusing mainly on the early days of KISS before the masks came off."

Tip for Beating This Record

To make songs easier to remember, try grouping them by theme, first letter, or album. You could also pick more distinctive categories, such as "Monosyllabic Titles" ("Deuce"; "Rain"; "Hate"), "Evening Serenades" ("Creatures of the Night"; "Thief in the Night"; "Crazy Crazy Nights") or "Traits of a Superhero" ("Strutter"; "Almost Human"; "Radioactive").

CRITERIA

☐ Song titles must be recited from memory.

☐ Songs from KISS band members' solo careers don't count.

RELATED RECORDS

▶ Most Kisses in 10 Seconds: 51

▶ Largest Group Eskimo Kiss: 5 people

▶ Longest Tongue Extension Past Lower Teeth: 2.5 inches

RECORD BEGGING TO BE SET

☐ Fastest Guitar Rendition of "Detroit Rock City"

Most Sips of Eggnog Taken in 30 Seconds While Listening to Neil Diamond

RECORD: 39

NAME: Cory Cavin

LOCATION: New York, New York

DATE: December 10, 2009

TOOLS: Eggnog, *Neil Diamond's Greatest Hits,* holiday spirit

Why celebrate Christmas cozily at home, swigging eggnog whilst listening to Neil Diamond, when you can do so onstage and claim a world record in the process? Comedian Cory Cavin bravely knocked back thirty-nine sips of the potent punch while grooving to Diamond's smooth timbre in "Girl, You'll Be a Woman Soon." In constructing the record, Cavin recognized that a classic background track was critical: "That could only be Diamond, a man as smooth to the ears as eggnog is to the throat." But Cavin now realizes that setting the record has influenced him on a deeper level. "Up there on stage, my mind wandered away from the eggnog and began considering the essence of Neil Diamond," he says. "I realized he is a role model for me in terms of who I aspire to become professionally: a man with a deep tan and sultry voice."

RecordSetter officials scrutinizing each sip.

CRITERIA

☐ Any song in Neil Diamond's library is acceptable.

☐ Eggnog must be sipped through pursed lips, not poured into mouth.

Tips for Beating This Record

Cavin has compiled a list for would-be "Diamond-noggers":

1. Relax into the song like it is a big, soft bed.

2. Focus on the tune as if it is a Tibetan chant. Let it take you away into a Diamond trance.

3. Keep sipping the eggnog. Push it past the point of where it is supposed to go. The eggnog may come out of your nose. Do not be alarmed. The glory is worth it.

RELATED RECORDS

► Fastest Rendition of "Sleigh Ride" While Accompanying Oneself on Cowbell, Kazoo, and Jingle Bells: 59.41 seconds

► Tallest Human Christmas Tree: 80 inches

RECORDS BEGGING TO BE SET

☐ Most People Sitting on Santa's Lap at Once

☐ Most Gift Requests Asked of Santa in 1 Minute

Most Times Smiling While Listening to "Beat It"

RECORD: 302

NAME: Krysta Nelson

LOCATION: Grapevine, Texas

DATE: July 5, 2009

TOOLS: "Beat It" (any audio format), strong cheek muscles

CRITERIA

- ☐ Must return to placid face between each smile.
- ☐ Must use original version of song, 4 minutes, 17 seconds in length.

RELATED RECORDS

▶ Most Graphic Designers Dancing to "Thriller": 7

▶ Most Socks Put on a Left Foot While Listening to "Beat It": 57

RECORD BEGGING TO BE SET

☐ Fastest Time to Eat a BLT While Listening to "P.Y.T." ("Pretty Young Thing")

Michael Jackson's death shook the world. For Allison Harris of Philadelphia, Pennsylvania, however, it inspired her to set a joyful record in the King of Pop's memory. She smiled along with "Beat It" exactly 283 times. Eight days later, Krysta Nelson took the song title as a literal challenge and beat Harris's record by a sunny nineteen smiles. Wanna be startin' somethin'? Try to break the record, and you'll have a thriller of a competition on your hands.

Yellow Jacket Comment

DAN: If Bubbles the Chimpanzee ever tries to beat this record, my life will be complete.

Largest Nose Flute Orchestra

RECORD: 109 people

CONDUCTOR: Opus Moreschi

LOCATION: New York, New York

DATE: March 17, 2010

TOOLS: Nose flutes (available at http://www.nashco.com/noseflutes.html)

"As a child," reminisces Opus Moreschi, "I was just the type to seek out nose flutes, jaw harps, and other such goofiness." The majority of participants in this record, however, did not share his familiarity with the nasal instrument. "I spent quite a bit of time trying to figure out how to explain the process best to a room full of people." In the end it was a matter of demonstrating the mouth placement and breathing technique, waiting 5 minutes while everyone got the hang of it, and then leading the crowd in a spirited rendition of "Mary Had a Little Lamb."

CRITERIA

☐ Orchestra must play one full verse of a song.

Tip for Beating This Record

Choose a short, well-known song with a limited note range to cater for novice nose flautists. "Mary Had a Little Lamb" consists of just four notes within one octave—tunes with a similarly small range include "Ode to Joy," "Row, Row, Row Your Boat," and "Jingle Bells."

RELATED RECORDS

▶ Longest Party Horn Toot: 12.51 seconds
▶ Longest Single Breath Beatbox: 1 minute, 6.8 seconds

RECORD BEGGING TO BE SET

☐ Largest Kazoo Orchestra

Members of newly minted nasal orchestra.

Most TV Channels Watched in 30 Seconds

RECORD: 32

NAME: Larry Francisco

LOCATION: Dallas, Texas

DATE: July 29, 2010

TOOLS: Television, remote control, comfy chair or couch

CRITERIA

☐ Only channels that show actual content are counted.

RELATED RECORDS

▶ Most Fresca Cans Glued Together While Watching *Battlestar Galactica*: 5

▶ Most Images of "Uncle Jesse" Viewed on a Web Browser at Once: 92

RECORD BEGGING TO BE SET

☐ Most Infomercial Products Named in 30 Seconds

arry Francisco is no couch potato. Sitting in his Texas living room just feet from a widescreen television, Francisco bravely pushed the limits of human endeavor to the max. Remote control in hand, he cycled through an extraordinary thirty-two television channels in 30 seconds, setting a high bar for cable connoisseurs. Most impressive of all, he found none of the shows sufficiently engaging for him to abort the record attempt, zone out, and fall into a vegetative state.

Yellow Jacket Comment

COREY: I'd like to use this space to ask a very important question: "Where the heck is *my* remote?"

Tip for Beating This Record

It's best to attempt this record in the wee hours of the morning when TV entertainment levels are at their lowest.

STEP 1:
Cool, calm, collected.

STEP 2:
Click, click, click, click, click.

STEP 3:
Crikey! Channel champion!

Fastest Time to Name All *Star Trek* TV Episodes in Broadcast Order

RECORD: 1 minute, 38.9 seconds

NAME: Mack Elder

LOCATION: New York, New York

DATE: February 16, 2010

TOOLS: Deep *Star Trek* knowledge, Vulcan ancestry

Clad in the United Federation of Planets uniform, Mack Elder proved his dedication to the original *Star Trek* series by reciting all seventy-nine episodes in the order they appeared on TV.

Though he credits the record as a "wonderful conversation starter at cocktail parties," Elder is most impressed by the effect his achievement has had on his online identity. Having received attention from Trekkie websites—both praise and criticism for his pronunciation of more esoteric episode titles—he is now something of an online celebrity. "If you search for my name on Google, the first several results all have to do with the *Star Trek* episode record," he says. "As far as things that could be tied to my permanent file on the Internet, a spectacularly geeky world record is pretty good."

CRITERIA

☐ Episodes must be recited from memory.
☐ Must be episodes from the original series.

RELATED RECORD

▶ Fastest Time to Name All *Star Trek* Movies in Chronological Order: 10.31 seconds

RECORD BEGGING TO BE SET

☐ Longest Conversation in Klingon

Fastest Solo Viewing of Every Episode of *LOST*

RECORD: 145 hours

NAME: Peter Wilson

LOCATION: Montreal, Quebec, Canada

DATE: May 23, 2010

TOOLS: Every episode of *LOST,* TV, extremely comfortable couch or chair

Peter Wilson wanted to show the world that his obsession with the television show *LOST* outstripped that of any ordinarily ardent fanboy. And so he set the world record for the fastest solo viewing of the 121 episodes of the show, live streaming himself watching the mysterious and often maddening 5,500-minute series. "I've always been a fan of a long-drawn-out story," Peter explains. "The problem with 'long and drawn-out' is that only rarely do you ever sit down and experience the whole story from beginning to end." Peter set the record with minimal breaks—switching out DVDs, using the bathroom, eating quick meals (TV dinners, naturally), and sleeping for a few hours at a time. As a theatrical masterstroke, he timed the attempt to culminate in the live broadcast of the much ballyhooed 2-hour finale. "Viewing a new episode to end the marathon made my adrenaline pump. Though the broadcast finished at 11:30 P.M., I couldn't fall asleep until around 6:30 the next morning. It wasn't just the excitement; my body had trained itself to not sleep for long periods of time."

CRITERIA

- ☐ Must watch all episodes in broadcast order.
- ☐ Must live stream attempt and have viewers tuned in throughout.
- ☐ Sleeping and eating breaks permitted.

RELATED RECORDS

- ▸ Most Chicken Wings Eaten by Two Brothers While Watching a UFC Pay-Per-View Fight: 46
- ▸ Most Karate Kicks While Listening to the Theme Song from *Walker, Texas Ranger*: 25

RECORDS BEGGING TO BE SET

- ☐ Most *LOST* Characters Named in 1 Minute
- ☐ Fastest Solo Viewing of Every Episode of *Twin Peaks*

Most Questions Answered About *LOST* in 2 Minutes by Someone Who's Never Seen the Show

RECORD: 18

NAME: Morgan Murphy

LOCATION: New York, New York

DATE: May 25, 2010

TOOLS: Zero knowledge of *LOST*, people to ask you questions

Looking for answers to J. J. Abrams's famously vague television drama *LOST*? Too bad. Morgan Murphy's never seen it. She did, however, offer to address the unanswerable by answering the most questions about *LOST* by someone who's never seen the show. Wondering how the Man in Black turned into the Smoke Monster? "Costume change," Murphy retorted. Even though she managed to pull creatively incorrect answers out of nowhere, one question stumped her: "What's up with the polar bears?" someone asked. "I don't freakin' know, man," she replied. Though her exasperated response matched most fan reactions to the bears' appearance, the answer wasn't counted.

CRITERIA

☐ Must never have seen an episode of *LOST*.
☐ Must be asked genuine questions about *LOST*.
☐ Must attempt to give genuine answers.

RELATED RECORDS

▶ Most TV Shows Named in 1 Minute Replacing One Word in Title with "Horse": 17
▶ Shortest Late-Night Talk Show: 2 minutes, 52.4 seconds

RECORD BEGGING TO BE SET

☐ Largest Collection of Lottery Tickets with the Numbers 4, 8, 15, 16, 23, and 42

16, 23, 42

Most Network News Sign-Offs in 30 Seconds

RECORD: 27

NAME: John Berman

LOCATION: New York, New York

DATE: August 19, 2009

TOOLS: Strong enunciation, relatively short name

As a news correspondent for ABC, John Berman signs off every report with his signature "John Berman, ABC News, New York." As Berman explains, "In my business, we say our names, and we say them a *lot*. My goal was to say it more in a burst of 30 seconds than anyone has ever said it in history." A RecordSetter event provided the opportunity, with Berman setting the bar at nineteen. After a coworker, ABC Radio correspondent Aaron Katersky, beat his record by one, Berman brought his A-Game and ruthlessly riffed off a resounding twenty-seven sign-offs. "I defy any network news correspondent out there to beat this," he crowed. Bring it, Blitzer!

CRITERIA

☐ Not necessary to be a network news correspondent.

☐ Must use "first name, last name, network name" format.

Tip for Beating This Record

Warm up your mouth muscles by reciting some tongue twisters prior to the attempt. Phrases that will loosen your jaw include "How can a clam cram in a clean cream can?" and "Seventy-seven benevolent elephants."

RELATED RECORDS

▶ Most News Team Members Dressed On-Air in Halloween Costumes: 11

▶ Longest Time to Balance a Boom Microphone on Two Fingers: 2 minutes, 9.9 seconds

RECORD BEGGING TO BE SET

☐ Most Lavalier Microphones Worn at Once

Most Knock-Knock Jokes Told in 1 Minute

RECORD: 16

NAME: Debbie Hampton

LOCATION: New York, New York

DATE: May 20, 2009

TOOLS: List of jokes, someone to say "Who's there?"

San Francisco's Debbie Hampton has a thing for good old-fashioned knock-knock jokes. To demonstrate the breadth of her comedy library, she cracked up the RecordSetter community by telling an unprecedented fourteen knock-knock jokes in 1 minute. That feat caught the eye of CNN, who invited her to try and beat her mark during a live interview with Eric Landsford. Hampton raised her own comedy bar, machine-gunning a gut-busting sixteen jokes with Landsford as her partner. "Knock, knock?" "Who's there?" "Debbie." "Debbie who?" "Debbie 'World Record Holder' Hampton, that's who."

CRITERIA

☐ All jokes must use traditional "Knock, knock?" "Who's there?" format.

☐ May not repeat jokes.

☐ Only jokes completed within time limit are counted.

RELATED RECORDS

▶ Most "Yo Mama" Jokes Told with a Helium Voice in 1 Minute: 9

▶ Longest Line of People Telling Knock-Knock Jokes in Succession: 31

RECORD BEGGING TO BE SET

☐ Most Stand-Up Comedians Named in 30 Seconds

KNOCK, KNOCK!

IS THAT YOU AGAIN, DEBBIE HAMPTON?

RECORDSETTER LEGEND

Opus Moreschi

Writer, Mirth Maker, Initiator of Crowd-Sourced Spectacles

Opus Moreschi, a comedy writer for *The Colbert Report,* describes himself modestly as a 6-foot-4 mammal who loves the smell of Band-Aids. He is also one of RecordSetter's most imaginative record holders, inventing titles that bring new meaning to the phrase "audience participation."

Moreschi's world record career began in November 2008 when his friend Elna Baker convinced him to attend the first-ever RecordSetter live event in New York. Sitting in the basement of a Chinese-Italian fusion karaoke bar, his cranial gears whirred as he watched twenty-three people—including passersby on the sidewalk who had been solicited by audience members—shave off RecordSetter cofounder Corey Henderson's beard.

Inspired by the collaborative spirit of the night, Moreschi took to the stage during the open-mike portion of the proceedings. He describes what happened next: "My first instinct, being propless and with no planning, was to try to insult people. But I wanted to keep with the positive atmosphere of the night, so I chose Most People Complimented in 1 Minute." His sixteen ensuing niceties were personalized, including such gems as "Your chin is well shaped" and "Your sweater reminds me of a simpler time."

Humble but heartfelt beginnings gave way to more ambitious records offering a sense of spectacle.

Moreschi's next attempt, Most Neckties Worn at Once, ended with him standing before a crowd, head lolling atop 7.4 pounds of silk and polyester. (Noticing that his face was beginning to turn purple during the tie-adding process, Henderson dispatched an assistant to monitor his pulse.)

His well-honed crowd-pleasing approach was employed to spectacular effect for one of RecordSetter's most visually splendid records: Most Unique Adjectives Affixed to a Person. Distributing pens and Post-Its, Moreschi asked people to write descriptive words that would turn him into a human Mad Lib. The resulting 356 terms allowed him to get closure from a childhood difficulty: being unable to distinguish between adverbs and adjectives. "Over and over again," he says, reflecting on his struggle, "if a Mad Lib called for an adjective, I reflexively gave 'bumpy' as my answer. So, when I saw somebody that night wrote 'bumpy' on a Post-It and stuck it to me, I actually got goosebumps. Which, I know, is sorta perfect."

Moreschi's method for coming up with world record topics is founded on two principles: procrastination and panic. The process begins with him committing to a day on which he will attempt a feat. "Then," he says, "as the date approaches, a rising sense of dread fills my soul as I realize I have no ideas. Usually the night before I have worked myself into such a panicked state that a new record is all I can think about."

The anxiety always gives way to a eureka moment, but putting things off until the last minute has occasionally been costly, especially in the case of his nasal orchestra record. "I paid some small family-run company on the Internet a ton of money to overnight me all those nose flutes," he confesses.

With record attempts that rally a crowd and present them with a captivating scene, Moreschi is, to use three adjectives once stuck to him on Post-Its: brainy, whimsical, spectacular.

CHAPTER 2

Food and Drink

Were you ever told not to play with your food? Well, forget that. In this chapter, you'll find cereal stuck to faces, bananas down pants, watermelons being driven through a car wash, and cream pies flying everywhere. There's also a smorgasbord of gastronomic creations, which combine the crafty flair of Martha Stewart with the prep methods of the Swedish Chef—equal parts culinary majesty and havoc. From the Most Images of Fish Sandwiches Looked at in 1 Minute to the Fastest Time to Drink a 2-Ounce Bottle of Tabasco Sauce Through a Coffee Stirrer, there is something for everyone, whether carnivore, vegan, or fruitarian.

Most Eggs Crushed with Head in 30 Seconds

RECORD: 56

NAME: Sam Stilson

LOCATION: Toronto, Ontario, Canada

DATE: April 25, 2009

TOOLS: Iron head, reliable egg source, friends who love forehead-flavored omelettes

Sam Stilson is a headbanger with a purpose. His forehead is a finely calibrated egg-crushing machine. With one hundred small white targets lined up on a table before him on a fateful day in Toronto, he launched his head into each one in rapid succession, shells smashing and slimy egg innards flying all over the place. Stilson twitches as he recalls the experience: "It was pretty painful slamming my head onto a table and cutting it up on those eggshells." But his recovery was quick. Starving in the wake of destruction he had exacted, Stilson gathered up the unused food and got cooking: "We ended up using the leftovers to set a second record—the Fastest Time to Eat a Fried Egg Sandwich."

When the timer began, Stilson got cracking.

CRITERIA

- ☐ Must crush eggs one at a time.
- ☐ Eggshells must crack enough to reveal white and yolk.

RELATED RECORDS

- ► Most Pencils Broken with Forehead in 1 Minute: 34
- ► Most Eggs Balanced on Chin: 68
- ► Most Hen Eggs Held in Hand at Once: 14

RECORDS BEGGING TO BE SET

- ☐ Fastest Time to Break and Separate Ten Egg Yolks
- ☐ Most Chickens Kissed in 10 Seconds

Largest Collection of Jack-O'-Lantern Grapes

RECORD: 14

NAME: Madeleine Daepp

LOCATION: Clayton, Missouri

DATE: January 20, 2010

TOOLS: Large bunch of grapes, precision carving device, steady hands

CRITERIA

☐ Jack-o'-lanterns must be hand carved.

☐ Each one must include two eyes and a mouth.

Yellow Jacket Comment

COREY: I hope this sparks a jack-o'-lantern revolution. I'd like to see some made of peas . . . jelly beans . . . cucumbers . . . endless possibilities.

RELATED RECORDS

▶ Longest Time to Wear Hollowed-Out Pumpkin on Head: 13 hours, 18 minutes

▶ Fastest Time to Shoot a Face onto a Pumpkin from 82 Feet Away: 5 minutes, 31.38 seconds

RECORDS BEGGING TO BE SET

☐ Most Eyes Carved into a Jack-O'-Lantern

☐ Largest Collection of Jack-O'-Lanterns Resembling Justin Bieber

P umpkin Schmumpkin. To really challenge yourself next Halloween, try carving jack-o'-lantern grapes. Madeleine Daepp did just that when she hollowed out fourteen ruby red grapes—beating out creator Caitlin Ropers's mark by eight—with just enough structural integrity to carefully carve tiny faces into them. (Sadly there wasn't enough room to fit a candle inside each one, but their smiles provided plenty of illumination.) A new world record, and a great Halloween decorating option for those stricken with cucurbitophobia*.

Tips for Beating This Record

Daepp shares some wisdom gleaned from her experience:

1. A good grape carver needs good tools. I use a Swiss Army Knife (the corkscrew is great for eyeholes) and a small spoon to scoop out the inside of my grapes.

2. Use high-quality materials; squishy or rotten grapes won't hold their shape properly.

3. Do not let others too close to your masterpiece. I had a rather traumatic experience losing one of my best works to a hungry roommate.

*CUCURBITOPHOBIA IS A FEAR OF PUMPKINS.

Most Grapes Consecutively Tossed and Caught in Mouth

RECORD: 23

NAME: Brian Pankey

LOCATION: Springfield, Illinois

DATE: September 20, 2010

TOOLS: Large bunch of grapes, proficiency with projectiles

To set this record, Brian Pankey combined skills he honed crafting two tricks: juggling two Ping-Pong balls with his mouth, and orally catching M&M'S (performed separately, of course). He reports that although M&M'S and grapes have a similar velocity, grapes are larger and more slippery, making them harder to catch. Pankey is presently in training for his next attempt at fruit play: juggling two grapes with his mouth. Holy spit!

CRITERIA

☐ Each grape must be tossed at least 12 inches above mouth.

☐ Grapes must be tossed by record attempter.

RELATED RECORD

▶ Most Toothpicks Stuck in a Grape in 30 Seconds: 20

RECORD BEGGING TO BE SET

☐ Fastest Time to Extract One Cup of Grape Juice by Stomping on Grapes

Tip for Beating This Record

"Curve your lips into an 'O' shape so they guard your teeth," says Pankey. "Keep your tongue out of harm's way and slightly extend your jaw to prevent the grape from dropping straight down your throat. Finally, to get the best angle, position your head so the grape threatens to land on the tip of your nose."

12"

KEEP YOUR EYES OPEN FOR DURATION OF ATTEMPT. REMEMBER, THEY'RE JUST GRAPES.

Slowest Time to Eat a Bowl of Cereal

RECORD: 22 minutes, 47.4 seconds

NAME: Matt Stringenz

LOCATION: Papillion, Nebraska

DATE: August 12, 2010

TOOLS: Cereal, milk, bowl, spoon, no plans for the day

A leisurely breakfast is a decadent way to start the day, but it need not involve bacon and eggs, pancakes, or waffles. Matt Stringenz keeps things simple, preferring to tuck into whole-grain Total cereal at a very relaxed speed. Stringenz took 22 minutes, 47.4 seconds to eat his way to the bottom of the bowl. That's the length of your standard sitcom, minus the ad breaks. Should you attempt to beat this record, take note: If you take too long, your milk might ferment into cheese.

Slowman Stringenz shows off his technique.

CRITERIA

□ Must use regular-sized cereal bowl.

□ Bowl must be at least two-thirds filled with cereal.

□ Must continuously chew or swallow cereal.

RELATED RECORDS

► Fastest Consumption of a Bowl of Cereal: 24.2 seconds

► Fastest Time to Spell "The Record Collection" Using Alpha-Bits: 1 minute, 55.8 seconds

RECORDS BEGGING TO BE SET

□ Most Cereal Mascots Named in 10 Seconds

□ Most Varieties of Cereal in a Bowl

□ Fastest Time to Find All Raisins in a Box of Raisin Bran

Tallest Frosted Mini-Wheat Tower

RECORD: 8 Mini-Wheats

NAME: Erin Browes

LOCATION: Vancouver, British Columbia, Canada

DATE: October 16, 2009

TOOLS: Frosted Mini-Wheats, discerning eye

Frosted Mini-Wheats stacking is a technically challenging sport. The nutritious cereal pieces, like snowflakes, are all unique, making construction an exhausting pursuit. "Those that are lopsided or chipped are very hard to stack," explained software engineer Erin Browes. The eight she forged into a record-breaking tower had smooth sides, allowing them to nestle against one another, Tetris-style. Rejected pieces, however, served a crucial role in fueling her record attempt. "Mini-Wheats are the perfect snack for the hardworking Mini-Wheat stacker," Browes admitted. "Those little suckers are full of quick-burning carbs and long-lasting proteins."

CRITERIA

☐ Frosted Mini-Wheats must be completely dry.

☐ No adhesives or external support permitted.

☐ Tower must stand at least 3 seconds without toppling.

Yellow Jacket Comment

DAN: An inspiring category. I'd have a go at beating it myself, but I'm more of a granola man.

Tip for Beating This Record

When shopping for cereal, Browes suggests buying the family-sized box. Not only will you have a great selection of Frosted Mini-Wheats to train with, but it's also a better deal.

RELATED RECORD

▶ Fastest Time to Stack Ten Cheerios: 14 seconds

RECORDS BEGGING TO BE SET

☐ Most Froot Loops Consecutively Tossed and Caught in Mouth

☐ Longest Time Juggling Three Boxes of Cereal

Largest Lucky Charms Beard

RECORD:
61 charms

NAME: Justin Gignac

LOCATION: New York, New York

DATE: March 17, 2010

TOOLS: Box of Lucky Charms, milk, ability to remain stone-faced while getting a cereal facial

Justin Gignac adores Lucky Charms. "I love that cereal, as I do most traditional Irish cuisine," he explains. Gignac's wife, Christine, used milk as an adhesive to attach the breakfast marshmallows to his face, creating a sweet, rainbow-hued beard. "As the cereal was glued to my face, I felt wet, sticky, and drippy like a balloon being covered with papier-mâché." Poise and inner calm were the secrets to this record. "I tried my hardest not to move. I think I reached level two or three of Zen."

CRITERIA

- ☐ Must use Lucky Charms marshmallows.
- ☐ Marshmallows must all be placed within beard region.
- ☐ Only adhesive permitted is milk.

Tip for Beating This Record

Gignac warns against getting overly enthusiastic with the adhesive: "Don't use too much milk," he says, "or the cereal doesn't stick and slides down the face."

RELATED RECORDS

- ▶ Largest Cocktail Umbrella Beard: 17 umbrellas
- ▶ Largest Toothpick Beard: 2,222 toothpicks

Fastest Time to Make a Turkey Sandwich

RECORD: 11.20 seconds

NAME: Thomas Hansell

LOCATION: Suffern, New York

DATE: August 10, 2010

TOOLS: Sliced turkey, bread, condiment of choice

Thomas Hansell's crusade to fast-track his food preparation was not without its obstacles. During his first attempt at making a turkey sandwich as quickly as possible, he pulled the fridge door open so fast, and with such might, that bottles and cartons came tumbling off the shelves, making a huge mess on the kitchen floor. Learning from his reckless haste, Hansell reattempted the record using a gentler touch and beat Jacob Martin's previous mark of 12.2 seconds. The sandwich, a simple turkey and mustard combo, was reportedly delicious.

CRITERIA

☐ Must pull plate from cupboard and turkey, bread, and condiment(s) from fridge.

☐ Must use at least one condiment.

☐ Must be a traditional-style sandwich (not open-face).

Yellow Jacket Comment

COREY: This would be a great post-Thanksgiving record. While grown-ups sleep off the meal, kids could clean up the table with speed-sandwich challenges.

Tip for Beating This Record

For the condiment, use a substance that comes in a squeeze bottle. It's much faster to squish a blob of mustard onto a sandwich than waste precious time digging in a jar with a knife.

RELATED RECORD

▶ Most Frozen Turkeys Fit in a Ford and Delivered to a Food Bank: 183

RECORDS BEGGING TO BE SET

☐ Most Handprint Turkeys Drawn in 30 Seconds

☐ Most "BLT" Acronyms Invented in 1 Minute

☐ Fastest Time to Eat a Subway Sandwich on a Subway

Most Images of Fish Sandwiches Looked at in 1 Minute

RECORD: 60

NAME: Todd Lamb

LOCATION: New York, New York

DATE: February 11, 2009

TOOLS: Sheets of cardboard, pictures of fish sandwiches, a fleet-fingered assistant

Todd Lamb spent his whole life believing there wasn't much to say about fish sandwiches. Then he saw some pictures online and realized he had been living a lie. "It turns out there are millions of different kinds," he says. Fascinated by his findings, Lamb needed to find a way to make the public aware of the variety of fish sandwiches in the world. The answer was a RecordSetter world record. Lamb recruited an assistant to flip through photos of sandwiches as he studied them intensely, saying "Fish!" for every one.

RECORD HISTORY

- ▶ Todd Lamb—New York, New York: 54 Fish Sandwiches
- ▶ Carlos Montoya—San Diego, California: 57 Fish Sandwiches
- ▶ Todd Lamb— New York, New York: 60 Fish Sandwiches

CRITERIA

- ☐ Pictures must be mounted on card stock and held by an assistant.
- ☐ Assistant must flip through cards one at a time.
- ☐ Record setter must say "Fish" for every card.

Tip for Beating This Record

Lamb says the most important thing is to find an assistant who can meet the physical demands of the task. "The key is to keep a tight grip on the images of fish sandwiches," he advises. "You need someone with strong fingers." It also helps to have the right accessories: "I make my assistants wear powdered gloves."

RELATED RECORD

- ▶ Most Goldfish Crackers Chicken Pecked off a Table in 1 Minute: 50

RECORD BEGGING TO BE SET

- ☐ Most Foods Deep-Fried in 5 Minutes

Most Jewish Delis Named in 1 Minute

RECORD: 30

NAME: David Sax

LOCATION: New York, New York

DATE: February 11, 2009

TOOLS: Extensive deli knowledge, ability to talk fast, hankering for pastrami on rye

After years spent traveling the globe to write an award-winning book about delicatessen culture, *Save the Deli*, many consider writer David Sax the undisputed pastrami expert of his generation. Sax's skills were put to the test when he attempted to utilize his meat knowledge in front of a rowdy live audience at a RecordSetter event in New York City. A lone heckler tried to throw him off his matzoh ball game by repeatedly shrieking, "Carnegie! Carnegie! Carnegie!" in reference to the landmark deli. Sax, however, was equal to the test. "I never found out who he was, but I would guess he was some guy from Katz's Deli down the street. They're bitter rivals."

CRITERIA

☐ All delis must be named from memory.

☐ May not include delis that are no longer in business.

DELIS NAMED: Liebman's, Loeser's, Lansky's, Fine and Shapiro, Zabar's, Artie's, Carnegie, Stage, Katz's, Second Avenue Deli, Ben's, Sarge's, Gottlieb's, Adelman's, Mill Basin, Caplansky's, Kat'z, Coleman's, Center Street, Schwartz's, Main, Smoked Meat Pete, Snowdon Deli, Nate 'n Al's, Kantor's, Langer's, Junior's, Goldberg's, Goldman's, Maison David.

Yellow Jacket Comment

DAN: This record has "Rolaids marketing campaign" written all over it.

RELATED RECORDS

▶ Most Times Saying "I'll Have What She's Having" in 30 Seconds: 45

▶ Most Complaints to a Deli Waiter In 30 Seconds: 8

Fastest Time to Peel a Clementine with Peel Kept Intact

RECORD: 11.39 seconds

NAME: Sujay Kulshrestha

LOCATION: St. Louis, Missouri

DATE: February 14, 2010

TOOLS: Clementine, long fingernails

WHEN COMPLETE, TOSS AND CATCH CLEMENTINE IN MOUTH FOR EXTRA SHOWBOAT INTIMIDATION.

Tip for Beating This Record

According to Kulshrestha, the secret is in the citrus choice. "If you choose a clementine with skin that hugs the fruit," he says, "it's much harder to start and peel quickly. Some clementines have a little air pocket in between the peel and the fruit, giving it an easy place to start peeling and a way to really get inside and take the rest of the peel off with minimal effort."

Speed peeler and college student Sujay Kulshrestha cites two sources of inspiration for his record: boredom and an upcoming chemistry exam. "Rather than going to a tutoring session, I decided to set a world record, probably because it's so much more productive and important in the long run." Recruiting his roommate to be the timekeeper, Kulshrestha was confident enough to launch straight into the attempt without practicing first. Just over 11 seconds later, he held a world record, a single peel, and a tasty fruit to enjoy in celebration of his victory. "It created a great story for the rest of the semester," Kulshrestha remembers fondly.

CRITERIA

☐ May only use hands to peel clementine.

RELATED RECORDS

▸ Fastest Time to Peel a Banana: 0.85 seconds

▸ Most Screws Screwed into a Banana: 550

RECORDS BEGGING TO BE SET

☐ Most Watermelon Seeds Spit in 30 Seconds

☐ Most Clementine Pieces Fed to a Friend in 1 Minute While Singing "My Darling Clementine"

Fastest Time to Eat an Apple Without Front Teeth

RECORD: 1 minute, 17.60 seconds

NAME: Toby Gradin Petersen

LOCATION: Brooklyn, New York

DATE: February 21, 2010

TOOLS: Apple, missing front teeth, resilient jaw

Six-year-old Toby Gradin Petersen stepped up to the makeshift stage at Beam Camp's Second Annual Brooklyn World Record Day determined to make her mark. Armed with a shiny red apple and lacking her two front teeth, she was in perfect fighting form. Petersen's choppers had fallen out just a few weeks earlier, giving her a "phantom tooth" feeling that made her attack the apple more aggressively. Readers should note that there are few more vulnerable record holders in this book. As her mother proudly informed us, Toby is now the proud owner of two front teeth. Shatter this record and the first-grader will not be reclaiming it.

CRITERIA

☐ Record setter must be missing two front upper teeth.

☐ Must eat apple until seeds are visible.

Yellow Jacket Comment

DAN: Ideal candidates to beat this record: young children, bar brawlers, senior citizens who don't floss.

RELATED RECORD

▶ Most People Simultaneously Flossing with Same Piece of Dental Floss: 428

RECORD BEGGING TO BE SET

☐ Most Teeth Placed Beneath a Pillow

BIRDS OF A FEATHER

Fruit

Smushing, stacking, stuffing, simultaneous sipping—these records take fruit and use it in ways you never learned at the dining table. The beauty of attempting these records is that, win or lose, you're left with a delicious snack afterwards. Just wash your hands before smushing those grapes.

WARNING
DO NOT ATTEMPT
THIS RECORD IF
MONKEYS ARE NEARBY.

Most Screws Screwed into a Banana

RECORD: 550

NAME: Liza Pliss and Steven Jenkins

LOCATION: New York, New York

DATE: May 29, 2010

Most Bananas Fit Inside a Pair of Pants While Wearing Them

RECORD: 148

NAME: Henri Mazza

LOCATION: Austin, Texas

DATE: August 27, 2010

Most Grapes Smushed with Hands in 1 Minute

RECORD: 63

NAME: Wyatt Accardi

LOCATION: Brooklyn, New York

DATE: April 4, 2009

TWENTY-FIVE MORE PEOPLE AND WE'LL HAVE A WORLD RECORD.

OR WE COULD JUST DRINK IT.

Most Watermelons Driven Through a Car Wash

RECORD: 455
NAME: Dianna Gunn
LOCATION: Houston, Texas
DATE: December 13, 2009

Most People Simultaneously Drinking out of a Pineapple

RECORD: 26
NAME: Andrea Carr and friends
LOCATION: Houston, Texas
DATE: September 18, 2009

Tallest Apple Tower

RECORD: 10 apples
NAME: Joe Kan
LOCATION: Melbourne, Australia
DATE: April 10, 2010

Largest Collection of Miniature Cows Made from Spam

RECORD: 36 cows

NAME: Arsenio Santos

LOCATION: San Francisco, California

DATE: January 16, 2007

TOOLS: Spam, carving tool, knowledge of bovine anatomy

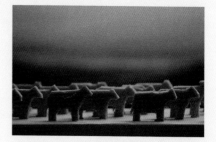

The elements of Spam are primarily porcine: ham, pork, and several shakes of salt with bits of starch, sugar, spice, and sodium nitrate to round things off. Cows are nowhere to be seen on the list of ingredients, which makes Arsenio Santos's decision to craft a miniature cattle herd a little curious. "I know Spam is an unusual medium," he acknowledges, "but it seemed to be the most artistic of meats. I mean, it's basically clay, right?" Before carving the thirty-six–cow "Spampede," as he affectionately calls it, Santos froze the blocks of Spam, which made the notoriously gelatinous substance easier to work with.

I'D BEAT THIS RECORD, BUT MY HOOVES MAKE CARVING DIFFICULT.

CRITERIA

☐ Cows must each be individually handcarved.

☐ May not use materials other than Spam.

RELATED RECORDS

▶ Most Spam E-mails in an Inbox: 96,899

▶ Largest Collection of Milk Jug Lids: 429

▶ Shortest Mechanical Bull Ride: 3.12 seconds

RECORD BEGGING TO BE SET

☐ Most "Moos" Directed Toward a Cow in 30 Seconds

Loudest Sound Made Using a Bag of Chips

RECORD: 88 decibels

NAME: Reverend Matthew Nunnery

LOCATION: Shreveport, Louisiana

DATE: September 18, 2010

TOOLS: Bag of chips, decibel meter

=ATTENTION=
BEATING THIS RECORD
MAY REQUIRE TIME TRAVEL.

Matthew Nunnery has always had a taste for Sun Chips, but his love for the healthy snack food reached new levels when he crushed a bag of them with superhuman force. The innocent-looking package roared like a lion, making a sound Nunnery called "the most incredibly loud thing in the history of human events."

A nearby decibel meter recorded a hefty 88 decibels. To put that in perspective, any sustained sound above 85 decibels is considered dangerous to the human ear.

Frito-Lay withdrew the special compostable packaging Nunnery used from the market after complaints that the loud noise it made when rustling "affected the consumer experience." As a result, this record may never be broken.

CRITERIA
☐ Any bag size permissible.
☐ Sound must be measured with a decibel meter.

RELATED RECORDS
▶ Loudest Cluck: 6 decibels
▶ Most Pringles Crunched in One Bite: 25
▶ Loudest Pop Rocks Chorus: 72.7 decibels

RECORD BEGGING TO BE SET
☐ Most Alarm Clocks Used to Wake a Sleeping Person

It's best to attempt this record on an empty stomach, when your desire for food is fierce.

Most Potatoes Held in Hand

RECORD: 11

NAME: Tomer Salton

LOCATION: Mishmeret, Israel

DATE: October 20, 2009

TOOLS: Sack of potatoes, sizable hand span

Tip for Beating This Record

Fret not if you weren't born with giant paws, says Salton. Strength and technique play an important role. "It helps if you have big hands, but most of the potatoes are held between the fingers, so make sure you spread them wide and have powerful inter-finger grip."

Looking around his friend's kitchen for record-setting inspiration, Israeli Tomer Salton stumbled upon a bowl of potatoes. Instantly he knew what he had to do: hold as many in one hand as humanly possible. Following a cursory visual inspection of Salton's mitts, his friend predicted that six taters would fit in his right hand. Living up to his nickname of "The Man Who Can," Salton blew his buddy's mind by clutching eleven spuds at once.

CRITERIA

☐ Must be uncut and complete potatoes.

☐ May not use baby potatoes.

RELATED RECORD

▶ Heaviest Mass of Potatoes Stuffed Inside Pants While Wearing Them in 1 Minute: 21 pounds

RECORDS BEGGING TO BE SET

☐ Fastest Time to Attach All Parts to a Mr. Potato Head Toy

☐ Largest Group to Play "Hot Potato"

Most Cheeses Named in 10 Seconds

RECORD: 23

NAME: Colton Carnahan

LOCATION: Franklin, Tennessee

DATE: December 28, 2009

TOOLS: Comprehensive cheese knowledge, lactose tolerance (preferred)

With a confident air and a brain full of dairy products, 12-year-old cheese recitation prodigy Colton Carnahan speed-talked his way through twenty-three varieties in a mere 10 seconds. The list was a veritable world tour of cheese and included popular Dutch export Gouda; American Monterey Jack; Longhorn, an English form of cheddar; and provolone, the pride of Italy. Carnahan also had time to mention smooth, nutty Edam. According to Cheese.com, this Dutch semi-hard variety goes down very nicely with a glass of pinot noir—a pleasure Carnahan will get to experience for himself in approximately 9 years.

Yellow Jacket Comment

COREY: I'd love to see this category added to culinary school curriculum.

DAN: Culinary school, schmulinary school. I'd just like to eat a sandwich with twenty-three cheeses on it.

CRITERIA

☐ Varietals are acceptable, that is, "aged cheddar," "sharp cheddar."

☐ Processed cheese foods (e.g., Cheez Whiz, string cheese) are not permitted.

RELATED RECORD

▸ Most Cheesecakes Named in 30 Seconds: 24

RECORD BEGGING TO BE SET

☐ Farthest Distance to Roll a Wheel of Cheese

Most Ketchup Packets Squeezed Open in 30 Seconds

RECORD: 7

NAME: Craig Morrison

LOCATION: Toronto, Ontario, Canada

DATE: February 15, 2010

TOOLS: Ketchup packets, old clothes, protective tarp

Craig Morrison is head over heels in love with ketchup packets. He loves them because they are free, easily accessible, and unbelievably useful for pranks (among his favorites: placing them under a toilet seat so that when people sit down, ketchup shoots all over the back of their legs).

To prepare for this record, Morrison crashed fast food joints in downtown Toronto, hitting the jackpot at Hero Burger, a chain with big bowlfuls of condiments located far from the cash registers. Weighed down by a hundred packets, Morrison was ready to set this record. "Going into it I really thought it would be easy," he says. "My goal was an ambitious fifty in 30 seconds." But Morrison had overlooked an important characteristic of his beloved condiment. "Once I started, ketchup got all over my hands, making them slippery and wet. My fingers just slid off the packets." At the end of the allocated 30 seconds, Morrison's kitchen looked like a crime scene. He has since stockpiled the ninety-three remaining packets in case of a future ketchup supply crisis.

CRITERIA

☐ Packets must be squeezed open, not torn.

☐ Packets must be squeezed open entirely by hand.

☐ All packets must be sealed at start of record.

RELATED RECORD

▶ Fastest Time to Dip Two Hands in Barbecue Sauce and Lick Them Clean: 37.1 seconds

RECORD BEGGING TO BE SET

☐ Farthest Distance to Shoot Ketchup from a Squeeze Bottle

Most Questions Asked During a Single Drive-Through Visit

RECORD: 33

NAME: Steve Fester

LOCATION: Denver, Colorado

DATE: January 25, 2010

TOOLS: Car, drive-through restaurant, lack of empathy for its employees

Morning radio DJ Steve Fester squeezed out thirty-three questions in a single drive-through visit, ranging from the sublime to the ridiculous. Rest assured, after persisting through the questions, this merry prankster at least had the kindness to order and pay for a small, black coffee.

PICK-UP WINDOW

CRITERIA

☐ All questions must be asked during a single visit.

☐ Only the driver's questions count.

☐ May not repeat questions.

QUESTIONS FESTER ASKED:

1. HOW ARE YOU TODAY?
2. ARE YOU STAYING WARM?
3. WHAT TIME DO YOU SERVE BREAKFAST 'TIL?
4. CAN I ORDER LUNCH?
5. WHAT'S ON A McMUFFIN?
6. HAVE YOU SERVED ANYONE FOR THE FIRST TIME AT McDONALD'S BEFORE?
7. IF I BUY AN EXTRA VALUE MEAL, HOW MUCH CHEAPER IS IT?
8. CAN I GET MORE THAN ONE VALUE MEAL?
9. CAN I GET FRIES WITH THAT?
10. CAN I GET FRIES WITHOUT SALT?
11. DO YOU SERVE BEER?
12. WHAT DO YOU RECOMMEND?
13. AND I CAN'T GET FRIES WITH THAT?
14. DO YOU HAVE FRESH FRIES?
15. DO YOU HAVE VEGAN ITEMS?
16. ARE YOUR BUNS GLUTEN FREE?
17. ARE YOU THERE?
18. DO YOU HAVE SUGAR-FREE SYRUP?
19. DOES YOUR MANAGER MAKE SURE YOU WASH YOUR HANDS AFTER YOU USE THE RESTROOM?
20. DO YOU HAVE COKE?
21. DO YOU HAVE PEPSI?
22. DO YOU HAVE FROSTIES?
23. CAN I GET A BIG MAC McMUFFIN?
24. HOW LARGE IS YOUR ORANGE JUICE?
25. ARE THEY THE SAME SIZE AS YOUR SODAS?
26. HOW MUCH ARE YOUR BURRITOS?
27. IS THAT WITH TAX?
28. HOW MUCH IS YOUR TAX HERE?
29. IS TAX THE SAME AT ALL McDONALD'S?
30. IS THAT STATE OR FEDERAL TAX?
31. CAN I HAVE THAT TAX WAIVED?
32. WHAT SIZES ARE YOUR COFFEES?
33. ARE THEY THE SAME SIZE AS THE McFLURRIES?

Fastest Time to Shuck a Lobster, Make a Lobster Roll, and Have Someone Take a Bite

RECORD: 2 minutes, 20.03 seconds

NAME: Tony DeLois

LOCATION: New York, New York

DATE: July 27, 2010

TOOLS: Hard-shell lobster, celery, lemon, mayo, salt, spices, lobster cracker, pick, knife, hot dog roll or regular roll

Tony DeLois is a chef hailing from Maine, proud home of the original lobster roll. The New England delicacy consists of just a few crucial ingredients, making it perfect for cooking at the speed of light. "The best roll needs just lobster, a little mayo or butter, squeezed on lemon, celery, and paprika," DeLois advises. A simple recipe it may be, but attempting this record offers its fair share of danger, as our intrepid chef discovered. "The first shell I cracked open led to lobster juice shooting right into my eye. From then on, I was handicapped."

CRITERIA

☐ Must use hard-shell lobster, celery, lemon, mayo, salt, and spices

☐ Must shuck one tail, two claws, and lobster knuckles.

☐ Only tools allowed are a knife, cracker, and pick.

☐ Ingredients may not be pre-chopped.

Yellow Jacket Comment

COREY: There are two main types of lobster rolls: Maine style—served cold, with mayo on a hot dog bun—and Connecticut style—warm, served with butter on a roll.

DAN: As long as one is brought to me in record time, I'm not picky.

Rock! Lobster!

Fastest Time to Shuck and Eat an Oyster

RECORD: 12.70 seconds

NAME: Tim Adams

LOCATION: Portland, Maine

DATE: October 1, 2010

TOOLS: Oyster, oyster knife, willingness to experience aphrodisiac effects

CRITERIA

☐ Oyster must be completely shut at start of record.

☐ May use oyster knife to open oyster.

☐ Timing stops once oyster has been swallowed.

Yellow Jacket Comment

DAN: If only all meals could be prepared and served in under 13 seconds.

RELATED RECORD

▶ Fastest Time to Eat Forty Chicken McNuggets: 4 minutes, 14.45 seconds

RECORDS BEGGING TO BE SET

☐ Largest Collection of Oyster Forks

☐ Most Pearls on a Necklace

Tim Adams lives in mid-coastal Maine, home to the sumptuously flavorsome Pemaquid variety of oysters. ("It's hard to believe an oyster that substantial could taste so clean," raves oysterguide.com.) Adams, a brewer and owner of the Oxbow Brewing Co., has a simple technique when it comes to shucking: "I find the sweet spot and crank on it." Once the sweet spot (read: weak spot) has been located, he pries open the shell, separates the meat, and slurps. He considers himself an oyster purist, but ever the brewer, he says, "I use no garnishes or additions, even when I'm not going for a record. Just raw Pemaquids accompanied by a big, rich stout."

Largest Soda Can Pyramid

RECORD: 120 cans

NAME: Anthony Rodriguez and Andrew Rodriguez

LOCATION: Phoenix, Arizona

DATE: October 11, 2009

TOOLS: An abundance of empty soda cans, experience stocking supermarket shelves

CRITERIA

☐ Each tier must have fewer cans than the one below it.

☐ Adhesives may not be used.

☐ Must use standard 12-ounce cans.

Yellow Jacket Comment

DAN: Let's hope this inspires Loudest Human Burp.

This is a record Frank Gehry would be proud of. Step one: Invite a group of friends over and serve copious quantities of soda. Step two: Instruct them to leave their empty cans and go home. Step three: Find a level surface and build a museum-worthy installation of unprecedented heights. That's exactly what brothers Anthony and Andrew Rodriguez did, building up a thirteen-story masterpiece before gleefully toppling it. Let's hope they remembered step four: Recycle when complete.

RELATED RECORDS

▶ Largest Solo Cup Pyramid: 3,311 cups

▶ Tallest Toilet-Paper Roll Pyramid: 66 rolls

▶ Longest Time to Balance Six Unopened Soda Cans on Chin: 12.57 seconds

RECORD BEGGING TO BE SET

☐ Most People to "Walk Like an Egyptian" at Once

ANYBODY HAVE A STRAW?

Most Strangers' Drinks Sipped out of in 15 Seconds

ALWAYS ATTEMPT RECORD WITH A FULL WALLET, AS BUYING REPLACEMENT DRINKS MAY BE REQUIRED.

RECORD: 15

NAME: Henri Mazza

LOCATION: Austin, Texas

DATE: August 27, 2010

TOOLS: Strangers with drinks, straw, charming personality

When setting a world record, it's important to articulate specific criteria. Otherwise, your mark could be stolen right out from under you, and you won't even see it coming. This happened to Jake Bronstein, who, after sneakily sipping from five unknowing strangers' drinks in 15 seconds, thought he'd created an achievement rude enough to last forever. Henri Mazza thought differently. He spotted a legal loophole in Bronstein's somewhat vague criteria. "The rules didn't specify the strangers had to be unaware of the impending threat to their drinks." With that knowledge in place, Mazza invited a large group of strangers to participate. This creative shortcut provided Mazza with a heavy advantage. He succeeded, but not without a last-second panic. Says Mazza, "When I was running out of time, I did what any world champion would do: grabbed beer out of a stranger's hands and took a huge slurp."

CRITERIA

☐ Must use own straw for all sips.

☐ Strangers may hold up to two drinks each.

☐ Only drinks sipped through a straw are counted.

RELATED RECORDS

▶ Most Times Unscrewing a Plastic Bottle Cap While Listening to *Perfect Strangers* Theme Song: 20

▶ Most Autographs Signed on a Stranger's Torso in 1 Minute: 34

RECORDS BEGGING TO BE SET

☐ Most Swizzle Sticks in a Cocktail

☐ Most Haircuts Given to Strangers in 1 Hour

Longest Straw Used to Drink a Coca-Cola

RECORD: 56.5 feet

NAME: Mel Sampson

LOCATION: New Minas, Nova Scotia, Canada

DATE: September 21, 2010

TOOLS: Long straw, can of Coke, Houdini-esque lung capacity

How do you drink from a can of Coke that's in another room? It's not a riddle or a trick question—it's the premise for this world record. After her 14.3-foot Longest Straw Used to Drink a Coca-Cola record was usurped by rival Eric Thiem, Mel Sampson reclaimed it in spectacular style, creating a 56.5-foot tube that snaked out of a Coke can, down a hallway, and into her mouth. This new mark more than doubled Thiem's straw length, apparently sending him into retirement. He has not been heard from since.

CRITERIA

☐ Must drink and spit out soda to prove straw is functional.

Tip for Beating This Record

Long straw-suckers risk light-headedness. Sampson advises aspiring extreme slurpers to "take a break while you're sucking the Coca-Cola through," or else you "suffer a full-fledged head rush."

RELATED RECORD

▶ Longest Stick Used to Roast a Marshmallow: 6 feet, 12 inches

RECORD BEGGING TO BE SET

☐ Longest Pair of Chopsticks Used to Pick Up a Grain of Rice

Most Types of Beverages Consumed in 30 Seconds

RECORD: 12

NAME: Marc Tatarsky

LOCATION: Suffern, New York

DATE: August 14, 2010

TOOLS: Variety of beverages

club soda   pink lemonade   chocolate milk

Gatorade   iced tea   milk

orange juice   Coke   water

To steal this world record from Nolan Ross, who had set the mark at ten drinks, grand-scale guzzler Marc Tatarsky lined up a parade of beverages that included club soda, seltzer, chocolate milk, Gatorade, Coke, apple juice, Fresca, pink lemonade, orange juice, milk, iced tea, and water. Thankfully, after he'd finished setting this extraordinarily impressive record, there was no line for the bathroom.

CRITERIA

☐ Must taste each drink independently.

☐ Minor variations of the same drink (e.g., skim milk and whole milk) do not count.

Yellow Jacket Comment

DAN: You know what they say: "Apple juice before Fresca and you won't feel grotesque-a."

RELATED RECORDS

▶ Largest Snapple Cap Collection: 5,016 caps

▶ Most Glasses Clinked in 1 Minute: 102

RECORDS BEGGING TO BE SET

☐ Most Types of Soda Served at a Bar Mitzvah

☐ Most Gatorade Coolers Dumped on a Coach's Head at Once

Most Items Read off a Chinese Take-Out Menu in 1 Minute

RECORD: 82 items

NAME: Maggie Doyle

LOCATION: London, England

DATE: May 26, 2010

TOOLS: Chinese restaurant menu, familiarity with Szechuan or Cantonese cuisine

London radio host Maggie Doyle proved she could whip up a meal for a ravenous crowd, reciting eighty-two items off the Turnham Green Chinese food take-out menu in just 1 minute. Listeners to her breakfast show were treated to an audacious listing of thirteen varieties of noodles, twenty-two types of chicken, fourteen styles of beef, and thirty-three other Chinese specialties. Maggie attributes her quick but eloquent pronunciation to her nationality. "Being Irish, I am known to speak fast anyway," she says. "As a broadcaster on national radio, I open my mouth and blurt lots of stuff out, fast."

CRITERIA

☐ May use menu from any Chinese food restaurant.

☐ Every item must be articulated clearly.

Yellow Jacket Comment

DAN: Turnham Green Chinese has an excellent-sounding menu. If anyone knows the owners, please tell them we'll stop by for a meal next time we're in London.

COREY: And Maggie—you're welcome to join.

Tip for Beating This Record

Preparation and attention to detail are critical. Maggie claims to have eaten Singapore Noodles every day for lunch as part of her training regimen. As someone who naturally speaks at a rapid clip, focus is all important for Maggie, who advises, "The secret to speed reading is simple: slow down."

RELATED RECORDS

▶ Most Fortune Cookies Eaten and Read Aloud in 1 Minute: 5

▶ Most Women Named Wendy to Eat at a Wendy's: 23

RECORDS BEGGING TO BE SET

☐ Longest Drumroll Using Chopsticks

☐ Largest Collection of Take-Out Menus

Most Pizza Slice Face Slaps in 15 Seconds

RECORD: 210

NAME: Mel Sampson

LOCATION: New Minas, Nova Scotia, Canada

DATE: September 20, 2010

TOOLS: 2 pizza slices, partner (ideally a drummer)

CRITERIA

- ☐ Any variety of pizza can be used.
- ☐ Slaps must be directed to face.
- ☐ May not use more than two slices of pizza.

RELATED RECORDS

- ▶ Most College Students in an Inflatable Pool Eating Pizza with Snow on the Ground: 15
- ▶ Most Times Slapped in Face in 1 Minute: 628

RECORD BEGGING TO BE SET

- ☐ Most Times Spinning a Pizza Dough in Air in 30 Seconds

Radio host Mel Sampson only endorses violence when the weapon of choice is pizza. Inspired after watching record creator Jon Friedman repeatedly cop a Meat Lovers' Special to his face on *Late Night with Jimmy Fallon*, Sampson asked her boyfriend, Angus Stuart, to pick up some slices and get slapping. "He's a drummer," she notes, "so I knew he would be able to move his hands quickly." The sauce and cheese flew everywhere, but Sampson soldiered on, braving both the heat of the pizza and the crust's vicious scratch. Record in hand, lessons were learned: "If I ever have to reclaim this record, I'll be using softer-crusted, room temperature pizza."

ATTENTION
BEWARE TROUBLESOME TOPPINGS!

O N I O N S

Although tasty, this topping is a risky choice—it could leave you in tears even if you clinch a world record victory.

ANCHOVIES

Beware this toothsome choice. The force of the slap may leave you with a fish-stache.

G A R L I C

Avoid this pungent topping, especially if you expect post-record hugs and kisses.

Fastest Time to Open a Can of Alphabet Soup and Spell "PANTYHOSE"

RECORD: 1 minute, 25.77 seconds

NAME: Colin Nissan

LOCATION: New York, New York

DATE: January 7, 2009

TOOLS: Can of alphabet soup, ability to spell "pantyhose"

When Colin Nissan set out to spell a word in alphabet soup noodles, "pantyhose" was not his first choice. "Chimpanzee" was the original target, but spelling this jungle primate proved challenging in trials. "I was flabbergasted to discover there were no C's in my entire can of soup," explains Nissan, "and not one could be found in the next three cans." Shocked but not deterred, he soldiered on. After a bout of furious soup sifting, the word "pantyhose" became immortalized in the RecordSetter canon, not to mention the name "Colin Nissan."

CRITERIA

☐ Must use 10.5-ounce can of alphabet soup with ring-pull lid.

☐ Must use hands to find and arrange letters.

RELATED RECORDS

▶ Fastest Time to Open Bag of Skittles and Sort Them by Color: 21.95 seconds

▶ Fastest Time to Spell "Ball" Using M&M'S: 15.28 seconds

RECORD BEGGING TO BE SET

☐ Fastest Time to Eat a Can of Alphabet Soup While Wearing Pantyhose

Greatest Height to Drop a Hot Dog into a Hot Dog Bun

RECORD: 59 feet, 4 inches

NAME: David Neevel

LOCATION: Portland, Oregon

DATE: April 1, 2010

TOOLS: Hot dog, hot dog bun, tall building, an outfit to which you are not emotionally attached

Hot dogs have long been a creative muse for advertising executive David Neevel. Among the weiner-related ideas Neevel has gifted upon the world are The Hot Dog Gun and The Hot Dog Online Web Ring, which features a working virtual clock with hot dog parts for hands. Topping both of those, however, is RecordSetter's first-ever hot dog–related record. Neevel bravely used a simple bun to catch a plummeting frankfurter dropped from five stories above. Sadly, he learned that when squeezed from great heights, ketchup and mustard plummet down in drops, not in a steady stream.

CRITERIA
- ☐ Must use standard-size hot dog and bun.
- ☐ Must successfully catch hot dog in bun.

Yellow Jacket Comment

DAN: This is a truly awesome feat. If David could perfect this preparation method and make it the centerpiece of a restaurant experience, I think riches wouldn't be far away.

RELATED RECORD
► Most Hot Dogs Stuffed in a T-Shirt in 30 Seconds: 185

RECORD BEGGING TO BE SET
☐ Most Times to Say "Hot Dog!" in 1 Minute While at a Dog Show

59 FEET, 4 INCHES
55 FEET
50 FEET
45 FEET
40 FEET
35 FEET
30 FEET
25 FEET
20 FEET
15 FEET
10 FEET
5 FEET
0 FEET

Fastest Time to Drink a 2-Ounce Bottle of Tabasco Sauce Through a Coffee Stirrer

RECORD: 9.97 seconds

NAME: Steve Shirley

LOCATION: New York, New York

DATE: December 10, 2009

TOOLS: Bottle of Tabasco, coffee stirrer, fondness for spice

CRITERIA

☐ May link two coffee stirrers to reach bottom of bottle.

☐ Bottle cap may be removed before timing begins.

RELATED RECORDS

▶ Fastest Time to Drink a Milkshake Through a Vuvuzela: 59.21 seconds

▶ Most Taco Bell Hot Sauce Packets Funneled at Once: 40

RECORD BEGGING TO BE SET

☐ Most Poblano Peppers Eaten in 30 Seconds

While setting a record at RecordSetter's much-ballyhooed tenth live event, Steve Shirley had two objectives. The first was to drink an entire bottle of Tabasco sauce through a coffee stirrer. The second was not to projectile vomit on the audience, packed on benches mere feet from his stage. Rest assured, no audience members had to schedule an emergency visit to the dry cleaner. Beyond achieving his objectives, this act of digestive strength would ultimately help land Shirley the job of a lifetime—and shockingly, not at a circus freak show. Soon after the event, the iron-throated wonder found himself in a job interview at Google. When asked for a "fun fact" about himself, he told his world record story. Two years later, he still works there.

HOW YOU FEELIN'?

HOT, HOT, HOT.

Fastest Time to Open a Bag of Skittles and Sort Them by Color

RECORD: 21.95 seconds

NAME: Caitie McMekin and Melanie Crampton

LOCATION: Washington, New Jersey

DATE: July 25, 2010

TOOLS: Bag of Skittles, flair for organization

The summer before they left home for college, Caitie McMekin and Melanie Crampton made a list of one hundred things they wanted to do before starting school. On the list were "send a message in a bottle," "visit Central Park," and "go laser tagging." Also included: "set a world record." So they did, choosing to organize the fractured rainbow found in a Skittles bag into separate colors. Cue a world record, a triumphant bucket list strike-through, and perhaps, even better, the perfect freshman icebreaker. "It was pretty cool to introduce ourselves at college as world record holders," said McMekin.

CRITERIA

- ☐ Bag must be unopened at start of record.
- ☐ Any flavor of Skittles in 2.17-ounce bag is permitted.

Yellow Jacket Comment

COREY: I pity the colorblind person who dreams of beating this record.

Tip for Beating This Record

Don't just grab the first bag of Skittles in the store—gently squeeze the packets to make sure you don't end up with conjoined candy pieces.

This record is excellent for band tour managers who've spent careers fulfilling the dressing room riders of diva performers.

RELATED RECORD

▶ Fastest Time to Sort a Deck of Cards by Suit and Number: 1 minute, 17.8 seconds

RECORD BEGGING TO BE SET

- ☐ Most Bags of Skittles Given to a Teacher on Last Day of Class

Longest Time to Dissolve Pep-O-Mint Lifesaver on Tongue

RECORD: 13 minutes, 4.75 seconds

NAME: Bill Geist

LOCATION: New York, New York

DATE: March 31, 2009

TOOLS: Pep-O-Mint Lifesaver, idle tongue

CRITERIA

☐ Sticking tongue out of mouth during record permitted.

☐ Talking while setting record permitted.

☐ Must use standard-size Pep-O-Mint Lifesaver.

RELATED RECORDS

▸ Most Polo Mints Fit Inside a Closed Mouth: 43

▸ Longest Time Balancing a Machete on Tongue: 1 minute, 19.6 seconds

RECORD BEGGING TO BE SET

☐ Longest Distance to Roll a Lifesaver

In the days before iPods, CBS News correspondent Bill Geist would keep his two children occupied during road trips by giving them each a Pep-O-Mint Lifesaver and challenging them to see who could keep it in their mouth the longest. The kids are now adults, but Geist's competitive Pep-O-Minting lives on in the form of this RecordSetter record. As part of a field report for *CBS News Sunday Morning*, Geist demonstrated remarkable self-restraint, keeping the candy on his tongue for over 13 minutes. Don't let his calm demeanor fool you—his low-key facade is just there to lure would-be competitors into a false sense of security so that they might be humiliated by defeat later on.

AFTER BREAKING THIS RECORD, YOU'LL HAVE FRESH BREATH FOR ALL THE MEET-AND-GREET (AND MAYBE KISSING) YOU'LL HAVE TO DO AS A NEW WORLD CHAMPION.

Longest Tootsie Roll Midgee

RECORD: 8 inches

NAME: Sean Patrick Bailey

LOCATION: Pittsburgh, Pennsylvania

DATE: August 29, 2009

TOOLS: Tootsie Roll Midgee

Tootsie Roll Midgees, the baby brother of the standard Tootsie Roll, are about 1.2 inches long. That is simply too short for hobbyist candy-roller Sean Patrick Bailey. The Pennsylvanian power-stretcher lengthened the piece of candy with his bare hands, expanding it to almost seven times its original length.

CRITERIA

☐ Tootsie Roll may not break at any point during the attempt.

Tip for Beating This Record

Run your hands together to warm them up before rolling the Midgee. The heat will soften the candy and allow it to stretch more easily. (Sticky hands are a small price to pay to become a world champion.)

RELATED RECORDS

▶ Most People to Blow Bubble Gum Bubbles at Once: 87

▶ Most Stomach Rolls in 30 Seconds: 47

RECORD BEGGING TO BE SET

☐ Most People Rolling Rolling Pins at Once

BEFORE

AFTER

I'D LOVE TO SEE BAILEY'S INVENTION MARKETED AS A "TOOTSIE ROLL STRETCHEE."

OR NOT.

Most Birthday Candles Fit on a Cupcake and Lit

RECORD: 235

NAME: David Ross

LOCATION: New York, New York

DATE: July 4, 2010

TOOLS: Cupcake, birthday candles, matches or lighter, fire extinguisher within reach

It helps to be celebrating someone who is 236 years old.

CRITERIA
☐ Must use standard-sized cupcake.
☐ All candles must be lit at once.

RELATED RECORDS
▶ Fastest Time to Blow out 107 Birthday Candles: 4.03 seconds
▶ Most Times Whistling "Happy Birthday" in 1 Minute: 18

RECORD BEGGING TO BE SET
☐ Most Words Iced on a Birthday Cake

What is the perfect way to end a thirty-third birthday celebrated with a world-record-themed party? "I was thinking of themes because I like theme parties. I saw RecordSetter and thought, 'Why don't I throw a theme party where everyone breaks a world record?'" says David Ross. And so he did, providing props and encouraging guests to set their own records. As a dramatic finale, he intended to break Mike and Jane Sweeney's existing record of thirty-seven candles fit on a cupcake. He and his friends crammed as many candles as possible onto the little cake, but after blowing out the resulting inferno and counting each one, they realized they had only used thirty-five. Come Fourth of July, Ross was fully prepared to annihilate the record, requesting a cupcake at his party with 235 candles. "America turned 234 years old, and then we added one for good luck," he says. Though the cake was a mini-fire hazard, Ross wasn't worried. One of his guests was a firefighter.

ATTENTION
ONLY YOU CAN PREVENT
CUPCAKE FIRES.

Most Doughnut Holes Stuffed in Doughnuts in 15 Seconds

RECORD: 9

NAME: Craig Mangan

LOCATION: San Francisco, California

DATE: March 23, 2009

TOOLS: Doughnuts, doughnut holes, emotional investment in reuniting estranged baked goods

Craig Mangan is a doughnut philosopher. Walking past a bakery one evening, he spied a stack of doughnuts piled on a tray. To his horror, their little holes were a mere two trays down from them. "Who knows how long the holes had been separated?" he wondered. Their orphan state was emotionally overwhelming, and Mangan knew immediately what had to be done. Partially to impress his then-girlfriend Jocelyn, but mostly to strike a victory for baked goods' rights, he leaped into action, reuniting doughnut and hole. Channeling his inner Bono, Mangan feels he made a political statement some may not be comfortable with. "I'm okay with that," he reveals, "and so was my girlfriend. In fact, she's now my wife."

CRITERIA
- [ ] May use store-bought or homemade doughnuts.
- [ ] Doughnuts and doughnut holes must be standard size.

RELATED RECORDS
- ▶ Most Women Eating Doughnuts and Drinking Coffee While Dressed in Black: 21
- ▶ Tallest Carrot Cake: 18 inches (21 layers)

RECORD BEGGING TO BE SET
- [ ] Most Doughnuts Tasted in 30 Seconds

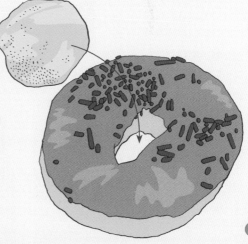

Most Homemade Pies Donated to a Mission

RECORD: 9

NAME: Amber Marlow Blatt

LOCATION: Brooklyn, New York

DATE: November 24, 2010

TOOLS: Pie ingredients, oven, transportation, Martha Stewart-esque baking ability

After learning of RecordSetter at the World's Largest Connect Four tournament in Brooklyn, Amber Marlow Blatt had an idea for her own record. "I decided to take my plans to bake for charity on Thanksgiving and evolve it into a world record," she says. On Thanksgiving eve 2009, Marlow Blatt stayed up late and made six pumpkin pies from scratch. The next day she delivered them to the Bowery Mission homeless shelter on Manhattan's Lower East Side. She raised the bar on Thanksgiving 2010, baking nine pies for Greenpoint Church in Brooklyn. "I'm really excited to have a tradition of making pies on Thanksgiving Eve now," she says. "Maybe I'll keep going, year after year, until I'm known as that crazy lady who makes one hundred pies and gives them away."

CRITERIA

☐ Must be fresh, homemade pies.

☐ Pies must be delivered on same day.

☐ Premade crust is acceptable, though not encouraged.

RELATED RECORDS

▶ Smallest Homemade Chocolate Chip Cookie: 0.39 inches

▶ Most Candy Bars Named in 30 Seconds While Being Tickled: 25

RECORDS BEGGING TO BE SET

☐ Most Items of Clothing Donated to a Clothing Shelter at Once

☐ Most Hours Volunteered at a Soup Kitchen in 1 Week

Most Fortune Cookies Eaten and Read Aloud in 1 Minute

RECORD: 5

NAME: Justin Gignac

LOCATION: New York, New York

DATE: July 14, 2009

TOOLS: Fortune cookies, glass of water, impeccable diction

Reflecting on his fortunes, Justin Gignac describes his mind-set going into this record attempt as overly optimistic. Other than buying a box of cookies, he didn't do anything special to prepare for the speed-eating endeavor. "I had never done any competitive eating before," he says, "so I didn't truly understand the skill that goes into it. I figured if I had a glass of water for dunking, I would be unstoppable."

Gignac's confidence, however, was short-lived. "As soon as I started eating that first cookie, I knew I was in trouble," he remembers. "The pieces were way too big and were cutting the roof of my mouth." Struggling to chew, swallow, and read out the fortunes coherently, Gignac made it through five cookies in his allotted minute. The funny part? He'd bought one hundred.

CRITERIA

☐ May dip cookies in water.

☐ Each fortune must be read aloud clearly.

Tip for Beating This Record

"I don't want to give away all of my secrets, but if you're gonna try to do a speed-eating record, you should do whatever you can to make it pain-free. Eating fast and talking with your mouth full is already hard enough," says Gignac.

RELATED RECORDS

▶ Tallest Oreo Tower: 48 cookies

▶ Fastest Time to Eat Fifteen Chocolate Mini Doughnuts: 2 minutes, 59.41 seconds

RECORDS BEGGING TO BE SET

☐ Most Palm Readers Visited in 1 Day

☐ Most Fortune Cookies Fit in a Pair of Pants While Wearing Them

"CHEW BEFORE YOU SWALLOW."
—CONFUCIOUS

Fastest Time to Lick a Candy Cane to a Sharp Point

RECORD: 2 minutes, 54.84 seconds

NAME: Emily Wilson

LOCATION: New York, New York

DATE: March 7, 2009

TOOLS: Candy cane, pregnancy (optional)

Food cravings during pregnancy are frequent fodder for sitcom scripts: pickles and ice cream? Zany! But Emily Wilson's cravings led to a serious accomplishment: a legitimate spot in the annals of human achievement. "I hungered for something I could taste without feeling full, sick, or spending a lot of money," she remembers. Candy canes ticked all the boxes. The greatest barrier was actually finding some. While the sticky treats flood stores at Christmastime, they were almost impossible to find when Wilson set the record in March. Fortunately, a discount dollar store provided the candy cane.

CRITERIA

☐ Must pop a balloon with the point to prove its sharpness.

☐ Must use a standard-size candy cane (no miniatures).

RELATED RECORDS

▸ Most Candy Bars Named in 30 Seconds While Being Tickled: 25

▸ Fastest Time to Vacuum 1 Pound of Sugar: 1 minute, 5.25 seconds

▸ Most Pencils Sharpened with Pencil Sharpener in 1 Minute: 5

RECORDS BEGGING TO BE SET

☐ Most Balloons Popped with a Pin in 30 Seconds

☐ Most Cherry Stems Knotted in Mouth in 2 Minutes

CAUTION: ALWAYS WALK WITH CANDY CANE SHARP POINTS FACING DOWN (UNLESS SOMEONE IS TRYING TO STEAL YOUR CHRISTMAS PRESENTS).

Most People Hit in Face with Pies in 30 Seconds While on Roller Skates

RECORD: 13

NAME: Drew Barrymore

LOCATION: New York, New York

DATE: October 2, 2009

TOOLS: Roller skates, cream pies, people whose idea of a good time includes being facially assaulted with baked goods

After directing and starring in the Roller Derby film, *Whip It,* Drew Barrymore suited up (skates, kneepads, and elbow pads) on *Late Night with Jimmy Fallon* to attempt this record. Audience members in ponchos lined the *Late Night* hallways, holding pies in front of them. Despite all the protective measures, technical difficulties soon kicked in. As Barrymore barreled down the hallway, pie cream flew everywhere, and the floor became a slippery mess. "A little harder than it looks!" she yelled out as she smashed thirteen faces before wiping out. "I'm not going down like that!" Barrymore said, before rising one last time to smash Fallon square in the kisser with her final pie. Though her 30 seconds were up and Dan and Corey were done counting, the satisfactory splat of pie against that famous face was worth it.

CRITERIA

☐ No more than one pie may be thrown at any person.

☐ Pies must be thrown one at a time.

RELATED RECORDS

▶ Most Show Tunes Sung While Roller Skating Down Carnaby Street: 7

▶ Most People Jumped Over While Wearing Roller Skates: 10

RECORD BEGGING TO BE SET

☐ Fastest Time to Sing "I've Got a Brand-New Pair of Roller Skates" While Wearing a Brand-New Pair of Roller Skates

Most Pies Thrown in One Face by a Clown in 1 Minute

RECORD: 41

NAME: Lawson Clarke

LOCATION: New York, New York

DATE: July 27, 2010

TOOLS: A pie-throwing partner dressed in clown attire, 41+ pie crusts, a lot of whipped cream, sense of humor

Lawson Clarke's circus-inspired record was not without its challenges—the first being the acquisition of appropriate wardrobe items. Having decided that he would wear stars-and-stripes, Speedos, and a pink shower cap while getting pies smushed into his face, Clarke had to sort out a costume for the clown who would be doing the throwing. "Tracking down a clown suit amid the sweltering heat of July in Manhattan was surprisingly hard," he said. Keeping a steady hand while applying clown makeup was also difficult. "Until you have to sit in a dressing room and attempt to paint another human being as a clown, knowing he'll soon be throwing pies in your face, you'll never understand what pressure really is." Lastly, a challenge discovered mid-performance was Clarke's biggest foe of all: breathing. "It never occurred to me that I'd have to hold my breath. When my airways were obstructed by a continuous wall of whipped cream, I was more than a little taken aback."

Though Clarke got drenched, victory reigned supreme.

CRITERIA

☐ Must use pies with 8-inch diameters.

☐ Only pies that hit the face are counted.

☐ Pies must be thrown one at a time.

RELATED RECORDS

▶ Most Pies Named in 10 Seconds While Hula-Hooping: 22

▶ Most Howls Elicited from a Dog Wearing a Clown Wig in 30 Seconds: 22

RECORD BEGGING TO BE SET

☐ Largest Collection of Sad Clown Paintings

IMPRESSIVE AS IT WAS, WITNESSING THIS RECORD LIVE REIGNITED MY CHILDHOOD FEAR OF CLOWNS. PLEASE CHANGE IMMEDIATELY.

Tallest Carrot Cake

RECORD: 18 inches (21 layers)

NAME: Cynthia Kueppers and Dave Bredesen

LOCATION: New York, New York

DATE: May 20, 2009

TOOLS: Carrot cake ingredients, clean hands

Some record-setting creations last forever. Some burn brightly but are gone in the blink of an eye. The 15 pounds of carrots and 6 pounds of cream cheese frosting Cynthia Kueppers and Dave Bredesen baked into eighteen layers of carrot cake fall into the latter category. The master bakers stacked the cake onstage in front of a live audience at the sixth RecordSetter LIVE! event in New York City. Just as the final layer was gingerly lowered into position, their ever-tilting creation gave way. Audience members scavenged over the messy but delicious debris, eventually consuming the entire thing.

CRITERIA

☐ Cake must be baked by record setters.

☐ Cake layers must be interspersed with layers of frosting.

☐ Each layer may be no more than 3 inches in height.

RELATED RECORD

► Tallest Pillow Tower Built Inside a Walmart: 28 pillows

RECORDS BEGGING TO BE SET

☐ Tallest Wedding Cake

☐ Tallest Tower of CDs by the Band "Cake"

Tallest Homemade Cookie Tower

RECORD: 28 cookies

NAME: Ashley Klinger

LOCATION: Cuyahoga Falls, Ohio

DATE: May 9, 2009

TOOLS: Cookie components, enough mental fortitude to resist eating your tools

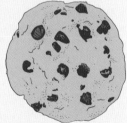

Ashley Klinger learned two lessons while attempting to build the tallest cookie tower the world has ever seen. First, the act demands a lot of willpower. Klinger had to bake "several extra batches" after discovering she would rather eat than build. But the extra time needed in the kitchen was put to good use. Klinger uncovered a hidden secret for perfect cookie building: "softer, chewier cookies that have baked for less time are easier to stack." Warm, fresh cookies, emanating a delectable scent, their chocolate chips melting ever so slightly into a delicious goo—compare that to plain old bricks and mortar and you can easily see why she ate her construction materials.

CRITERIA

☐ No adhesives or external support permitted.

Tip for Beating This Record

Don't use cookies that have rough, uneven textures or protrusions. Instead of oatmeal or chocolate chip, try sugar cookies or snickerdoodles. Their flatter surfaces stack more easily.

RELATED RECORDS

▸ Longest Cupcake Kebab: 33.5 inches
▸ Largest Cookie: 102 feet in diameter
▸ Most Deep-Fried Oreos Eaten in 1 Day: 5

RECORD BEGGING TO BE SET

☐ Most Chocolate Chips Held in Hand at Once

DID YOU KNOW?

THE OFFICIAL STATE COOKIE OF OHIO IS THE BUCKEYE COOKIE, WHICH HAS A TASTY PEANUT BUTTER VIBE.

Tallest Marshmallow Tower

RECORD: 5 marshmallows

NAME: Amber Franklin

LOCATION: Citrus Heights, California

DATE: September 16, 2009

TOOLS: Marshmallows, flat surface, restraint from eating marshmallows

CRITERIA

☐ No adhesives or external support permitted.

☐ Mini marshmallows not permitted.

RELATED RECORDS

▶ Most Times Setting a Marshmallow on Fire in 30 Seconds: 13

▶ Fastest Time to Eat Eight Tablespoons of Marshmallow Fluff While Standing on One Foot Dressed Like a Flamingo: 3 minutes, 25.07 seconds

RECORDS BEGGING TO BE SET

☐ Farthest Distance to Slingshot a Marshmallow

☐ Most Consecutive Nights Using Bag of Marshmallows as a Pillow

The third most rewarding marshmallow-related activity—after campfire toasting and playing Chubby Bunny—is stacking the gelatinous globs to form a squishy, pastel tower. Amber Franklin's five-story confectionery creation may look soft and nonthreatening, but attempts to beat her record have felled the mightiest of men. RecordSetter veteran Darryl Learie, who has logged eighty-one world records including Most One-Armed Push-Ups on a Raw Egg, expressed his frustration over a failed attempt: "What makes it hard is that the bottom marshmallows actually change shape under the weight, and thus the column becomes unstable." Stale marshmallows may be the key to success here—if you can avoid eating them for long enough.

ALTERNATING THE MARSHMALLOW COLORS ISN'T A REQUIREMENT, BUT IT DOES MAKE A PRETTIER TOWER.

Tallest S'more

RECORD: 10.2 inches

NAME: Clint Cantwell

LOCATION: New York, New York

DATE: August 12, 2009

TOOLS: Graham crackers, Hershey's chocolate, marshmallows, Marshmallow Fluff, cooking device (microwave, bonfire, or stovetop)

Clint Cantwell, a self-proclaimed BBQ hobbyist, faced some logistical complications when preparing for his record. Unable to set up a campfire at the indoor venue he was performing in, Cantwell went to Plan B and brought a blowtorch. Despite some major wobbles as the tower cleared the 10-inch mark, the blowtorch and a secret ingredient, Marshmallow Fluff, made the record his. "The fluff is like glue," he says. When added to your s'more, it helps make it steady.

CRITERIA

☐ S'more must stand alone without external support.

RELATED RECORD

▶ Longest Stick Used to Roast a Marshmallow: 78 inches

RECORDS BEGGING TO BE SET

☐ Most People Roasting Marshmallows Around a Fire at Once

☐ Most S'mores Made in 5 Minutes

Corey narrowly avoids blowtorched-fluff blowback.

RECORDSETTER LEGEND

Mel Sampson

Radio DJ, Woman of the People, Jill of All Trades

M el Sampson came of age in the vast wilderness of Happy Valley-Goose Bay in Labrador, Canada. Life in an isolated small town was idyllic but quiet—too quiet for Sampson, who from an early age was a bit of a motormouth. In addition to making fake radio shows for her mother, the verbal youngster liked to chat nonstop in the classroom. "My kindergarten report card alleged I talked too much!" she says.

At the first opportunity, young Sampson fled sleepy small-town living and headed to the relatively big city of New Minas, Nova Scotia. With a population of 4,300, it wasn't exactly a booming metropolis, but it was still thousands of miles and a world away from her birthplace. Sampson was studying for a career in mining at Acadia University until a single haircut changed her life. Making conversation while layering her locks, her hairstylist chatted about his girlfriend, who was enrolled in a radio and television program. Hearing about all the cool things she got to do gave Sampson a twinge of longing. By the end of her hair session, she had decided to apply for radio school.

After graduating and honing her DJ skills at a few smaller radio stations, Sampson scored her current dream job: drive-time presenter for a brand-new station, New Minas's K-Rock 89.3. Perks of the gig include being able to rock out to bands like ZZ Top, as well being able to focus on a community of listeners who aren't shy about calling in. Sampson's world record aspirations kicked in when she saw Jimmy Fallon run a RecordSetter segment on his show. "I thought, if [Cameron Diaz] can cuddle with bunnies, I can do that," she says. Her brain lit up with a bright idea: a full week of record-breaking attempts, live on radio.

The week began with an attempt to construct the Longest Straw Used to Drink a Coca-Cola. "It took ten of us to build the straw in our board room," she says. The 14.3-foot tool allowed her to take the record from Phil Covitz, but little did she know she would be constructing a straw four times that size within a year, to reclaim the record on-air after it had been wrested away. At the end of record-breaking week, Sampson held four new RecordSetter world records, including Farthest Distance to Throw a Vinyl Record, Tallest Shaving Cream Wig, and Most Radio Listeners to Call in and Say "Booya" in 1 Minute—a shared feat with her loyal listeners.

A year later, Sampson embarked on another record-breaking week, claiming Most Candy Bars Named in 30 Seconds While Being Tickled and Most Pizza Slice Face Slaps in 15 Seconds, which she shattered at first attempt. "I hope nobody breaks that record," she confides. "My face got scratched up by the pepperoni. I just don't want to do it again." The record she remains most proud of is the Most People to "Boo" Cancer at Once—a 346-person feat achieved at a Race for the Cure event to benefit breast cancer research.

Sampson's RecordSetter radio marathon is now an annual event, with the listeners defining the categories. "We run a record-breaking democracy here in New Minas," she says. Her fans are demanding: "They always ensure I reclaim any records that have tumbled during the year. If a kid in Terre Haute, Indiana, takes my record, it becomes a matter of regional pride."

Despite her successes, Sampson still experiences fear of failure during her attempts. "I do all my records live on the radio," she says. "Anything can go wrong. I have bombed badly. I have failed. To know I am creating bad radio makes the fear even worse." But the upside is irresistible. "To be introduced as 'The Record-Breaking Mel Sampson' everywhere I go makes everything worth it."

CHAPTER 3

Sports and Games

Olympic competitors strive for a form of excellence captured in the Latin motto *Citius, Altius, Fortius*—faster, higher, stronger. The achievements of RecordSetter athletes, however, go beyond such a narrow definition of sporting excellence. Speed, height, and strength are just the beginning; to capture the essence of the RecordSetter competitor, you'd have to add originality, imagination, and "Did that really just happen?"

From dry-land waterskiers to invisible hula-hoopers, each one of these record holders is a finely calibrated contender performing at the peak of her or his game.

Largest Handheld Yo-Yo

RECORD: 35 inches in diameter

NAME: Chris Allen

LOCATION: Chico, California

DATE: September 18, 2010

TOOLS: 2 dog pools, 2 pizza pans, axle, weight rings, duct tape, rope

Chris Allen has dedicated his life to promoting all things yo-yo. From the years he spent traveling with a barnstorming yo-yo team to the present day, where he proudly runs the world's largest yo-yo news site at yoyoskills.com. To set this record, Allen fashioned a massive yo-yo out of doggie bathing pools and pizza pans. He flung it from the top of a fire station training tower, bracing his body to ensure he did not get pulled to the ground and headplant into unforgiving concrete. As Allen explains, "A yo-yo always feels four times as heavy when dropped from a great height. Get the weight wrong and it will pull your arm out of your socket." Though his record-setting creation plummeted downward and came up again, Allen stayed put.

CRITERIA

- ☐ Must drop yo-yo by hand.
- ☐ Yo-yo string must be at least 32 feet in length.
- ☐ Yo-yo must roll to end of string and return at least ⅔ of the way back up.

Tip for Beating This Record

"The yo-yo must be heavy enough to generate sufficient drag to spin back up, but light enough so you don't follow it over the ledge." No matter what your toy weighs, you'll need to brace yourself for a jolt when it hits the end of the string.

RELATED RECORDS

- ▸ Most Consecutive Under the Leg Yo-Yo Loops: 148
- ▸ Most Times Saying "Yo" in 15 Seconds: 123

RECORD BEGGING TO BE SET

- ☐ Most "Around the Worlds" in 30 Seconds

Most Consecutive Yo-Yo Revolutions While Doing Splits

RECORD: 122

NAME: Malachy Quinn

LOCATION: New York, New York

DATE: August 9, 2008

TOOLS: Yo-yo, extreme lower-body flexibility

Yo, check this out! Equal parts flex master and yo-yo warrior, Malachy Quinn brought together two rarely connected skill sets to achieve this truly revolutionary (cough) feat. Quinn casually lowered himself into a split without so much as a wince, then spun his yo-yo in a vertical circle, lasso style, 122 consecutive times. Quinn captured the record at the International Yo-Yo Open, using an extremely deluxe YoYoFactory eight8eight yo-yo. (Retail value around $100, but you can't put a price on being a world record holder.)

CRITERIA

☐ Must get into splits position before attempt begins.

RELATED RECORDS

▶ Most Yo-Yo Gravity Pulls in 1 Minute: 9

▶ Most Consecutive Forward Yo-Yo Passes While Standing on One Foot: 4

RECORDS BEGGING TO BE SET

☐ Most Episodes of *Yo! MTV Raps* Watched While Doing Splits

☐ Most Consecutive Yo-Yo Revolutions While Eating a Banana Split

Most Trivial Pursuit Questions Answered Incorrectly in 1 Minute

RECORD: 18

NAME: Mick Cullen

LOCATION: Round Lake Heights, Illinois

DATE: August 13, 2010

TOOLS: Trivial Pursuit cards, partner to read cards, desire to underachieve

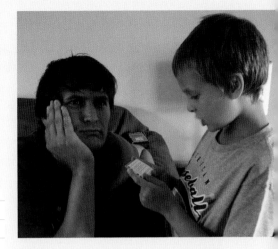

Mick Cullen is a Trivial Pursuit champion, but not in the way you might expect. Instead of studying up on general knowledge and pop culture, he harnessed the power of willful ignorance to swipe this record from originator Nathaniel Lawlor. "I had a game plan of coming up with a brief answer in my mind (flan, false, my face) without even listening to the question," says Mick. "It worked gangbusters." In response to the question "What Beatles song is reportedly the most recorded song of all time?" Cullen responded, "My face." His guess for the most popular crop in U.S. home vegetable gardens? "Lipstick." Sometimes, in the words of Albert Einstein, imagination is more important than knowledge.

CRITERIA

- ☐ Must hear each question in entirety before answering.
- ☐ Questions must be read off Trivial Pursuit cards.
- ☐ May not read questions before attempt.

RELATED RECORDS

- ▶ Most Trivial Pursuit '90s Edition "Viewing" Questions Answered Correctly in 1 Minute: 15
- ▶ Most Questions Tweeted to One Person in 24 Hours: 111

RECORD BEGGING TO BE SET

- ☐ Fastest Time to Insert All Wedges into Six Trivial Pursuit Game Pieces

BIRDS OF A FEATHER

Rubik's Cube Records

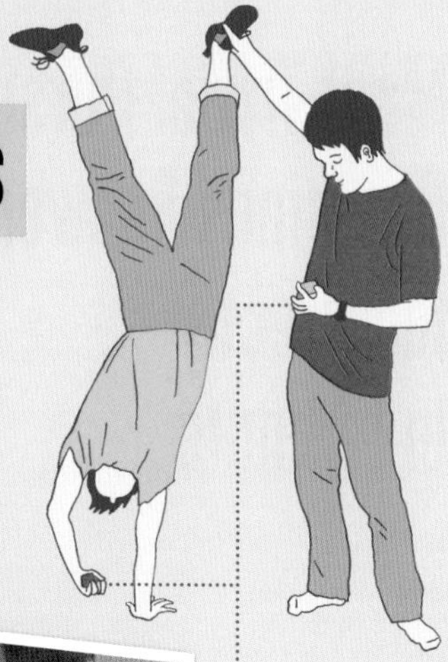

S aying you can solve a Rubik's Cube is shorthand for telling the world you are brainy, patient, and great entertainment at '80s-themed parties. So what does it mean if you can solve a Cube with your nose, while playing Guitar Hero, or with one hand, while upside down? Clearly you should go become some sort of space adventurer. (After beating one of these records, of course.)

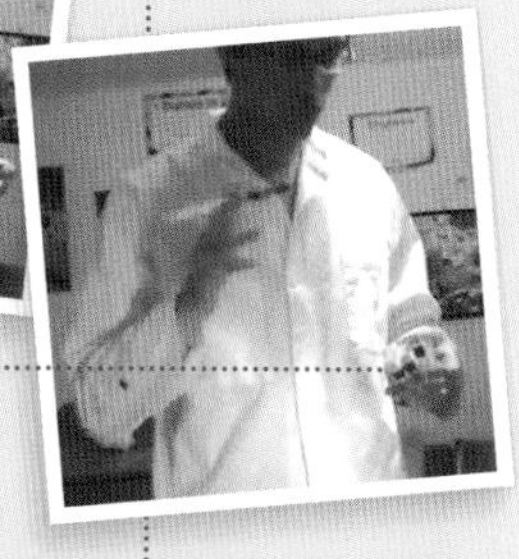

Tallest Tower of Solved Rubik's Cubes

RECORD: 10 Cubes

NAME: Sean Kladek

LOCATION: Bloomington, Minnesota

DATE: December 30, 2010

Fastest Time to Solve a Rubik's Cube While Spinning a Pen

RECORD: 57.48 seconds

NAME: Rémi Duboué-Dijon

LOCATION: Larressore, France

DATE: January 22, 2011

Fastest Time for Two People to Each Solve a Rubik's Cube with One Hand While One of Them Is Upside Down

RECORD: 56.27 seconds

NAME: Antton Curutchet and Rémi Duboué-Dijon

LOCATION: Bayonne, France

DATE: January 14, 2011

Fastest Time to Solve a Rubik's Cube While Riding a Unicycle

RECORD: 1 minute, 9.44 seconds

NAME: Caleb Stultz

LOCATION: Happy Valley, Oregon

DATE: March 21, 2009

TOOLS: Rubik's Cube, unicycle, family lineage that includes many clowns

CRITERIA

☐ Must use a standard 3 x 3 x 3 Rubik's Cube.

☐ Timing begins when record setter sits on unicycle.

☐ Timing stops when Cube has been solved.

RELATED RECORD

▶ Most Consecutive Football Receptions on a Unicycle: 70

RECORD BEGGING TO BE SET

☐ Most Rubik's Cubes Solved In 1 Hour

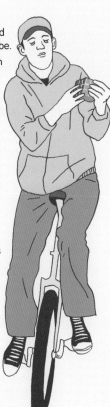

Caleb Stultz can answer a question that has puzzled sages since the 1980s: If one ever finds oneself riding a unicycle while attempting to solve a Rubik's Cube, which skill is more difficult? "It's undoubtedly unicycling," advises Stultz, who took just over a minute to solve the Cube while balancing on a single wheel. "When I'm solving the Rubik's Cube, I can't use my hands to help balance myself," he explains. The record attempt had a couple of unforeseen obstacles: The weather was so frigid Stultz's fingers locked up, making it a gargantuan task to turn the puzzle. Even worse, the record setter's pet cat, Hunter, caused chaos by crawling dangerously close to the unicycle wheel throughout the attempt. Record challengers, take note: Beware of oncoming traffic—animal or vehicular.

Fastest Time to Sort a Deck of Cards by Suit and Number

RECORD: 1 minute, 17.8 seconds

NAME: Daniel Downes

LOCATION: Wrexham, Wales, U.K.

DATE: October 21, 2010

TOOLS: Deck of cards, ability to quickly distinguish between spades and clubs

D aniel Downes barely needed to practice before embarking on his world record attempt. Playing cards are his equivalent of a security blanket to insulate him from life's challenges. "I find them very calming—kind of like my version of a cigarette," he says. A cigarette without the health hazards. "I've been handling cards for about 5 years and have never had any injuries," he proudly reports.

CRITERIA

☐ Deck must be shuffled at beginning.

☐ Aces can be high or low.

☐ Must clearly show cards in order after feat is complete.

Yellow Jacket Comment

COREY: I could see this category becoming huge in Vegas. Feels like an ideal hobby for card sharks and poker pros.

RELATED RECORDS

▶ Most Card Shuffles by Four People in 1 Minute: 10

▶ Most One-Handed Card Shuffles in 1 Minute: 9

RECORD BEGGING TO BE SET

☐ Fastest Time to Build a House of Cards Using 52 Cards

Largest Connect Four Tournament

RECORD: 97 participants

NAME: The Bell House

LOCATION: Brooklyn, New York

DATE: November 24, 2009

TOOLS: Connect Four sets, fiercely competitive people

Brooklyn tavern The Bell House took the classic kids' game of Connect Four a step further by organizing the world's largest Connect Four tournament. Ninety-seven participants emerged from all five boroughs of New York City, determined to take each other down via precision placement of black-and-red plastic discs. Visionary organizer Heather Dunsmoor admitted securing the world record was finger-aching work: "Opening the boxes and snapping together dozens of Connect Four boards was a real test of stamina."

Tips for Beating This Record

Is your Connect Four technique in need of an overhaul? Tournament victor Keith Sanders has hints for when you're playing at a bar:

1. Google "Connect Four strategy." I did before the tournament and discovered there are a slew of pages offering up game wisdom. A few are doctoral thesis level, but a simple rule of thumb is "when in doubt of what move to play, go in the middle row."

2. "Ignore the open bar. Many of my opponents took advantage of it and they fell by the wayside. Stay off the booze unless you are toasting victory."

CRITERIA

☐ All participants must play at least one full game.

☐ Tournament must ultimately have a champion.

RELATED RECORDS

► Most Connect Four Pieces Held in Hand at Once: 76

► Fastest Tandem Connect Four Checkerboard: 29.44 seconds

RECORDS BEGGING TO BE SET

☐ Largest Settlers of Catan Tournament

☐ Most Times for a Child to Ask a Babysitter to Play Candyland in 30 Seconds

Most Lunch Foods Named in 1 Minute While Jumping on a Pogo Stick

RECORD: 33

NAME: Gabriel Mauch

LOCATION: Chicago, Illinois

DATE: July 19, 2009

TOOLS: Pogo stick, encyclopedic knowledge of lunchtime eats

CRITERIA

☐ Falling off pogo stick isn't grounds for disqualification, but foods may not be named until jumping resumes.

Yellow Jacket Comment

DAN: I'd like to see someone set a record for most lunch foods *eaten* while jumping on a pogo stick.

RELATED RECORDS

▶ Most Burrito Ingredients Named in 1 Minute While Jumping on a Pogo Stick: 35

▶ Most Balls Juggled While Jumping No-Handed on a Pogo Stick: 5

RECORD BEGGING TO BE SET

☐ Longest Single Pogo Stick Jump

To become a world record holder, Gabriel Mauch fused two skills he had mastered a decade apart. After summers spent pogoing in his driveway, Mauch packed up his toys and went off to culinary school. But he soon found a way to combine the old hobby with his newly acquired food knowledge. In Mauch's words, "The two skills combined to make a perfect storm of awesome." His list of lunch foods included grilled cheese, chicken nuggets, a steak sandwich, cheese fries, and chicken strips. Kangaroo meat, however, did not make the cut.

Fastest Time to Run 50 Miles While Juggling

RECORD: 8 hours, 23 minutes, 52 seconds

NAME: Perry Romanowski

LOCATION: Chicago, Illinois

DATE: October 27, 2007

TOOLS: Running shoes, cardiovascular endurance, physical fitness, juggling balls, cheering supporters (optional, but makes a big difference)

Joggling is a sport that showcases the most handsome elements of long-distance running and juggling, allowing its leading practitioners two ways to excel. Take Chicago's Perry Romanowski. A research chemist who has been joggling for 18 years, Perry admits, "I may never be the fastest runner or the most dexterous juggler, but I might just be the fastest joggler." Clocking in at just under 8 hours, 30 minutes, Romanowski powered his way through 50 joggled miles. Romanowski's mantra aptly captures the RecordSetter philosophy: "You can't pick what you're good at in life, but once you uncover it, no matter how silly, go out and be great!"

CRITERIA

- ☐ Balls must be juggled every step.
- ☐ If any objects are dropped or touch the ground, record setter must stop to pick them up before carrying on.

Yellow Jacket Comment

DAN: This book has been aerodynamically engineered to function as a juggling device. Buy two more copies and a pair of running shoes, and you'll be on your way to toppling Romanowski.

RELATED RECORDS

- ▸ Longest Time Juggling Three Torches While Hopping on One Foot: 1 minute, 5.55 seconds
- ▸ Most Times Saying "Hey" Loudly in 30 Seconds While Jogging in a Store: 41
- ▸ Longest Time to Juggle Three Beanbag Chairs: 57.1 seconds

RECORD BEGGING TO BE SET

- ☐ Longest Time Juggling While Bouncing on a Trampoline

Longest Time Hula-Hooping While Standing on One Leg

RECORD: 12 minutes, 1.45 seconds

NAME: Ella Morton

LOCATION: New York, New York

DATE: July 1, 2010

TOOLS: Hula-hoop, balance, calves of steel

Ella Morton's monumental 12-minute "hula-hoop while standing on one leg" did not come without a struggle. Despite training monastically, her first attempt, live on stage at Joe's Pub—a legendary Manhattan venue—was a disaster. "The shame of failing in front of over 150 people crushed my spirits," she says. But Morton would not be deterred. After securing a slot for a repeat attempt at the following month's RecordSetter event, she used the next 30 days to focus without respite. "I would stand with one leg bent, flamingo-style, at pedestrian crossings, on the subway, or while riding elevators," she says. This regime paid off. In front of another packed house, Morton was triumphant: The record was hers at 3 minutes, 7 seconds.

The glory, however, proved to be fleeting. Three months later, Thomas Pringle of Orlando, Florida, shattered her record at 5 minutes, 10.12 seconds. Goaded, Morton did not waste time. She knew there was only one thing for her to do. "That very night I got home, fired up the webcam, and crushed Pringle's record with over 12 minutes of stubborn, calf-muscle-searing, one-legged hooping. I couldn't walk the next day, but it was totally worth it."

CRITERIA

☐ Timer stops when hula-hooping stops or foot touches ground.

Tip for Beating This Record

"When choosing a hoop, don't settle for a lightweight kids' version from a 99-cent store," says Morton. "Use a big, heavy hoop—the kind you see at circuses and Burning Man. They are easier to rotate, which allows you to conserve precious energy."

RELATED RECORDS

► Fastest Time to Sing "Itsy-Bitsy Spider" While Hula-Hooping: 8.62 seconds

► Most Consecutive Catches Juggling Four Hula-Hoops: 52

RECORDS BEGGING TO BE SET

☐ Most Hula-Hoops Rotated Around Body at Once

☐ Longest Time Hula-Hooping in a Principal's Office

Most People Invisible-Hula-Hooping at Once

RECORD: 27 people

NAME: iD Tech Camp

LOCATION: Villanova, Pennsylvania

DATE: July 26, 2010

TOOLS: Well-oiled hip joints, overactive imagination

CRITERIA
☐ Participants must rotate hips simultaneously for at least 10 seconds.

RELATED RECORDS
▸ Most Jump-Rope Jumps Using an Invisible Jump Rope in 30 Seconds: 106

▸ Most Times Coaxing a Dog Through a Hoop in 30 Seconds: 22

▸ Most People Standing in a Hula-Hoop with a Cat: 3

RECORD BEGGING TO BE SET
☐ Most People Doing the "Hokey Pokey" While Hula-Hooping

HEY COREY, WHERE ARE YOU?

I'M RIGHT HERE. I JUST PUT AN INVISIBLE JUMPSUIT ON OVER MY YELLOW JACKET. NOW I CAN INVISIBLY HULA-HOOP WITHOUT FEELING SELF-CONSCIOUS.

After a summer spent at a Pennsylvania computer camp, the participants in this group record were looking for a way to ease back into the nonvirtual world. They claim this idea was simply the first one that came to mind. A warning, perhaps, of what will occur if you spend too much time in dark rooms behind a computer monitor. But watching the erstwhile hula-hoopers execute this surreal feat in the open air of the plaza is to see some of America's finest young minds united by a common goal: gyrating their hips in pursuit of world record glory.

Fastest One-Quarter-Mile Roller Skate Sprint with Dog

RECORD: 1 minute, 55.06 seconds

NAME: Art Hoffman

LOCATION: Louisville, Kentucky

DATE: October 26, 2009

TOOLS: Dog with a sense of humor, collar, and lead, roller skates

Wear protective gear in case your pooch speeds up suddenly.

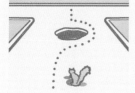

Avoid potholes and curious wildlife.

Choose a long-legged dog for maximum speed.

Art Hoffman and his dog, Chenji, completed a quarter-mile roller skate sprint in a breathtaking 1 minute, 55.06 seconds. Hoffman, who was sixty-two at the time the record was set, claims his feat to be a victory for an entire generation. "It feels great to represent the 'old farts.' More and more of us seniors are blessed with good health, and I am grateful for the chance to showcase our talents." Hoffman trained assiduously for this event, even lifting weights in his basement as Chenji worked a treadmill alongside him. Living proof that while you may not be able to teach an old dog new tricks, you can teach an old man a new trick involving a dog.

CRITERIA

☐ May not be pulled by dog.

☐ Must be attempted on a flat surface.

RELATED RECORDS

► Fastest Time to Write "The Quick Brown Fox Jumps over the Lazy Dog" Five Times: 1 minute, 6.41 seconds

► Most Balloon Dogs Created in 1 Minute: 6

RECORD BEGGING TO BE SET

☐ Most Times Coaxing a Dog to Roll Over in 1 Minute

ATTENTION
RECORD SHOULD ONLY BE ATTEMPTED IN AN EMPTY PARKING LOT OR STREET WITH EXTREMELY LIGHT TRAFFIC.

Longest Bicycle Ride with Feet on Handlebars

RECORD: 2 minutes, 40.45 seconds

NAME: Alexander Paul Kleinschmidt

LOCATION: McKinney, Texas

DATE: June 28, 2009

TOOLS: Bicycle, nostalgic fondness for childlike whimsy

NEW SPORT: BIKE YOGA!

Coasting around a suburban parking lot with his feet caressing the handlebars of his mountain bike is a trick Alexander Paul Kleinschmidt cultivated back as a 9-year-old loitering around the neighborhood with his buddies. "I've gained 12 years and 170 pounds since then, but the trick works all the same," he says. "It's just like riding a bike."

CRITERIA
☐ Must keep feet on handlebars for duration of attempt.

Tip for Beating This Record
Kleinschmidt breaks the record down into manageable pieces, offering three rules to follow:

1. **Speed:** Make sure the bike is going at least 5 miles per hour before you raise your feet. The wheels need to have enough angular momentum to keep the bicycle straight while you swing your legs up.

2. **Direction:** Be sure that the bike is going in a straight line while you pull your legs up. Once your feet are on the handlebars, keep them toward the center, away from the hand grips.

3. **Momentum:** Make sure you begin on a gentle slope with enough room away from cars so you can move freely and safely. Always have a spotter on hand.

RELATED RECORD
▶ Largest Bicycle Pile on Top of a Person: 9

RECORD BEGGING TO BE SET
☐ Fastest Time to Replace a Bicycle Tire

Most Consecutive Stationary 360 Underflips on a Skateboard While Blindfolded

RECORD: 27

NAME: Brett Moser

LOCATION: Dallas, Texas

DATE: June 26, 2010

TOOLS: Skateboard, blindfold, insomnia (optional)

Imagine standing on a skateboard. Now imagine popping the board off the ground and making it do a 360-degree revolution beneath you while you are airborne. Now imagine doing it twenty-seven times in a row, in front of a baying crowd of thousands, while blindfolded. That's what professional skateboarder Brett Moser did in setting this extreme sport world record. Perhaps most impressively of all, his attempt came while sleep deprived. Moser had been traveling and slept for just 2 of the previous 72 hours.

CRITERIA

☐ Must remain on skateboard for entire attempt.

Yellow Jacket Comment

DAN: I could totally crush this record by, like, 10,000 underflips, but, um, I don't own a blindfold.

RELATED RECORDS

▶ Longest Fingerboard Rail Grind: 110 Inches
▶ Most Consecutive Pop Shuvits: 37

RECORDS BEGGING TO BE SET

☐ Most Consecutive McTwists on a Halfpipe
☐ Most Ollies in 1 Minute

Perform in front of children for maximum impact.

Youngest Person to Ride a Motorcycle in the "Globe of Death"

RECORD: 4 years, 6 months, and 28 days old

NAME: Maximus Garcia

LOCATION: Altoona, Iowa

DATE: August 16, 2006

TOOLS: Death globe, motorcycle, unconventional childhood

CRITERIA

☐ Must wear helmet while on motorcycle.

☐ To be attempted by trained professionals only.

RELATED RECORDS

▶ Longest Office-Chair Train Pulled by a Motorcycle: 19 chairs

▶ Fastest Time to Make a Sphere out of a Pile of Buckyballs: 1 minute, 45.2 seconds

▶ Youngest Person to Fly Around the World: 6 months

RECORD BEGGING TO BE SET

☐ Youngest Person to Say "Motorcycle"

ALERT!
DO NOT ATTEMPT
THIS RECORD UNLESS YOUR
LAST NAME IS KNIEVEL

At exactly 4 years, 6 months, and 28 days old, an age when most kids are still unable to ride a bike, Maximus Garcia mounted a motorcycle and survived a trip around "The Globe of Death." On the off chance you are not familiar with the Globe, it is a circular metal cage, 13 feet in diameter, that was first ridden by Garcia's parents, circus performers Leo and Getti Garcia. "Watching Mom and Dad perform in the circus made me want to do the same," says Garcia, who followed in their footsteps as a seventh-generation circus daredevil. Maximus, now 9, has been a fixture in the family act ever since. His parents are proud to report that he has yet to take a fall of any kind.

Longest Dryland Waterski Session

RECORD: 17.34 seconds

NAME: Steve Sandholm

LOCATION: Payne Lake, Michigan

DATE: July 11, 2009

TOOLS: Water skis, rope, tractor, grassy field, trust in driver

Steve Sandholm is so obsessed with waterskiing that a lack of water will not deter him from strapping on the planks and taking a ride. That's right: he skied on land, being pulled by a tractor instead of a boat. Despite initial fears, Sandholm's arms managed to stay in their sockets.

CRITERIA

- ☐ Timing stops when person falls or lets go of rope.
- ☐ Must remain in forward progress for duration of feat.
- ☐ Must be pulled by a motor vehicle.

Yellow Jacket Comment

COREY: Steve should take this sport to Ethiopia, the most populous landlocked country in the world. It has over 73 million people, but no ocean access.

RELATED RECORDS

- ▶ Largest Group of People to Waterski Barefoot Behind the Same Boat: 4
- ▶ Most People to Inflate Lifejackets at Once: 1,154 people

RECORD BEGGING TO BE SET

- ☐ Longest Barefoot Waterskiing Session

Fastest Time to Complete a Game of Labyrinth

RECORD: 21.69 seconds

NAME: Alon Mass

LOCATION: Ithaca, New York

DATE: October 17, 2007

TOOLS: Labyrinth, neurosurgeon-like hands

CRITERIA

☐ Must be on a flat surface.

☐ Must use regulation-sized game.

Yellow Jacket Comment

DAN: As if finishing a game of Labyrinth in less than 22 seconds wasn't impressive enough, Alon also holds the record for Fastest Time to Complete a Backwards Game of Labyrinth (22.53 seconds) and Fastest Time to Complete a Two-Ball Game of Labyrinth (2 minutes, 37.8 seconds).

Tip for Beating This Record

"For speed," says Mass, "clean the dust off the board before your run. For a two-ball run, however, dust is good—you want the balls to stick to have more control over the movement of the balls relative to one another."

RELATED RECORDS

▶ Fastest Time to Type Every European Country Name: 1 minute, 3.74 seconds

▶ Fastest Game of 52-Pickup: 5.47 seconds

RECORD BEGGING TO BE SET

☐ Fastest Time to Complete a Game of Labyrinth Using Feet

L abyrinth is an epic game of skill in which a player steers a steel marble through a carved maze, artfully avoiding numerous holes through which the ball could plunge. It's an addictive challenge that is thrilling and frustrating in equal measure. Medical student Alon Mass, who began playing when he was 10 years old, is now a master of the medium, turning the rudimentary controls with tantric focus. As Mass has discovered, the secret lies in a minimalist approach. "The ball moves faster than you think, so you should control it with less hand movement than you would naturally anticipate."

Most Foam Fingers Worn at Once

RECORD: 29

NAME: Marty Farris

LOCATION: Norman, Oklahoma

DATE: June 27, 2009

TOOLS: Foam fingers, love of sports bordering on fanatacism

When it comes to sporting paraphernalia, nothing says "We're number one!" like a giant foam index finger pointing skyward. A fixture at basketball matches, gridiron games, and the more serious little league tournaments, foam fingers show team spirit and encourage athletes to strive for their best. In setting this record, Marty Farris demonstrated his pride in the University of Oklahoma's (OU) sporting teams by dressing himself in twenty-nine of the college's trademark red hands. OU is the alma mater of five Heisman Trophy winners. With Farris's support, that number may soon become six.

Tip for Beating This Record

Tie enough fingers together to create a belt around your waist, then cram as many fingers as possible under it. Do the same around your head, then stack fingers on top of each other before having an assistant place them on your hands. All that foam against your body will probably make you hot and itchy, so work quickly!

CRITERIA

☐ May not use any adhesive to attach fingers to body.

☐ May use an assistant to put fingers on.

RELATED RECORDS

▶ Most Finger Snaps in 1 Minute: 172

▶ Most Mouse Clicks in 30 Seconds: 832

RECORDS BEGGING TO BE SET

☐ Most Fans Hugged by a Sports Mascot in 1 Minute

☐ Most Balloons Attached to Body with Static Electricity

THIS MAN LOOKS LIKE A VERY CONFUSING DIRECTIONAL SIGNPOST.

Longest Time to Spin a Basketball on a Pinky While Wearing a 5-Foot Fake Mustache

RECORD: 11.14 seconds

NAME: Matt Parker

LOCATION: Cheraw, South Carolina

DATE: July 1, 2009

TOOLS: Basketball, 5-foot-wide false mustache, adhesion method strong enough to keep it on your face, muscular pinkie

CRITERIA

☐ Mustache must remain in place for entire record.

☐ Must spin ball yourself.

Tip for Beating This Record

It's all about putting in the hours, says Parker. "To learn how to spin the ball on your finger, you have to practice, practice, practice," he says. "Hold the ball with your fingers, twist your wrist, and aim your pointer finger to the sky, beneath the center of the ball. Do this a few hundred times—trimming your fingernails before you start—and you'll soon be spinning with ease."

RELATED RECORDS

▶ Longest Time Spinning Pillow on Finger: 5 minutes, 29.93 seconds

▶ Most Clothespins Attached to a Mustache: 10

Matt Parker is a rare mix of attributes—a former high school basketball standout turned ninth-grade science teacher who lives to make short films in his spare time. This world record stems from one of his scripts, which, in Parker's words, was "a time travel/alternate universe short film in which a friend and I build a time machine out of a Krispy Kreme delivery van." Due to a time travel malfunction, the characters were to encounter evil versions of themselves who sported giant mustaches. The film never progressed beyond preproduction, but one of the 5-foot-long prop mustaches lingered in Parker's bedroom. When it came to record setting, Parker knew he wanted to play to his basketball strengths. The mustache is a surreal twist to ward off all challengers. Keeping it glued on was Parker's greatest achievement.

Most Times Circling Basketball Around Waist in 30 Seconds

RECORD: 56

NAME: Aaron Jones

LOCATION: Omaha, Nebraska

DATE: August 6, 2009

TOOLS: Basketball, nimble torso

Many elite record setters train for hours in the leadup to their big moment, but for Aaron Jones, prolonged practice of this feat was physically impossible. His shoulders were so sore after just two 30-second rehearsals that he would have to wait 24 hours between training sessions. (Speed-spinning a basketball around your body is very rough on the rotator cuffs.) Eventually, Jones crushed previous record holder Chris Rivers's mark of forty-nine circulations, whipping the basketball around his torso at an unprecedented rate of almost two circulations per second.

CRITERIA

☐ Circulations must be consecutive—no dropping of the ball permitted.

Tip for Beating This Record

Jones says that staying in peak physical condition is essential. "Stay limber," he suggests. "Relax your shoulders and keep your fingers as spread out as possible. The hardest part is the soreness in your shoulders afterward, so make sure to stretch well and warm-down." A svelte body is also an advantage: "Don't get a fat gut like me. It makes the orbit of the ball that much bigger."

RELATED RECORDS

► Most Times Bouncing Basketball Against Forehead in 1 Minute: 143

► Most Images of Charles Barkley on a Cookie: 1

RECORDS BEGGING TO BE SET

☐ Most Karate Belts Tied Around Waist in 1 Minute

☐ Fastest Time to Run Ten Circles Around an NBA Player

Most Consecutive "Behind the Back" Golf Ball Bounces Using a Golf Club

RECORD: 406

NAME: Dylan Porter

LOCATION: Coffeyville, Kansas

DATE: March 30, 2010

TOOLS: Golf ball, golf club, supple wrist

Golfing attire isn't required, but it does help set the mood.

CRITERIA

☐ May only use one hand to hold club.

RELATED RECORDS

▶ Most Consecutive Golf Ball Bounces Using Alternating Sides of a Skillet: 138

▶ Most Golf Balls Hit off Human Tee in 1 Minute: 23

▶ Most Radio Listeners to Call in and Say "Tiger Woods" in 1 Minute: 15

RECORDS BEGGING TO BE SET

☐ Most Golf Balls Balanced on a Forearm

☐ Most Piñatas Hit with a Golf Club in 30 Seconds

Golf can be an agonizing sport—a momentary lapse in concentration may mean kissing your chances of victory good-bye and consigning yourself to shot after embarrassing shot in the sand trap. The combatants in this category are all too familiar with the fine-tuned focus required to come out on top. Dylan Porter, who swept in and stole the record from Jon Birdsong after a four-attempt tussle between Birdsong and Michael Lavery, tells what's involved in bouncing a ball on a golf club—behind the back—an astonishing 406 times. "Just concentrating for that long is kinda tough," he says. "Your arm starts to hurt, your contact lenses start to dry up, people are talking to you—it all throws off your concentration."

Most Golf Balls Hit in 10 Seconds

RECORD: 20

NAME: Ryan Deaton

LOCATION: Chelsea, Michigan

DATE: August 24, 2009

TOOLS: Golf balls, golf club, brawny shoulders

CRITERIA
- ☐ Must hit each ball individually.
- ☐ Must drive, not putt, each ball.

RELATED RECORDS
- ► Longest Time to Balance Twelve Golf Clubs on Chin: 1 minute, 58.36 seconds
- ► Fastest Time to Tear a Miniature Golf Scorecard into Four Pieces: 2.9 seconds
- ► Most Consecutive Annual Golf Bets: 30

RECORDS BEGGING TO BE SET
- ☐ Fastest Time to Complete 18 Holes of Mini-Golf
- ☐ Most Golf Balls Retrieved from the Bottom of a Pool in 2 Minutes

Ten seconds is long enough for your average rookie golfer to take a few swings at a golf ball, miss, get embarrassed, kick at the grass in frustration, and finally hit the ball a few meager yards down the fairway. Not so for Ryan Deaton. Proving his prowess with a putter, the young gun from Michigan lined up twenty balls and thwacked them individually in 10 seconds. And we're not talking little taps here. Deaton sent each ball sailing into the air with a force that would blow the spikes off Phil Mickelson's golf shoes. Perhaps this speedy approach to the green is the shake-up that the staid world of golfing needs. A 30-minute version of the PGA Tour could be just around the corner.

REMEMBER THIS MAN'S NAME. HE'S TIGER WOODS MEETS ARNOLD PALMER WITH A SIDE DISH OF CHI-CHI RODRIGUEZ.

IN FACT, CALL HIM CHI-CHI PALMER-WOODS.

Most Vertical Feet Skied Uphill in 24 Hours

RECORD: 34,546 feet

NAME: Dina Mishev

LOCATION: Glenwood Springs, Colorado

DATE: February 8, 2009

TOOLS: Skis, climbing skins, Chapstick

DINA'S RECORD DWARFS MOUNT EVEREST!

34,546 FEET

29,029 FEET

Mount Everest   Sunlight Mountain

Dina Mishev broke through the pain barrier to scale Colorado's Sunlight Mountain Resort, a one and one-half mile ski run spanning 1,500 feet of vertical gain. Such a feat is hard to achieve once. Mishev performed it twenty-three times over the course of many hours. She reels off the list of the indignities she suffered: "Peeing on myself about 13 hours into it, my lips getting so dry they cracked every time I tried to talk, the skin behind my fingernails peeling back." Despite all this, her most difficult challenge was of the musical variety. "Every time I ended a lap, they'd play Survivor's 'Eye of the Tiger.' You try listening to that twenty-three times without losing your focus and just rocking out."

CRITERIA

☐ Uphill and downhill trails must be rated Intermediate (blue), according to the North American grading scheme.

☐ May take rest breaks as needed.

RELATED RECORDS

▶ Farthest Distance to Throw a Snowball: 223 feet

▶ Highest Tap Dance: 17,598 feet

RECORD BEGGING TO BE SET

☐ Most Ski-Lift Tickets Attached to a Ski Jacket

Longest Yoga Pose Held on a Moving Escalator

RECORD: 20.19 seconds

NAME: Raymond Kwong

LOCATION: Bloomington, Minnesota

DATE: June 25, 2009

TOOLS: Escalator, flexibility, well-functioning chakras

CRITERIA

☐ Must remain on escalator continuously, without stops.

☐ May use any yoga pose.

RELATED RECORDS

▸ Longest Time to Hold Yoga Tree Pose While Being Tickled with a Feather: 6 minutes, 57.50 seconds

▸ Longest Crow Pose: 1 minute, 8.18 seconds

RECORD BEGGING TO BE SET

☐ Most People Dancing "The Chicken Dance" on an Escalator

With his arms stretched out like eagle's wings and knees splayed across three slowly moving steps, Raymond Kwong performed his finest Warrior II pose while descending an escalator on the second floor at the legendary Mall of America. Anyone wishing to defeat Kwong had better start practicing their poses and looking for a longer escalator. At the risk of instigating, might we suggest a trip to the Wheaton Metro station in Washington, DC. With an escalator running for a dizzying 230 feet, it takes 3 minutes to journey from top to bottom—the perfect amount of time to travel to Nirvana and back, not to mention crush a certain somebody's record.

STANDING POSES ARE BEST. HEADSTANDS NOT RECOMMENDED.

RECORDSETTER LEGEND

Mick Cullen

Father, Professor, World Record Machine

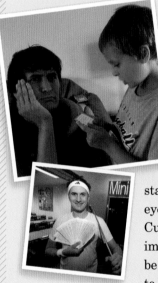

Mick Cullen's childhood was wrapped up in the *Guinness Book of Records*. Multiple record setters like champion beer drinker Peter Dowdeswell and the bicycle-eating "Monsieur Mangetout" loomed as large in his imagination as sports heroes did with his friends. Whereas other boys longed to become firemen, baseball players, or astronauts, young Mick clung to a different dream. "I wondered if someday I might be able to juggle while jogging, hop up stairs on a pogo stick, grow my thumbnail 12 inches long, or gather enough people to play softball for 75 hours straight."

His life changed when he bought tickets for the Pitchfork Music Festival in Chicago and stumbled across the RecordSetter stage. No sooner had the Yellow Jackets caught his eye when the carpe diem spirit that infuses Mick Cullen kicked in. "I wanted to do something truly impressive and not just set a silly record that could be easily broken by someone else." The Fastest Time to Name a Country Starting with Every Letter of the Alphabet Except "X" immediately sprung to mind. Cullen, a self-confessed "list obsessive," can reel off inventories of countries, elements, presidents, and Rock & Roll Hall of Fame inductees upon command. He began his verbal world tour, starting in Angola, stopping over in places like Ethiopia, Japan, Peru, and Suriname on the way to his final destination of Zambia. Twenty-five countries in a brazen 12.65 seconds: a record had been set. A childhood fantasy had been fulfilled.

Mick Cullen University Lecturer had become Mick the Record Setter. But he was only just getting started.

Over the past couple of years, Mick Cullen has become a record-setting junkie. He is the proud owner of twenty-eight records, including Most Erasers Balanced on Head at Once (an epic nineteen). The apex was a sixteen-record haul in a single day, a feat of stamina broadcast live on the radio show that he hosts on Round Lake, Illinois, station WRLR 98.3 FM. Such a triumph might exhaust mere mortals (both mentally and physically), but Cullen remains modest. "The most difficult part was combing through the RecordSetter website database to find the records I was going to break, then hauling all the necessary stuff into the radio station." Watching him effortlessly stuff nineteen CDs back in their cases while casually sitting on the floor is to witness a record-setting Zen Master in the zone.

Mick is not the only Cullen to be RecordSetter obsessed. Both of his sons, Xavier and Elijah, hold records—for Xavier it was Most Table Football Goals Scored in 1 Minute by a 7-Year-Old, while Elijah owns Most Toy Cars Fit Inside a Pair of Pants Worn by a 6-Year-Old. Mick admits he will be surprised if one of them has not surpassed his monumental achievement by the time they become teenagers. Unthreatened, he takes the long view: "I'll still be an eccentric college professor who has an underground rock radio show and likes to set world records." Fondly remembering the many childhood nights he spent under the covers immersed in world records, he proudly declares, "If you'd told me when I was 12 that's what I would be when I grew up, I would have taken it."

CHAPTER 4

Science and Technology

Records are set and broken at a feverish pace across all the RecordSetter categories, but none tumble so frequently as the feats in the technology section. Have a peek through the virtual pages and you'll see people getting poked, tweeted, and texted, often while solving a Rubik's Cube or reciting the first one hundred digits of Pi. This is the place where the smarties whose talents brought them mockery in the schoolyard get to step up, show off their skills, and receive the adulation they so richly deserve.

Fastest Time for Two People to Alternately Text the Words "O Romeo, Romeo, Wherefore Art Thou Romeo?" Back and Forth to One Another

RECORD: 1 minute, 7.13 seconds

NAME: Tim Sandlund and Tallie Nicola

LOCATION: Lima, Ohio

DATE: November 22, 2009

TOOLS: Two cell phones, good network coverage, appreciation of Shakespeare

CRITERIA

☐ Each participant must text one word per message.

☐ Must wait to receive text before typing new text.

☐ Spelling errors not permitted.

Yellow Jacket Comment

COREY: I wonder if this is what the future of theater looks like.

DAN: Probably, though instead of humans texting, it'll be robots exchanging Thought Messages.

RELATED RECORD

▶ Fastest Time to Recite "To Be, or Not to Be" Soliloquy While Shaking a Shake Weight: 3 minutes, 28.1 seconds

RECORDS BEGGING TO BE SET

☐ Fastest Time for a Theater Troupe to Act Out *Macbeth*

☐ Fastest Time to Text "Shakespeare Belongs on a Stage, Not in a Text Message!"

Armed with cell phones and dazzling finger dexterity, two friends texted each other Shakespeare's legendary line, one word per message, in lightning fashion. "We wanted to update *Romeo and Juliet* once again," record co-creator Tim Sandlund explains. "Conversations that would once have been held between the ground and a balcony would occur via text." As the Bard wrote in *Richard II,* "When words are scarce they are seldom spent in vain."

Most Text Messages Sent and Received in a Single Month

RECORD: 200,052

NAME: Andrew Acklin

LOCATION: North Olmsted, Ohio

DATE: September 1, 2010

TOOLS: Cell phone with easy-to-use keypad, callused thumbs

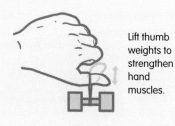

Lift thumb weights to strengthen hand muscles.

Rotate and stretch.

"Thumbs hurt. Omg!"

Using acronyms (OMG, LOL) reduces text time.

A s 19-year-old Andrew Acklin discovered when setting this record, being the world's best demands a thick skin. He texted so often in one month that his thumbs developed blisters. "I worked nearly twenty-four/ seven," he says, "except when I fell asleep in the act of texting." Pity the five hundred contacts in Acklin's cell phone who were the target of his messaging mania. When asked if he has any advice for aspiring challengers, his reply was pragmatic: "Get an unlimited texting plan."

CRITERIA

- ☐ Incoming and outgoing texts counted.
- ☐ One month defined as "length of a monthly billing period."
- ☐ Maximum of two phones may be used, both by the same person.

RELATED RECORD

- ▶ Most Text Messages Sent to One Person in 5 Minutes: 230

RECORDS BEGGING TO BE SET

- ☐ Most Cell Phones Run over by a Steamroller at Once
- ☐ Most Text Messages Sent to a Grandmother in 1 Minute

Fastest Time to Say First One Hundred Digits of Pi with Eyes Closed

RECORD: 13.10 seconds

NAME: Matt Parker

LOCATION: Cheraw, South Carolina

DATE: April 18, 2010

TOOLS: Mathematical mind, prodigious memory

CRITERIA

☐ Must be recited from memory.

☐ Must keep eyes shut for duration of attempt.

Yellow Jacket Comment

DAN: Whenever I close my eyes and think of Pi, I get too hungry to recite the numbers.

RELATED RECORD

▶ Fastest Time to Name All U.S. Presidents with Eyes Closed: 12.40 seconds

RECORD BEGGING TO BE SET

☐ Fastest Time to Eat 3.141592653589793238 4626433832795028841971693993751058 2097494459230781640628620899862803 48253421170679 Pieces of Pie

Matt Parker loves a dare. His girlfriend challenged him to learn the first fifty digits of Pi. Parker accepted the bet and raised it by fifty, aiming to test his numerical limits. His methodology was rigorous: "I memorized ten digits at a time. When I could get to where I could say the first ten digits without thinking about it, I would start learning the next ten and then practice all twenty together." Once Parker had attained his goal, it was time to move to phase two: speed recitation. For this, Parker, a teacher, enlisted the aid of his students in the ninth-grade science class. "I would practice in front of them," he says, "and they would time me." Perhaps not an official part of the South Carolina curriculum, but an exciting learning experience nonetheless.

Fastest Time to Say First One Hundred Digits of Pi While Twisting a Rubik's Cube and Balancing Fifteen Books on Head

RECORD: 30.12 seconds

NAME: Lauren Moore

LOCATION: Austin, Texas

DATE: November 9, 2009

TOOLS: Rubik's Cube, 15 books, exceptional aptitude for multitasking

Tip for Beating This Record

"Don't be afraid to move around when you are balancing," says Moore, adding that your focus should be "more about staying under the books than keeping the books over you."

If the world needed a triathlon for geeks, Lauren Moore may just have invented it. First she memorized a healthy chunk of Pi. Then she threw a Rubik's Cube into the mix. The cherry on the world record cake was the cranial book balancing, which she mastered with a little help from above. "I started by balancing bibles on my head," she says. "At first I couldn't even balance one, but by practicing every day I learned to center my balance under the books." Threaten her record and she will not be intimidated. "I've toyed with the idea of adding a fourth talent, maybe walking on a treadmill while doing it all."

CRITERIA

☐ Timing starts when first digit of Pi is recited.

☐ Timing stops when one-hundredth digit of Pi is recited.

☐ May not use hands to balance books.

RELATED RECORDS

▶ Tallest Book Tower Held in Hand While Balancing on a Rola Bola: 53 books

▶ Fastest Time to Eat an Apple with Deck of UNO Cards Balanced on Head: 1 minute, 7 seconds

RECORD BEGGING TO BE SET

☐ Tallest Tower of Rubik's Cubes Held in Hand

Most Mouse Clicks in 30 Seconds

RECORD: 832

NAME: Tom Andre Seppola

LOCATION: Honningsvåg, Norway

DATE: October 13, 2010

TOOLS: Mouse, eager trigger finger, supple forearms

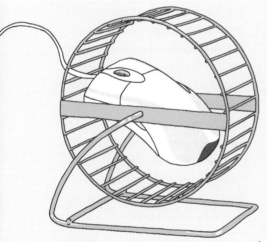

CRITERIA

☐ Must provide video evidence.

☐ Use of auto-clickers not permitted.

☐ Record must be set using a click counter such as TheClickGame.com.

RELATED RECORDS

▶ Most Pen Clicks in 1 Minute: 350

▶ Longest Time Spinning Pillow on Finger: 1 hour, 8 minutes, 58 seconds

RECORDS BEGGING TO BE SET

☐ Most Mouse Traps Set in 30 Seconds

☐ Largest Collection of Mickey Mouse Hats

Old gamers never die—they just become world record holders. Norway's Tom Andre Seppola has his old school Nintendo (NES) to thank for this record. He and his brother became addicted to Gold Medal Challenge '92, a vintage classic that challenged gamers to compete in the decathlon without leaving the comfort of their couch. Glory came to those who mastered the art of pressing the joystick buttons super fast. The Seppola brothers were overcome by a competitive zeal and dedicated the next 12 months to pushing the controller from every angle. "Victory came down to millimeters and milliseconds," says Seppola, "so I developed a method in which I only need to flex my arm muscle for the clicking motion to kick in." To win this record, Seppola just let his muscle memory do the work. After 30 seconds of intense clicking, it felt like his arm "was on fire," he says, "but in a good way."

Most Medical Symptoms Googled in 30 Seconds

RECORD: 7

NAME: Biana Fay

LOCATION: Brooklyn, New York

DATE: July 28, 2010

TOOLS: Internet browsing device, tendency to self-diagnose

CRITERIA

- ☐ Must use Google to perform the searches.
- ☐ May not use Google's auto-complete feature.
- ☐ Search queries must refer to a medical symptom or complaint.

RELATED RECORDS

- ▶ Most Human Bones Named in 30 Seconds: 27
- ▶ Fastest Time to Type English Alphabet Using One Hand: 2.89 seconds

RECORDS BEGGING TO BE SET

- ☐ Fastest Time to Google Every Member of N'SYNC
- ☐ Fastest Time to Look Up the Word "Google" in a Dictionary

Biana Fay is a self-described "low-grade hypochondriac" who delights in Googling minor bodily sensations after scaring herself into believing they might be the first signs of a serious illness. Years of practice freaking out about suspected malignant moles that turned out to be dropped flakes of chocolate gave her the confidence to set this record. Perfectly healthy as she prepared to type in a litany of symptoms from "funny poops" to "itchy ankles," she took a minute to reassure all viewers with words of calm: "If any of these things are happening to you, just know I have been through them and I am totally fine."

Google

Most Browser Windows Opened in 1 Minute

RECORD: 49

NAME: Brett Walling

LOCATION: Washington, DC

DATE: March 21, 2010

TOOLS: Computer, Internet connection, browser, speedy shortcut-key skills

CRITERIA

☐ Browser must be closed at start of attempt.

☐ Timing starts as soon as browser opens.

☐ Each browser window must open fully before next window may be opened.

Tip for Beating This Record

Internet speed is a factor, because each page must load before you can open the next window. Use the fastest connection you can find. Truly devoted record setters should hop on the next plane to South Korea, home of the world's speediest Internet.

RELATED RECORDS

▶ Farthest Distance to Throw a Laptop Computer: 80.3 feet

▶ Most Mozilla Firefox Tabs Open at Once: 101

RECORDS BEGGING TO BE SET

☐ Most Car Windows Opened in 1 Minute

☐ Most Window Panes Karate-Chopped in Half at Once

Who among us has the patience anymore to stick to just one webpage at a time when browsing the 'net? Certainly not Brett Walling. In homage to the short attention spans now cursing the tech-enhanced youth, Walling opened as many Safari windows as his bandwidth would allow in 60 seconds.

As the originator of this record, Walling faces a challenge common to all early adopters—being thwarted by new releases in the tech world. "At that time [of the record] there was no Google Chrome, so the jury is out on which browser might be best at this point," he says. Though a Safari man from way back, Walling invites challengers to try their luck using any browser they wish.

Most Images of "Uncle Jesse" Viewed on a Web Browser at Once

RECORD: 92

NAME: Dan Wiese

LOCATION: Pasadena, California

DATE: July 6, 2009

TOOLS: Photos of John Stamos, browser, early '90s childhood

It's easy to understand the appeal of Uncle Jesse of *Full House*, as portrayed by John Stamos. He's a nice guy with a dash of mischief, which is why so many members of Gen Y took him into their hearts as a surrogate uncle back in the early '90s.

For Stephen Jayne, the originator of this record, Jessemania lasted way beyond the era of Hammer Pants and scrunchies. Jayne located sixteen images of Stamos as Jesse online and viewed them simultaneously, laying down a challenge for *Full House* fans worldwide.

The RecordSetter community has chosen to honor submissions that incorporate shots of the actor outside of his Uncle Jesse character, including that of the current record holder, Dan Wiese. Should any *Full House* fans feel that this decision is a travesty, please signal your discontent by using Stephanie Tanner's catchphrase: "How rude!"

CRITERIA

☐ All images of John Stamos permitted, including those in which he's not depicting Uncle Jesse.

RELATED RECORD

▶ Fastest Time to Name All *Star Trek* TV Episodes in Broadcast Order: 1 minute, 38.90 seconds

RECORD BEGGING TO BE SET

☐ Most Consecutive Tweets to @JohnStamos

Most Instant Message Chats Open While on a Flight

RECORD: 12

NAME: Stephen Goldblatt

LOCATION: Somewhere over Albuquerque, New Mexico

DATE: March 26, 2009

TOOLS: Boarding pass for airplane with in-flight WiFi, at least 12 friends who use instant messaging

Airplanes used to be an oasis for the frazzled. Despite their cramped conditions, they offered a refuge from the relentless onslaught of telecommunications. Judging by the vast number of giddy IMs, tweets, and e-mails that in-flight Internet connectivity now inspires, those days are long over. Stephen Goldblatt demonstrated this when he used in-flight WiFi to open twelve simultaneous IM chats while 36,215 feet above Albuquerque, New Mexico. "I feel my record really demonstrated how fully connected with the earth you can still be, even while hovering in a metal aircraft over the nation," he says. Goldblatt is particularly proud of the way he kept calm throughout: "I was desperate not to create too much of a spectacle and tip off the air marshall," he remembers. "I would have hated to have been arrested for holding up my Flip camera on a flight."

CRITERIA

☐ May use any instant messaging application.

☐ Plane must be at cruising altitude during attempt.

RELATED RECORDS

► Longest Time Juggling Three Bags of JetBlue Cashews While Standing on One Foot: 1 minute, 21.65 seconds

► Most Paper Airplanes Constructed and Flown in 1 Minute: 7

RECORDS BEGGING TO BE SET

☐ Most In-Flight Duty-Free Items Purchased on a Flight

☐ Most People High-Fived on an Airplane

Most Plays of a Single Song in iTunes

RECORD: 65,363

NAME: Yoyo Markus

LOCATION: Plainview, New York

DATE: July 10, 2010

TOOLS: iTunes, infinitely tolerable song

Music is powerful, and not just in a make-you-dance kind of way. Playing the same song for hours on end can wear down the human spirit and lead to psychological breakdowns, especially if the song in question is a novelty tune or children's TV theme.

With this in mind, we recommend you choose your music carefully if you want to top this feat. The current record holder, Yoyo Markus, picked Panic! at the Disco's "Nine in the Afternoon"—a song whose title alone requires several minutes of thinking time. Markus listened to the tune for just under 3,577 hours, or 149 days. No ill effects have been observed, but it could be a while before the post-traumatic stress kicks in.

CRITERIA
☐ Plays do not need to be consecutive.

RELATED RECORD
▶ Most Metallica Songs Named in 30 Seconds: 25

RECORDS BEGGING TO BE SET
☐ Largest iTunes Music Library
☐ Most Consecutive Panic! at the Disco Songs Played at a Party

WARNING. THE FOLLOWING SONGS ARE NOT RECOMMENDED FOR THIS RECORD:

ALVIN AND THE CHIPMUNKS — "CHIPMUNK SONG"

AQUA — "BARBIE GIRL"

BAHA MEN — "WHO LET THE DOGS OUT"

CRAZY FROG — "AXEL F"

DANA LYONS — "COWS WITH GUNS"

BARNES & BARNES — "FISH HEADS"

RICK ASTLEY — "NEVER GONNA GIVE YOU UP"

Shortest Podcast

RECORD: 35.94 seconds

NAME: Mark Hartwell

LOCATION: Fort Myers, Florida

DATE: January 20, 2010

TOOLS: Microphone, online distribution method, conciseness

CRITERIA

☐ Podcast must have a defined topic or theme.

RELATED RECORDS

▶ Most Male Nipples Exposed on a Video Podcast: 19

▶ Shortest Late-Night Talk Show: 2 minutes, 52.4 seconds

RECORDS BEGGING TO BE SET

☐ Shortest TV Weather Report

☐ Shortest Blog Post

Podcasts offer anyone, anywhere the opportunity to talk to the world about anything. As the format is free, most 'casters have a tendency to fall in love with the sound of their own voice, droning on long past the point of interest. Not Mark Hartwell. The man behind the *World's Shortest Podcast* series crafts programs about technology that clock in at an average of 1 minute, 37 seconds. His longest stretched to 3 minutes, 32 seconds, an extravagance that continues to embarrass Hartwell. "I let my listeners down and cost them a couple of extra minutes from their already crowded schedules," he laments, standing firmly behind his belief that "brevity is the soul of wit."

Longest Active E-mail Address

RECORD: 411 characters

NAME: Zachary Reidell

LOCATION: Minneapolis, Minnesota

DATE: August 13, 2010

TOOLS: E-mail service offering "wildcard" addresses, robust keyboard

hi-this-is-the-longest-email-in-the-world-and-is-much-superior-to-contact-admin-hello-webmaster-info-services-peter-crazy-but-oh-so-ubber-cool-english-alphabet-loverer-abcdefghijklmnopqrstuvwxyz-at-please-try-to-send-me-an-email-if-you-can-possibly-begin-to-remember-this-coz.this-is-the-longest-email-address-known-to-man-but-to-be-honest.this-is-such-a-stupidly-long-sub-domain-it-could-go-on-forever@zcht.org

I n our world of oversaturation, overstimulation, and too much information, record setter Zachary Reidell found a technologically simple way to keep the Internet at arm's length: create a ridiculously long e-mail address that no one would remember. His clocked in at 411 characters and read: "hi-this-is-the-longest-email-in-the-world-and-is-much-superior-to-contact-admin-hello-webmaster-info-services-peter-crazy-but-oh-so-ubber-cool-english-alphabet-loverer-abcdefghijklmnopqrstuvwxyz-at-please-try-to-send-me-an-email-if-you-can-possibly-begin-to-remember-this-coz.this-is-the-longest-email-address-known-to-man-but-to-be-honest.this-is-such-a-stupidly-long-sub-domain-it-could-go-on-forever@zcht.org. Why not e-mail him to say congratulations?

CRITERIA
☐ Must be an active e-mail address.

RELATED RECORDS
► Most Unread E-mails in an Inbox: 326,548
► Longest Time to Balance a Computer Keyboard on Nose: 1 minute, 39.82 seconds

RECORD BEGGING TO BE SET
☐ Longest E-mail

HIS EMAIL ADDRESS IS SO LONG THAT HE HAD TO HIRE AN ASSISTANT JUST TO CARRY HIS BUSINESS CARDS.

ZING!

Shortest Active E-mail Address

RECORD: 7 characters

NAME: Benjamin Bailey

LOCATION: Kent, England, U.K.

DATE: January 31, 2011

E-MAIL: b@hh.la

TOOLS: Top-level domain expertise, teeny-tiny domain name

Back in the early days of the Internet, it was relatively easy to nab a short, memorable e-mail address. If you were an early convert to the whole Web thing, you could register a Hotmail account with your name as the username. As soon as your friends wrapped their heads around what e-mail actually was, they could easily remember the address for when they sent that momentous first digital letter. Well, times have changed. If you want to sign up for a popular e-mail service these days, be prepared to be known as recordsetter7201921943@gmail.com.

Annoyed by how messy this looks, some people are going rogue, registering their own domains, and creating teeny-tiny addresses. One such daredevil is Benjamin Bailey, who pounced on the Laotian .la domain and created b@hh.la. "Bahhla": simple to remember, fun to say, and an example of one man's triumph over technology.

Tip for Beating This Record

While a few one-letter domains are owned by large corporations—Exhibit A: Google's g.cn—the rest of us non-kazillionaires must settle for at least two characters before the dot. Beating Bailey's record requires a bold move: You'll need to establish your own country. Once you've done that, ask ICANN (the Internet Corporation for Assigned Names and Numbers) for a top-level domain and set up an e-mail address with a one-letter username. (Or pay a savvy 11-year-old with superior tech skills to do it for you.)

CRITERIA

☐ Must be an active e-mail address.

RELATED RECORDS

▸ Most Inside Jokes in an E-mail: 7

▸ Most E-mails Sent from a Gmail Account: 17,883

RECORDS BEGGING TO BE SET

☐ Shortest Mailing Address

☐ Largest Keyboard Collection

Most Spam E-mails in an Inbox

RECORD: 96,899

NAME: Tamlyn Rhodes

LOCATION: London, England

DATE: January 19, 2011

TOOLS: An e-mail address known to every possible online marketer and cyber swindler

CRITERIA

☐ Mail must be unsolicited, mass-sent spam.

RELATED RECORDS

▸ Fastest Time to Log into Gmail: 1.3 seconds

▸ Longest Skype Video Chat: 194 hours, 1 minute, 19 seconds

RECORDS BEGGING TO BE SET

☐ Most Nigerian Princes in an Elevator

☐ Largest Collection of Infomercial Products

TO: RecordSetter World Record Book Reader

SUBJECT: Thhis_offfer_willl_chaange__your__whhole__llife!

MESSAGE: CONGRATULATIONS! I am here to contacting you about business venture which I intend to establish in your country. You have the chance to buy cheap best-quality Xanax with bonus $1 million in lottery winnings and free iPhone with overnight shipping. To get this plus a free credit report that will MELT FAT AWAY and enroll in an online training program to become a Certified Nursing Assistant, send account details for release of funds and goods to Tamlyn Rhodes. He holds the RecordSetter world record for most spam in an inbox and therefore welcomes electronic correspondence from strangers.

IF YOU SEND ME A PERSONAL CHECK FOR $10,000, I CAN'T PROMISE I'LL TURN YOUR MONEY INTO BILLIONS, BUT I CAN PROMISE I'LL SEND A THANK-YOU NOTE.

Longest Time Using Only Social Media to Communicate

RECORD: 100 days

NAME: Clark Harris

LOCATION: Atlanta, Georgia

DATE: May 1, 2010

TOOLS: Ability to adhere to vow of silence, online omnipresence

CRITERIA

- ☐ May only use Twitter, Facebook, LinkedIn, YouTube, Flickr, and Google Chat.
- ☐ E-mail, talking, writing, text messaging, and use of sign language are not allowed.
- ☐ Simple yes/no questions may be answered with nod or head shake.

RELATED RECORD

- ▶ Longest Time to Remain Silent While Dressed as a Knight: 2 minutes, 40.12 seconds

RECORDS BEGGING TO BE SET

- ☐ Longest Instant Messaging Conversation
- ☐ Longest Time Remaining Silent at a Drive-Through Window

"Listening is the most overlooked tool for understanding." Those were the first words uttered by Clark Harris after his 100-day silence. "What better challenge for a guy who never shuts up than to not talk for a month?" said newly dubbed Silent Clark, who forced himself to communicate using only social media.

Harris was raising money for the Leukemia and Lymphoma Society in honor of his mother, Ruth Harris, whose 10-year battle with cancer had recently ended. Three weeks into the experiment, Harris's wife, Genna, suffered a health crisis. "I just wanted to hear his soothing voice to ease the panicking," she later wrote on the project's blog. "But of course, this was not an option. Instead I sent him a direct message on Twitter from my phone to tell him the details." His apologetic textual response brought home the value of verbal communication for conveying comfort and affection.

During the wrap party, Harris celebrated raising over $18,000 and named the most difficult part of the past 100 days: "Not being able to tell my wife 'I love you' for 3 months."

Most Facebook Friends on Facebook Chat at Once

RECORD: 507

NAME: Brad Silver

LOCATION: Sydney, Australia

DATE: May 1, 2011

TOOLS: Facebook account, chatty friends

Facebook has not only taken over the world—it's taken over world records. An endless flow of Facebook-related record attempts have been submitted to RecordSetter.com, and the addictive nature of Mark Zuckerberg's site ensures that individual titles are set and beaten faster than you can untag yourself in an unflattering party photo.

One Facebook fiend who has triumphed over a host of challengers is Brad Silver, whose Most Facebook Friends on Facebook Chat at Once record currently stands at 507. That's more than the population of Lime Springs, Iowa. (Shout-out to all the readers in Lime Springs!) Frequently challenged categories include the Most Pending Friend Requests; Most Comments on a Post, Video, or Photo; and Most Unread Notifications. You may have already broken one of these records. Quick, go look!

CRITERIA

☐ Must provide video evidence.

☐ Only friends who are online may be counted.

RELATED RECORDS

▶ Longest Comment Thread on a Facebook Photo: 50,779

▶ Most Facebook Photo Albums: 800

Most Facebook Pokes

RECORD: 601

NAME: Tyler Shuman

LOCATION: Philadelphia, Pennsylvania

DATE: October 9, 2010

TOOLS: Lots of Facebook friends who enjoy virtually prodding one another

CRITERIA

☐ Must provide video evidence.

☐ No time limit for pokes to accumulate.

RELATED RECORDS

▶ Largest Hokey Pokey Circle: 90 people

▶ Longest Comment Thread on a Facebook Status Update: 34,286 comments

RECORDS BEGGING TO BE SET

☐ Most Times Poking Someone in 30 Seconds

☐ Largest Group to Delete Facebook Accounts at Once

Facebook's creators discovered a simple way to dominate the world, but their success has not come without its share of failures. Take the Poke function. We defy you to find anyone who can actually explain its purpose, other than to fuel Poke Wars. Tyler Shuman breathed new meaning into the feature by using it to set a world record. "To me, poking on Facebook is like going to school. It can be very awkward and you hate half the people that do it with you," the popular vlogger explained, "but the joy is it gives you interaction with the click of a button." Shuman achieved his feat by unleashing a poking frenzy on his 2,500 Facebook friends but is realistic that the end may soon be nigh for his favorite device. "If one day Facebook decides to scrap the feature, I hope they award me the last poke before they do."

THAT'S THE WRONG KIND OF POKE, DAN.

Most Tweets Sent to MC Hammer in 1 Minute Using Cell Phone

RECORD: 6

NAME: Brian Ries

LOCATION: New York, New York

DATE: March 25, 2009

TOOLS: Cell phone, Twitter account, 1 minute of Hammer Time

CRITERIA
- ☐ Must be sent from a mobile device.

RELATED RECORDS
- ▶ Most Indie Hip-Hop Albums Released in 1 Year: 17
- ▶ Most Potato References in a Rap Song: 30

RECORD BEGGING TO BE SET
- ☐ Longest Parachute Jump While Wearing Parachute Pants and Listening to Coldplay's "Parachutes"

Twitter has become a de facto way for celebrities to communicate directly with the outside world. But way back in early 2009, the medium was still new and A-listers were scarce. One of the greatest luminaries in the Twittersphere was a legendary hip-hop visionary, known on Twitter as @MCHammer. Journalist Brian Ries took full advantage of the revolutionary social medium by repeatedly tweeting to his musical hero live. "Hello I miss Ure music luv ur jams" began his race against the clock. "My fingers were shaking, and my tweets were total jibberish," remembers Ries, unsure whether the nerves were caused by the nature of the challenge or the knowledge he was addressing an American musical giant. @moneyries shot out six tweets to Hammer and the superstar responded by retweeting him—the ultimate compliment in Twitterland. Ries is confident his record will never be broken, taunting all comers by quoting his inspiration: "U can't touch this."

Longest Word in a Tweet

1035874232565154

RECORD: 137 characters

NAME: Michael Wilson

LOCATION: Adelaide, Australia

DATE: June 18, 2010

TOOLS: Twitter account, knowledge of fancy mathematical words

Once numbers get really big, most of us resort to made-up words like "kazillion," "bajillion," or "rackalackadillion." Not Michael Wilson. The self-described skeptic and scientist secured his record for the longest word in a tweet by writing the term for 1035874232565154. That would be "Undecmillianmilliamilliam-millianongenoctoquinquaginmil-liamillianmilliaseptenseptuagi nmilliamilliamquingenunvigin milliaseptingenseptendecillion," naturally.

HEY, COREY, REMEMBER HOW YOU BORROWED TEN DOLLARS FOR LUNCH LAST WEEK? I FORGOT TO TELL YOU THAT I CHARGE INTEREST AT THE RATE OF UNDECMILLIANMILLIAMILLIAMMIL-LIANONGENOCTOQUINQUAGINMILLIA-MILLIANMILLIASEPTENSEPTUAGIN-MILLIAMILLIAMQUINGENUNVIGIN-MILLIASEPTINGENSEPTENDECILLION PERCENT PER YEAR.

SO WHAT DO I OWE YOU?

WELL, FOR STARTERS, YOU'RE GONNA NEED TO SELL YOUR CAR.

CRITERIA
☐ Word must be found in a dictionary.
☐ Any language permissible.
☐ Synthesized mathematical terms permitted.

RELATED RECORD
▶ Most Chemical Symbols from the Periodic Table of Elements in a Single Tweet: 77

RECORDS BEGGING TO BE SET
☐ Largest Abacus
☐ Fastest Time to Recite the Ten Times Tables

Most Consecutive Tweets Using Every Letter of the Alphabet

RECORD: 5

NAME: Tim Atkinson

LOCATION: Brooklyn, New York

DATE: October 18, 2010

TOOLS: Twitter account, full knowledge of the English alphabet

If tweeting is an art—packing everything you have to say into 140 characters or less—then consider Tim Atkinson the equivalent of Salvador Dali. He is a visionary in the medium, able to stretch its boundaries to new dimensions, crafting tweets that encompass hidden universes. Or in his case, entire alphabets. A master of the details, he then double-checks his creations using a computer application he programmed with his own hand. The only downside about such tweeting creativity? The alphabetical tweets did not get many retweets. As Atkinson explains, "I was close to or at the 140-character limit with each of the tweets, which is sort of a no-no when it comes to getting retweeted."

CRITERIA

☐ Each tweet must be unique and grammatically correct.

☐ Each tweet must use real words and/or known slang.

☐ Each tweet must be written in sentence form.

RELATED RECORDS

▶ Longest Twitter Hashtag: 417 characters (Really!)

▶ Fastest Time to Write the English Alphabet: 9.46 seconds

RECORDS BEGGING TO BE SET

☐ Most Consecutive Tweets Without Using Vowels

☐ Fastest Time to Spray Paint the English Alphabet on a Wall

Most Memes Mentioned in One Tweet

RECORD: 43

NAME: Matt Kempster

LOCATION: Sacramento, California

DATE: September 28, 2009

TOOLS: Twitter account, intimate familiarity with Internet culture

An Internet meme, according to online culture experts Mike Rugnetta, Stephen Bruckert, and Patrick Davison of MemeFactory, is "a piece of media with a set of identifiable characteristics which are changed or 'mutated' by users, then passed on." Think Lolcats, Chuck Norris facts, and viral videos like the *Dramatic Chipmunk*. Memes are spread like knock-knock jokes, with the format getting passed along, laughed at, and altered slightly to keep it fresh.

For this record, Matt Kempster, a big fan of memes, used his flair for abbreviation to stuff forty-three web trends into just one 140-character tweet.

CRITERIA

☐ Must reference established memes, as recognized by the Know Your Meme database (http://www.knowyourmeme.com).

RELATED RECORD

▶ Most People to Wear Internet Meme Costumes at a Party: 52

RECORD BEGGING TO BE SET

☐ Most People in Cat Costumes Playing a Keyboard

FULL LIST OF MEMES REFERENCED:

ASIAN PRINCE
TAY ZONDAY
ATE MY BALLS
RAINBOW STALIN
☐_☐ FACE
OVER 9,000
RAGEGUY
FLEA MARKET MONTGOMERY
SHOOP DA WOOP
ADVICE DOG
COURAGE WOLF
GENTLEMEN
RICH RAVEN
NUMA NUMA
YO DOG
SPAGHETTICAT
BEL-AIR
HA! HA! GUY
FLYING SPAGHETTI MONSTER
DANCING BABY
SOULJA BOY
CHUCK NORRIS
CREEPY KATARA
DIVIDE BY 0
HYPNOTOAD
CANDLEJACK
NO U
56 STARS
EXPLODING VAN
CHARLIE BIT ME
SNEEZING BABY PANDA
MUSTARD MAN
MAMA LUIGI
KEYBOARD CAT
HAPPYCAT
LONGCAT
PANCAKE BUNNY
SHINY PIDGEY
CEILING CAT
BUBB RUBB
SPARTA REMIX
RICKROLL
TOM GREEN

139

Most Toppings on a Scanned Sandwich

RECORD: 31

NAME: Jon Chonko

LOCATION: New York, New York

DATE: July 14, 2009

TOOLS: Bread, skewers, as many sandwich toppings you can cram neatly onto the surface of a flatbed scanner

Think of the most interesting thing you've done with a flatbed scanner. Chances are it can't compete with Jon Chonko's hobby of choice: scanning sandwiches and posting the high-res, hunger-inducing images on his website, www. scanwiches.com.

At a RecordSetter live event in the height of summer 2009, Chonko celebrated his love for the lunchtime staple by building the biggest sandwich his scanner could handle. Shirtless, and with his torso covered in sandwich tattoos drawn by friends, Chonko used six kinds of meat, seven varieties of cheese, four types of bread, and a heap of salad and condiments to create a massive, edible tower that just barely stayed intact long enough to set the record.

"I used skewers to hold it together, but keeping it upright as I worked was hard," says Chonko. "It kept toppling over. The audience came to the rescue, though—people came out of the crowd to help hold it up." Having solved the stability issue, Chonko ran into a tech problem. "Once I got it on and into a position to scan, I found out that I couldn't do the scanner's full-resolution at a scale that big." He settled for fewer dots per inch, which thankfully still made for an image that won accolades from his foodie followers. "People were coming by the table, helping me out and contributing ideas on how to build the sandwich," he remembers. "They were the reason I could even finish it. Without the crowd giving me a hand I might have never set the record."

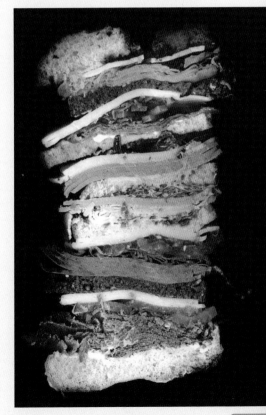

CRITERIA

☐ Must slice sandwich before scanning it.

☐ All toppings must be visible in scan.

RELATED RECORD

▶ Most Crustless Peanut Butter and Jelly Sandwiches Made by Seven People in 1 Minute: 14

RECORDS BEGGING TO BE SET

☐ Most Jelly Beans Photocopied at Once

☐ Fastest Time to Make Ten Grilled Cheese Sandwiches

Most Barrel Rolls on Star Fox 64 in 1 Minute

RECORD: 75

NAME: Brandon Roudebush

LOCATION: Pittsburgh, Pennsylvania

DATE: August 16, 2010

TOOLS: Star Fox 64, a Nintendo 64, immunity to dizziness

Star Fox 64 is a shooter game for the Nintendo 64 console. It was released in 1997 and is now considered a classic. For expert analysis of this record, we turn to Anthony Carboni, a lifelong gamer and host of the Web show *Bytejacker*. "I've been judging fictional-spaceship barrel-roll records for over 15 years—this is a stellar performance," says Carboni. The impressiveness comes from the difficulty of pressing the Nintendo 64 controller's shoulder bumper buttons, which suffer from what Carboni calls "weird mushiness." "A sustained rate of 1.25 rolls per second is phenomenal," says Carboni. "It can definitely be beaten, but it's not going to be an easy task on a standard-issue N64 controller."

Tip for Beating This Record

"You might have a better chance by alternating your barrel-roll directions—that way you're not trying to overload one shoulder button," advises Carboni. "Also, do whatever yoga stretches there are for fingers. And maybe use Chinese finger traps to build up strength."

A PILOT DOES A "BARREL ROLL" WHEN HE ROTATES A SPACESHIP 45 DEGREES AS HE'S ACCELERATING, CREATING A SPIRAL MOTION FORWARD.

CRITERIA

☐ Must attempt record using a Nintendo 64.

☐ No hacks or cheats allowed.

RELATED RECORDS

▶ Fastest Time to Complete First Level of Star Fox 64 on Nintendo 64: 2 minutes, 44.7 seconds

▶ Most Star Fox 64 Quotes Recited in 1 Minute: 25

RECORD BEGGING TO BE SET

☐ Fastest Time to Roll 100 Meters

Fastest Time to Solve Two Rubik's Cubes While Playing Guitar Hero

RECORD: 5 minutes, 2 seconds

NAME: Julian Aguirre

LOCATION: Los Angeles, California

DATE: August 6, 2009

TOOLS: Rubik's Cubes, Guitar Hero, super-human concentration

The "Multicolored Multitask" sounds like an activity a polo-shirted, khaki-clad manager might dream up at a corporate retreat. But it is so, *so* much cooler than that. Julian Aguirre, known in virtual worlds as JRefleX93, set the gaming world aflame when he uploaded a video of himself nonchalantly playing Ozzy Osbourne's "Mr. Crowley" on expert level while solving two Rubik's Cubes. The IQ (Impressiveness Quotient) of the setup was off the charts—Aguirre sat with his back to the TV, using a mirror to see the screen and strumming with his right elbow as his right hand worked the Cube. He switched Cubes mid-song with no break. Rubik's Number One was solved in 1 minute, 3 seconds, while Rubik's Number Two took 2 minutes, 36 seconds. (Aguirre had to briefly pause his Cube spinning in order to bust out a particularly gnarly guitar solo.)

CRITERIA

☐ Must play the song "Mr. Crowley" on Expert Mode.

☐ Timing begins with first note of song and ends at the completion of second Cube.

RELATED RECORD

▶ Fastest Time for Two People to Each Solve a Rubik's Cube with One Hand While One of Them Is Upside Down: 56.27 seconds

RECORD BEGGING TO BE SET

☐ Fastest Time to Floss Teeth While Playing Guitar Hero

Longest Printer Toss

RECORD: 26 feet, 6 inches

NAME: Josh Fleischer

LOCATION: Sarasota, Florida

DATE: July 22, 2009

TOOLS: Universally reviled printer, upper body strength

Working for a marketing company, Josh Fleischer witnessed printers break down at the rate of about three per month. "There was a pile of printers waiting to be thrown out," he says. "These printers used to drive us all crazy." The collective agitation found its outlet after Fleischer saw the film *Office Space,* in which disgruntled corporate drones take a malfunctioning printer into a field and beat it into shards with a baseball bat. Inspired by the cathartic destruction on display, Fleischer decided to see how far he could throw a 21.4-pound HP Officejet Pro K550. The 26.5-foot toss provided a fleeting infusion of calm but couldn't make up for an overall dislike of cubicle culture: "I have left the company since then and pursued another career."

CRITERIA

☐ Must measure distance from takeoff line to location where printer lands (not its final stopping point).

☐ Must toss printer on a flat surface.

RELATED RECORDS

▶ Farthest Distance to Throw a Soccer Ball: 82 yards

▶ Farthest Distance to Throw a Laptop Computer: 80 feet, 4 inches

RECORDS BEGGING TO BE SET

☐ Most People's Faces Photocopied at Once

☐ Most Printers Donated to a School

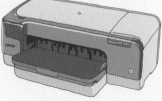

Most Video Game Consoles Played in 1 Minute

RECORD: 9

NAME: Jimmy Fallon

LOCATION: New York, New York

DATE: July 28, 2010

TOOLS: Current and vintage game consoles, TVs, favorite games from the last 25 years

CRITERIA

☐ Must make forward progress in each game.

RELATED RECORD

▶ Most Fireballs Thrown by Sagat in Super Street Fighter IV in 30 Seconds: 37

RECORDS BEGGING TO BE SET

☐ Most Board Games Played in 1 Minute
☐ Most Decks of Cards Shuffled in 1 Minute

CONSOLES AND GAMES IN FALLON'S LINEUP:
▶ NINTENDO ENTERTAINMENT SYSTEM — THE LEGEND OF ZELDA
▶ SEGA GENESIS — SONIC THE HEDGEHOG
▶ SUPER NINTENDO ENTERTAINMENT SYSTEM — DONKEY KONG COUNTRY
▶ SEGA DREAMCAST — CRAZY TAXI
▶ NINTENDO 64 — STAR FOX 64
▶ SONY PLAYSTATION — TOMB RAIDER
▶ SONY PLAYSTATION 2 — KATAMARI DAMACY
▶ XBOX — HALO
▶ PS3 — STREET FIGHTER IV
▶ WII — TIGER WOODS PGA TOUR
▶ XBOX 360 — MADDEN NFL

During the taping of his late-night NBC show, Jimmy Fallon became a hedgehog, a busty archaeologist, an intergalactic pilot, and an NFL player. All these transformations happened within virtual worlds—courtesy of eleven game consoles. With Dan and Corey on hand to officiate and 60 seconds on the clock, Fallon gleefully rushed between controllers. The final tally of nine was a chronologically accurate trip down memory lane for those who grew up mashing buttons and yelling at their televisions.

Tallest VHS Tape Tower

RECORD: 6 feet, 3 inches

NAME: Dan Kendall

LOCATION: Oakland, California

DATE: April 3, 2009

TOOLS: VHS tapes, high ceiling

CRITERIA

☐ Tower must be made of VHS tapes only.

☐ Must not use any adhesives.

Yellow Jacket Comment

DAN: VHS tapes make for solid construction materials, but I can think of a Beta option.

COREY: You might want to rewind that joke.

RELATED RECORDS

▸ Tallest Tower of Dominos: 133 inches

▸ Most CDs Held at Once: 194

RECORDS BEGGING TO BE SET

☐ Fastest Time to Wrap a Mummy Using VHS Tape

☐ Largest Collection of *Jerry Maguire* VHS Tapes

With the advent of DVDs, videocassettes dropped off the consumer radar. So when lumbered with 600 VHS tapes, film editor Dan Kendall stacked them in his cubicle. His office mate David saw the stack and was hit with a lightning bolt of inspiration. "A bridge!" he cried. "We must build a bridge." In the weeks that followed, the duo experimented with construction techniques. After building a dual-arch bridge on top of their adjacent cubicles, they had secured the confidence to take on an even more daunting project: a giant tape tower. Construction took place on top of Kendall's desk, with a final height of 6 feet, 3 inches— 8 foot 8, if you include the desk. Gazing at the creation, Kendall could not help himself. He leapt to the top of the tower and surveyed the world from its summit. In that moment, VHS stood for Very High Satisfaction.

Longest Time to Balance Twenty-Five VHS Tapes on Chin

RECORD: 7.15 seconds

NAME: Brian Pankey

LOCATION: Springfield, Illinois

DATE: May 7, 2010

TOOLS: VHS tapes, stable chin

Got a bunch of old videotapes gathering dust in a closet? Why not put them to good use by stacking them on your chin? Master balancer Brian Pankey gathered a library of twenty-five classics from the '90s such as *Home Alone* and piled them on his chin, keeping them there for more than 7 seconds before the tower collapsed. His technique was to use the bottom tape as a pillar, placing it vertically and stacking the other twenty-three cassettes horizontally on top. Adding to the challenge was the fact that Pankey remained seated the whole time. As he says in the video, balancing while sitting down is much harder than doing so standing because you can't move very far to stabilize the stack. This increases the likelihood of *Mrs. Doubtfire* falling onto your face.

CRITERIA

☐ No adhesives permitted.

☐ Must attempt while seated.

Yellow Jacket Comment

COREY: This planet is littered with millions of VHS tapes that will probably never be watched again. Kudos to Brian on taking an outdated artifact and evolving it into a world record tool.

RELATED RECORDS

► Most "Gallagher" VHS Tapes Smashed with a Sledgehammer in 1 Minute: 5

► Most Compact Discs Held at Once: 194

► Longest Time to Balance Eleven Highlighter Markers on Chin: 50.44 seconds

RECORDS BEGGING TO BE SET

☐ Longest VHS Tape Domino Chain

☐ Most VHS Tapes Held in Hand at Once

Brian Pankey

One Man, One Year, 750 World Records

There are jugglers. There are balancers. There are magicians. And then there is Brian Pankey. Not satisfied with choosing just one of those callings, Pankey has, from an early age, pursued all three. This one-man circus juggles knives, beanbag chairs, and hula-hoops. He balances wheelbarrows on his chin. He does card tricks and coin tricks and once made twelve balloon dogs while balancing a broom on his forehead. With more than 1,200 RecordSetter titles, Brian Pankey is, by far, the world's most prolific record setter.

Born in Springfield, Illinois, Pankey's early memories are of entertaining a crowd. "I was one of those kids who made television sets out of cardboard boxes or made sock puppets and performed for my family," he says. "I always knew I was going to be an entertainer."

Sitting in his eighth-grade history classroom years ago, Pankey watched, as his teacher amused the students by juggling three oranges. The kids were entertained, but Pankey was inspired. Soon the 13-year-old had devoted himself to juggling, going to the circus every year to scope out the performers, and find inspiration for his own burgeoning routines.

Juggling begat balancing. To teach himself the trade, Pankey began perching long, light objects on his forehead and chin. Once he'd mastered that, he progressed to bicycles, couches, and shopping carts.

After seeing a RecordSetter record-setting segment on *Late Night with Jimmy Fallon,* Pankey knew he'd found an opportunity to showcase his talents to the world. The first world record Pankey submitted was the Longest Time to Juggle Three Beanbag Chairs. There was no introduction to camera or an explanation of what was about to happen—he simply started juggling, while standing in front of a 7-foot-tall black box with a giant white question mark painted on it. So began the mystery and legend of Brian Pankey.

Following his first submission, record setting became something of an addiction, from Most Consecutive Golf Ball Bounces on Alternate Sides of a Rubber Mallet to Longest Time to Juggle Three Traffic Cones While Wearing an Orange Hat. Staff members became fascinated by the multitalented man with a bottomless reserve of enthusiasm for world records.

Though delighted to be racking up so many achievements, Pankey began to crave more of a challenge. He soon got his wish, finding a friendly rival in Australian Peter Craig. The duo frequently engage in frenzied battles for supremacy—Pankey's record of Most Consecutive Baseball Bounces on the Head of a Rubber Mallet went back and forth between them fifteen times in the space of 10 weeks. "Peter and I might be from opposite sides of the world, but we are far from opposite. When Peter beats me for a record, it inspires me to do better," he says.

Having set an astonishing 750 records in a year—including a 10-day spree during which he performed 126 records—Pankey is now looking to recruit the next generation of champions. "I want to help others achieve their goals," he says, citing school programs about goal setting as his preferred mode of passing on the "Way of the Pankey."

CHAPTER 5

Money and Style

Cash and clothing—they're what separate us from the animals (except for some of the more pampered poodles and a few chimps in tuxedos).

The fashion-forward folk in this section have come up with ingenious ways of stashing their cash—think belly buttons and noses used as wallets—and making old apparel seem new again. When faced with a stack of tired old T-shirts, they'll try to put them all on in 30 seconds, or transfer them to a partner as quickly as possible. A pair of pants is just asking to be stuffed with bananas, toy cars, or monkey wrenches, and as for party hats and cocktail umbrellas, well, let's just say they're accessorized in the most unexpected ways.

Fastest Time for Two People to Switch Pants

RECORD: 11.37 seconds

NAME: Matt Dalton and Sean Haley

LOCATION: Bohemia, New York

DATE: November 25, 2009

TOOLS: 2 people, 2 pairs of pants, 2 determined minds

Matt Dalton and his friend Sean Haley chanced upon the pants-switching record while browsing RecordSetter.com. "We turned to one another, noticed we both indeed were wearing pants, and decided to give it a shot," recalls Dalton. "We studied the technique of numerous people and the taking on and off of pants for a number of days before finally agreeing on the record-breaking methodology." There was just one obstacle: The two friends wore different pants sizes.

Refusing to be thwarted, they got creative. Sean Haley, the larger of the duo, ran 4 miles a day so he could fit into Dalton's pants. Meanwhile, Dalton ate a stream of snack foods to fatten up. Confident of victory after the mutual body modifications, Dalton's only worry was getting something important caught in the zipper. "We were both fearful for our lives the entire time," he says, "yet knowingly put them on the line for the sake of the record and the good people of RecordSetter."

CRITERIA

☐ Pants must be zipped/buttoned up before and after switch.

☐ Drawstring pants not permitted.

RELATED RECORD

► Most Times Unzipping Pants in 30 Seconds: 166

RECORDS BEGGING TO BE SET

☐ Most Pairs of Pants Worn at Once

☐ Fastest Time for Two People to Switch Airplane Seats

BIRDS OF A FEATHER

Pants

Pants—there's just something about them that's inherently entertaining. Even the word is fun to say. Go on, shout it out loud: PANTS! Now that you're warmed up, check out the parties going on in the pants of these record setters. Imagine the tingly feeling of cramming twenty-six monkey wrenches down your trousers. Or the incidental hamstring massage that comes with stuffing 21 pounds of potatoes into your pants. These are unique sensations that can be experienced by challenging one of the following feats.

Most Monkey Wrenches Fit Inside a Pair of Pants While Wearing Them in 30 Seconds

RECORD: 26

NAME: George Renfro

LOCATION: El Segundo, California

DATE: December 30, 2010

Fastest Time to Remove Pants, Turn Them Inside Out, and Put Them Back On

RECORD: 11.46 seconds

NAME: Nikolai Mayo-Pitts

LOCATION: Palmyra, Virginia

DATE: June 3, 2010

Most Times Unzipping Pants in 30 Seconds

RECORD: 166

NAME: Peter Craig

LOCATION: Blakeview, Australia

DATE: July 16, 2010

Most Toy Cars Fit Inside a Pair of Pants Worn by a 6-Year-Old

RECORD: 140

NAME: Eli Cullen

LOCATION: Lindenhurst, Illinois

DATE: March 25, 2010

Heaviest Mass of Potatoes Stuffed Inside Pants While Wearing Them in 1 Minute

RECORD: 21 pounds

NAME: Craig Morrison and Sam Stilson

LOCATION: New York, New York

DATE: March 17, 2010

Longest Time Lying on Back in Snow Wearing Only Boxers While Eating Ice Cream with Bare Hands

RECORD: 2 minutes, 33.4 seconds

NAME: Josh Graber

LOCATION: Roscoe, Illinois

DATE: December 19, 2010

Most Socks Put on a Left Foot While Listening to "Beat It"

RECORD: 57

NAME: Nat Locke

LOCATION: Perth, Australia

DATE: July 13, 2009

TOOLS: Socks, Michael Jackson's "Beat It"

CRITERIA

☐ Must put on socks one at a time.

☐ Nylon socks (e.g., knee highs) do not count.

Yellow Jacket Comment

COREY: I guess the trick for this record is to have small feet and big socks.

DAN: Doesn't sound like the category for me, then.

RELATED RECORDS

▸ Most Michael Jackson Songs Named in 30 Seconds: 26

▸ Most Socks on a Left Hand: 30

RECORD BEGGING TO BE SET

☐ Most Oven Mitts Fit in a Sleeping Bag While Listening to "Man in the Mirror"

No one wants to be defeated, but downfall was in the cards for Sami Freeman of Lake City, Florida. Her world record, in which she bundled forty-three socks onto her foot while listening to "Beat It," was moonwalked all over by Australian morning radio host Nat Locke of Nova 93.7. Showing how funky and strong was her fight, Locke ignored a gnawing ache in her ankle and kept cramming specially purchased socks onto her left tootsie while broadcasting her show. "It's like your foot was *born* to go in a sock," marveled cohost Nathan Morris as he watched the action. Reckon fifty-seven socks on a foot is an easy record? Then beat it. Just beat it.

Most T-Shirts Put on in 30 Seconds

RECORD: 13

NAME: Alex Kirchner

LOCATION: Brisbane, Australia

DATE: January 18, 2010

TOOLS: Large T-shirt collection, ability to distinguish armholes from head holes

Filmmaker Alex Kirchner was ready. Before him lay a desk and three sets of rolling luggage, all loaded to the gills with T-shirts. Kirchner, clad in a black tank top for the sake of modesty, was poised, like a cobra ready to strike. For the next 30 seconds he sped down the line, dragging garment after garment through his arms and over his head. After three failed attempts in which laughs or wardrobe malfunctions impeded his progress, Kirchner hit his stride, stuffing himself into a sensational thirteen shirts in just 30 seconds. After the thirteenth shirt, he felt a sense of comfort, later saying it felt like he was giving himself "a bit of a cuddle."

Tip for Beating This Record

Kirchner says the trick to trumping him is "organizing the shirts in progressively larger sizes and degree of stretchiness, and rolling them upward so that the sleeve holes are clearly visible and easily accessible."

CRITERIA

☐ T-shirts must be put on one at a time.

☐ Arms must go through sleeves and head must go through neck.

RELATED RECORD

▶ Fastest Time to Open a Suitcase and Put On a Suit: 17.24 seconds

RECORD BEGGING TO BE SET

☐ Most Used T-Shirts (in Good Condition!) Donated to a Clothing Bank at Once

Most T-Shirts Transferred Between Two People in 30 Seconds

RECORD: 11

NAMES: Karsyn Parker and Cassandra Saelee

LOCATION: Fresno, California

DATE: March 28, 2009

TOOLS: T-shirts that fit both participants, agile arms

CRITERIA

☐ Must transfer T-shirts one at a time.

RELATED RECORDS

▸ Fastest Time for Two People to Switch Shorts: 12.35 seconds

▸ Fastest Time for Two People to Hug 10 Times: 3.36 seconds

RECORD BEGGING TO BE SET

☐ Largest Collection of Band T-Shirts

Ever watched something on television and thought, "I could do that"? Karsyn Parker took that sentiment one step further. Watching a RecordSetter segment on *Late Night with Jimmy Fallon* one night, Parker witnessed Christine Santora and Justin Gignac transfer eight T-shirts between their bodies in half a minute's time. Santora began the record wearing all the shirts at once, removing them individually, and giving them to Gignac to pile onto his body. Parker instantly knew she could better the achievement. A text was hastily dashed off to her friend Cassandra Saelee. Before you could say "polyester," the two girls fit in hours of practice before ultimately reaching eleven world-record-breaking T-shirt transfers. "It was super hard to keep from laughing, and it would get really hot in the layers of shirts," says Parker. Switching on the AC and bringing multiple fans into the room helped ease the heat, but nothing could suppress their overwhelming joy.

Largest Collection of People Wearing Jean Shirts

RECORD: 62

NAME: Boston Beer Company

LOCATION: Boston, Massachusetts

DATE: January 14, 2009

TOOLS: Crowd of denim devotees, jean shirts

CRITERIA

☐ All participants must be in the same location.

☐ Shirts must be blue denim.

RELATED RECORDS

▶ Fastest Time to Put on Three Shirts While Balancing on Another Person's Shoulders: 22.23 seconds

▶ Most Brothers in a T-Shirt: 3

RECORD BEGGING TO BE SET

☐ Largest Group of People Named Jean Wearing T-Shirts

Jim Koch is well-known for two things: brewing Samuel Adams beer and wearing denim shirts. Legend has it that Koch even maintains a Batman-esque wardrobe of identical jean shirts so that he never has to deviate from his uniform.

At a Boston Beer Company function, Koch's employees paid tribute to their CEO's distinctive style by banding together and showing up in versions of his famous shirt. With their denim-and-khaki ensembles, the team unwittingly ignited a trend that Parisian fashion magazines dubbed "Old Navy Cowboy."

DID YOU KNOW?

YOU CAN ALSO CALL A JEAN SHIRT A DUNGAREE SHIRT.

I WONDER IF YOU GET A FREE JEAN SHIRT WHEN YOU WORK THERE.

WHO CARES ABOUT THE JEAN SHIRT? I WONDER IF YOU GET FREE BEER.

157

Most Neckties Worn at Once

RECORD: 97

NAME: Opus Moreschi

LOCATION: New York, New York

DATE: February 11, 2009

TOOLS: Ties, strong neck, good circulation

Opus Moreschi is a dapper dresser. No matter whether he's heading out for cocktails or popping into the grocery store for a cauliflower, it's highly likely he'll be clad in a suit and tie—he's just that sharp. In fact, Moreschi's necktie collection is so extensive that to wear it all at once puts him in physical peril. During this record attempt, in which he looped 7.4 pounds of ties around his neck, witnesses noticed a purple hue slowly creeping up Moreschi's face as the pressure on his jugular veins increased. Determined to get the best result possible, he insisted on continuing until he was wearing all ninety-seven ties. RecordSetter officials agreed, on the condition that his pulse was monitored. Moreschi reports no long-term medical effects and his record has yet to be beaten.

CRITERIA

☐ Ties must be worn around neck.

☐ Ties may be any width but must be tied in a standard knot (e.g., four-in-hand, half-Windsor).

Yellow Jacket Comment

DAN: He could rent himself out for weddings in case any attendees forget their ties.

COREY: Great idea. We should register the URL RentAGuyWearing97 NecktiesAtOnce.com.

RELATED RECORD

▶ Most Pairs of Underwear Worn on Head at Once: 47

RECORD BEGGING TO BE SET

☐ Most Bow Ties Worn at Once

Most Hats Worn at Once

RECORD: 51

NAME: Scott Reynen

LOCATION: Denver, Colorado

DATE: July 31, 2009

TOOLS: Stack of hats, friends with long arms

"Hats are surprisingly heavy," says Scott Reynen. Well, yes—when you're wearing fifty-one of them. Despite not being a hat wearer by nature, Reynen was inspired when his company did a project for a cap manufacturer and received a heaping pile of sample hats. He stacked them on his noggin until his arms could no longer reach the top of the tower, then roped his coworkers into finishing the job. "I had trouble keeping my neck straight enough to balance them," remembers Reynen. But his simple, fuss-free strategy—"First, get a lot of hats. Then, wear them"—allowed him to remain calm and still for long enough to capture the crucial photographic proof.

CRITERIA

☐ No adhesives or external support permitted.

☐ Assistance from others permitted.

RELATED RECORDS

▶ Longest Time to Balance a Fedora on Nose: 10.30 seconds

▶ Longest Visor Chain: 25

▶ Most Hats Put on in 30 Seconds: 24

RECORD BEGGING TO BE SET

☐ Fastest Time to Pump 10 Gallons of Gas While Wearing a 10-Gallon Hat

Tip for Beating This Record

Baseball caps are okay to use for stacking, but their unequal weight distribution can cause them to topple forward. A sturdier option is a hat with a brim around the whole crown, such as cowboy hats, porkpie hats, sombreros, and bowlers.

Most Pairs of Glasses Worn at Once

RECORD: 20

NAME: Holland Wich

LOCATION: Jensen Beach, Florida

DATE: January 23, 2011

TOOLS: Large glasses collection

CRITERIA

- ☐ All pairs must be worn on head.
- ☐ All pairs must face forward.
- ☐ No adhesives permitted.
- ☐ Assistance from others permitted.

RELATED RECORD

► Most Times to Ask "Where Are My Glasses?" to Someone Tuning a Guitar in 30 Seconds: 28

RECORDS BEGGING TO BE SET

- ☐ Fastest Time to Read an Eyechart
- ☐ Most Pairs of Eyeglasses Tried on in 10 Minutes

Jeepers creepers, Holland Wich loves to shade her peepers. This visionary young woman was on a mission to lead a more adventurous life, one achievement at a time. "I had recently started to keep a little journal of my bucket list," she says. "One of the items was 'Beat a world record.'" An avid collector of sunglasses, Wich perused RecordSetter for feats involving eyewear. She soon stumbled upon the entry for most pairs of glasses worn, which, after eight attempts by eight people, stood at eighteen. Eager to make a spectacle of herself, Wich grabbed her twenty favorite pairs from her collection of eighty-five and arranged them on her face. Not only did she break the record but she provided a creative new way to stay protected from UV radiation.

Tip for Beating This Record

"Use smaller glasses first, then build your way up to the bigger ones," advises Wich. "Also, it helps if someone puts the glasses on for you. Once you get to around eight, it's hard to see and even harder to find out where they will stay."

Most Party Hats Worn at Once

RECORD: 114

NAME: Elna Baker

LOCATION: New York, New York

DATE: March 17, 2010

TOOLS: Party hats, princess fantasies

arty hats make Elna Baker feel like royalty. "They remind me of fairy-tale princess hats," she says, "so whenever I put one on I am transformed into a pretty princess." Or sometimes, an animal. While dancing at a party one night, Baker was overwhelmed by the desire to slide one of the conical hats around her waist in order to "dance like a bumblebee with a stinger." The hat's elastic stretched around her waist without snapping, leading Baker to wonder how many would fit on her body. A RecordSetter live event offered the opportunity to find out. On stage, despite resembling a giant festive porcupine, Baker once again felt regal. "I'm just saying," she says, "only a real princess could set this kind of a record."

CRITERIA

☐ No stacking hats on top of each other.

☐ May not receive assistance from others.

Tip for Beating This Record

"Be patient," says Baker. "This isn't a time-based record, so feel free to go at your own pace. And finally, as the saying goes, 'The larger the party hat the longer the string,' so keep that in mind."

RELATED RECORDS

▶ Most People Wearing Dinner Napkins as Hats at a Dinner Party: 63

▶ Most Silly Bandz Worn at Once: 150

RECORD BEGGING TO BE SET

☐ Most Parties Attended in One Night

Longest Scarf Knit in 2 Hours

RECORD: 68 inches

NAME: Alexandra Young

LOCATION: New York, New York

DATE: May 20, 2009

TOOLS: Wool, knitting needles, ability to tell a garter stitch from a stockinette stitch

Super stitcher Alexandra Young first got the knitting bug while recuperating from wisdom teeth extraction. With a week of recovery time to endure, she picked up her mom's gear to pass the time. "When you look at my scarf you can pinpoint whenever I took my pain medication, because the stitches start to get messed up, then straighten out again," she says.

Soon after finishing her first garment, Young used her knitting powers to stitch her way into the record books, needling the world's longest 2-hour scarf. The colossal garment was put to even more meaningful use a week after its creation when Young's grandmother passed away. "There is a Chinese tradition in which every family member places a blanket over the deceased until they are completely covered," she explains. "I used the yarn from the scarf to knit the blanket and now it is buried with her in California."

CRITERIA

☐ Scarf must be at least 6 inches wide.

RELATED RECORDS

► Most Scarves Tied Around Neck in 30 Seconds: 7

► Largest Doily Crocheted in 1 Hour: 5 feet in diameter

RECORDS BEGGING TO BE SET

☐ Farthest Distance to Throw a Sewing Machine

☐ Most Knitting Needles Held in Hand at Once

Most Hangers Hung on a Body

RECORD: 142

NAME: Jovah Siegel

LOCATION: Portland, Oregon

DATE: November 22, 2010

TOOLS: Lots of hangers, somewhere to put your displaced clothing.

Wildland firefighter Jovah Siegel invented a world record category fit for U.S. Army Basic Training. "Most people probably wouldn't understand without personally experiencing this, but holding your arms up—even without weights—becomes excruciatingly painful after just a couple of minutes," he says. Upon becoming a world record holder, the pain dissipated and the strong man remains bullish about hanger records. "Hangers are something that everyone has. They are numerous and versatile," proclaims Siegel, predicting a bold future in which "there will soon be many other hanger records." The closet's your oyster, people. Get to it.

CRITERIA

- ☐ Hangers may be hung from both body and clothing.
- ☐ Holding hangers in hands prohibited.
- ☐ No hangers may touch floor.
- ☐ Must attempt record standing up.

RELATED RECORD

- ▶ Longest Time to Keep a Quarter Balanced on Spinning Coat Hanger: 2 minutes, 56.2 seconds

RECORD BEGGING TO BE SET

- ☐ Most Articles of Clothing Hung on a Hanger

Tip for Beating This Record

Siegel recommends wearing "button-up clothing," as it offers more protrusions on which to hook the hangers. The order of placement is another key factor. "Do your arms last and take a picture quickly," he warns. "Those hangers will not stay put forever."

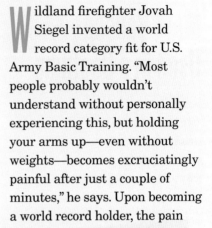

Most Balloons Used in a Costume

RECORD: 154

NAME: Mot Buchanan

LOCATION: Akron, Ohio

DATE: April 24, 2010

TOOLS: Balloons, a sense of style, voluminous lungs

BUCHANAN'S RECORD-SETTING CREATION

Yellow Jacket Comment

DAN: I want to set the record for Most Helium Balloons Worn at Once.

COREY: But what if you floated away?

DAN: You could hijack a blimp and come save me.

From bright red lobsters to (nonfunctioning) sniper rifles, Mot Buchanan can seemingly make anything out of a handful of balloons. Buchanan, a professional balloon entertainer, has been performing since he was 9 years old and recently started experimenting with the cutting-edge field of balloon fashion. "Lately my focus has been making dresses out of balloons for special occasions like proms or weddings," he says. This record-setting outfit comprised ninety-nine balloons topped with forty-nine more serving as a hat, three forming a purse, and two as a bracelet. Should we expect to see the style on *Project Runway* anytime soon? Only if straight pins are banned from the show.

CRITERIA

☐ Outfit must be made solely from balloons.

RELATED RECORDS

▶ Most Candles Lit Inside an Inflated Balloon: 2

▶ Most Inflated Balloons Fit Inside an Inflated Balloon: 4

RECORD BEGGING TO BE SET

☐ Most Balloon Animals Made in 2 Minutes

Largest Cocktail Umbrella Beard

RECORD: 17 umbrellas

NAME: Max Mendelsohn

LOCATION: Chicago, Illinois

DATE: March 17, 2010

TOOLS: Cocktail umbrellas, luxuriant beard

If your beverage is giving you the blues, just stick a mini-paper umbrella in it, and it will instantly improve the taste. And if your beard is feeling a little boring, you can liven it up using the same approach. Max Mendelsohn crammed seventeen pastel cocktail umbrellas into his whiskers, holding them in place using only the adhesive power of his hirsute masculinity. Cheers to your manly manliness, Max Mendelsohn.

AHA! THIS EXPLAINS THE HAIR IN MY DAIQUIRI.

IT DOESN'T EXPLAIN THE TOOTH IN MINE.

CRITERIA
☐ Cocktail umbrellas must be open.
☐ May not place umbrellas in mustache.

RELATED RECORDS
▸ Fastest Time to Make a ShamWow Cocktail: 28.52 seconds
▸ Most Consecutive Catches Juggling a Crutch, an Umbrella, and a Traffic Cone While Balancing on a Rola Bola: 63

RECORDS BEGGING TO BE SET
☐ Most Open Umbrellas Held at Once
☐ Most Skittles Fit in a Beard

CAUTION: BE ALERT! COCKTAIL UMBRELLAS MAY HAVE A MINI MARY POPPINS ATTACHED TO THEM.

Largest Toothpick Beard

RECORD: 2,222 toothpicks

NAME: George Gaspar

LOCATION: Sherman Oaks, California

DATE: February 4, 2009

TOOLS: Lustrous beard, toothpicks

BEFORE

AFTER

While growing his entry for the 2009 World Beard and Moustache Championships, George Gaspar was looking for ways to "play with it as it sprouted." Beard-based activities are often hard to come by, but after glimpsing a video clip featuring a man filling his whiskers with toothpicks, he knew his own impressive growth had found its true calling. The record attempt began well. As Gaspar remembers, "The first thousand went in fine, and the second thousand went in okay, but then as we started to add more they would push some out." After hitting 2,222, Gaspar called it a day, faced the bathroom mirror, and saw what he had become: a human toothpick dispenser for hors d'oeuvres hour. If you'd like to host a cocktail party with a difference, give him a call.

CRITERIA

- ☐ Toothpicks must be placed in beard, not mustache.
- ☐ Adhesives not permitted.

RELATED RECORDS

- ▶ Largest Lucky Charms Beard: 61
- ▶ Most Toothpicks Stuck in a Marshmallow in 15 Seconds: 16
- ▶ Tallest Toothpick Tower: 45 stories

RECORDS BEGGING TO BE SET

- ☐ Largest Toothpick Mustache
- ☐ Most Breath Mints Handed Out at a Garlic Festival

Most Fake Mustaches Worn at Once

RECORD: 8

NAME: Milo Kotis

LOCATION: Brooklyn, New York

DATE: April 4, 2009

TOOLS: False mustaches, face space

SUGGESTED MUSTACHES

THE SATAN

THE HULK HOGAN

THE CHAPLIN

THE DALÍ

THE VON BISMARCK

THE MAGNUM, P.I.

CRITERIA
☐ All mustaches must be attached to neck region and above.
☐ All mustaches must be attached directly to skin.

RELATED RECORDS
▶ Fastest Time to Shave off One's Mustache: 36.65 seconds
▶ Longest Time to Spin a Basketball on a Pinky While Wearing a 5-Foot Fake Mustache: 11.14 seconds

RECORDS BEGGING TO BE SET
☐ Most Fake Mustaches Worn by a Grandmother
☐ Most People Wearing Fake Mustaches in a Photo Booth

Milo Kotis is too young to grow a real mo, but that didn't stop him from setting a mustache-based world record. The then 8-year-old enlisted the help of some friends to adorn his face with a collection of mustaches that would knock the nose hairs off Tom Selleck.

Rather than sticking to the traditional top lip position, Kotis placed his 'staches all over his face—including one on each cheek, one behind an ear, and another on his chin.

Check back in approximately 12 years, when—our fingers are crossed—Kotis will have set another world record: Largest Real Mustache.

Tallest Shaving Cream Wig

RECORD: 14 inches

NAME: Mel Sampson

LOCATION: New Minas, Nova Scotia, Canada

DATE: September 24, 2009

TOOLS: Shaving cream, protective tarp

Having seen Jimmy Fallon set the record for tallest shaving cream wig on his TV show—then watched as it was broken twice within 3 months—Mel Sampson was determined to claim the title live on her radio show.

Sampson took a relaxed approach, choosing not to have a trial run before the big moment: "I have naturally curly hair so I just crossed my fingers and hoped that it could hold a lot of shaving cream," she says.

Sourcing three enthusiastic employees and five cans of dollar-store cream, Sampson awaited her new hairdo. After a minute of nonstop spraying, Sampson had added 15 inches of foam to her height. Washing it all out from her curly hair was no small task. Fallon, with his slick, short, TV hairdo, didn't have this problem. That said, he doesn't have this record now, either.

CRITERIA
☐ Must use canned shaving cream.
☐ Measurement determined by wig's peak height within time limit.

RELATED RECORD
▶ Fastest Time to Shave off One's Own Mustache: 36.65 seconds

RECORD BEGGING TO BE SET
☐ Largest Group of People Wearing Mullet Wigs

Tip for Beating This Record
Stock up on supplies, says Sampson. "Have lots of shaving cream available because you'll be shocked at how much you can use. Lots of garbage bags are a must, especially when attempting the record in the lobby of your workplace."

Most Afro Picks Fit in an Afro

RECORD: 101

NAME: Ahmir "Questlove" Thompson

LOCATION: New York, New York

DATE: June 25, 2009

TOOLS: Afro picks, large halo of hair

"**M**y mother's gonna kill me when she sees this on television!" laughed Roots drummer Questlove as he embarked upon his ambitious record backstage at *Late Night with Jimmy Fallon*. Despite sporting one of the most famous afros in the land, the Roots drummer was beginning to have doubts about using it to set a record. With less than half of the picks in place, he looked in the mirror and could hardly believe the transformation. "I look like Patti LaBelle, circa 1984!"

"One false move of my neck and it's curtains," he said, trying to place more combs in his 'fro without moving his head. As the growing sphere of picks transformed him into a kind of hip-hop cyborg, his spirits lifted. Questlove finally reached his goal of 101 and celebrated with a good old-fashioned, "Mama, I made it!"

CRITERIA

☐ May not receive assistance from others.

☐ Must use standard-sized fan-style picks with metal prongs.

RELATED RECORDS

▶ Longest Hair Twirl: 1 hour, 2 minutes, 2 seconds

▶ Most Cocktail Umbrellas Fit in Hair in 1 Minute: 56

▶ Most Paper Airplanes Stuck in Hair at Once: 32

RECORD BEGGING TO BE SET

☐ Most Hair Clips Worn in Hair at Once

Most Giraffe Tattoos on a Shoulder

RECORD: 4

NAME: Daniel Fowler

LOCATION: Perth, Australia

DATE: June 3, 2009

TOOLS: Tattoo artist, open shoulder space, parental permission

❝ I will be the shoulder-giraffe-tattoo record holder forever." A bold claim from Daniel Fowler, who currently has four giraffe tattoos on his shoulder. The first giraffe appeared on the Australian's shoulder after a wild night out in Amsterdam. He was shocked by an American challenger, Mike MacDonald, who got three giraffes stampeding across his left shoulder just to top Fowler's original mark. The Aussie wasted no time before striking back with his second, third, and record-breaking fourth giraffes, all for the sake of owning the record. MacDonald's reaction? He plans to reclaim his crown. "I'm pretty confident that Daniel's scrawny little shoulder will run out of space before mine does," he says.

CRITERIA

☐ Tattoos must display full giraffes.

☐ Tattoos must appear on the same shoulder.

Tip for Beating This Record

MacDonald rustled up these pointers for those planning a shoulder-based safari park:

1. Ideally, you should be single and prepared to live a life of celibacy. It can be challenging to convince a spouse (or a potential mate) that getting giraffes tattooed on your body is a good idea.

2. Stay away from elephants you might come across—they *hate* giraffe tattoos.

RELATED RECORD

▶ Most Bottles in a Tattoo of a Gnome Pushing a Wheelbarrow of Bottles: 5

RECORD BEGGING TO BE SET

☐ Largest Group of People Wearing Giraffe Costumes

Most Quarters Fit Inside a Belly Button

RECORD: 30

NAME: Randon Beasley

LOCATION: Fayetteville, Arkansas

DATE: August 31, 2010

TOOLS: Quarters, cavernous "innie" belly button

When it comes to belly buttons, there are two major types: innies and outies. University of Arkansas student Randon Beasley has been blessed with the Grand Canyon of innies—a cavern so deep, it appears purpose-built for quarter-stuffing. In August 2010, Beasley's friend Taylor Johnson barged into his dorm room, started jumping on his bed, and refused to stop until Beasley broke the RecordSetter quarters-in-a-belly-button record. It stood at sixteen coins. Beasley took on the challenge.

Once he began stuffing the quarters, word spread down the dorm hallway. Soon, a crowd of students arrived to cheer him on. Thirty coins later, Beasley had acquired a new nickname among his peers: "The Quarter Guy." He's since been invited to demonstrate his prodigious talent on several major talk shows.

CRITERIA
□ Must stand for duration of attempt.
□ Quarters must remain in belly button unassisted for at least 3 seconds.

RELATED RECORDS
▶ Most Blueberries Fit in a Belly Button: 10
▶ Most American Quarters Fit Inside a Nose: 18

RECORD BEGGING TO BE SET
□ Most Jelly Bellies Fit Inside a Belly Button

WITH A BELLY BUTTON LIKE THAT, RANDON DOESN'T EVEN NEED TO OWN A WALLET.

AMEN.

Most Quarters Fit Inside a Nose

RECORD: 18

NAME: Paul Green Jr.

LOCATION: Kerman, California

DATE: March 15, 2008

TOOLS: Wide and flexible nostrils, American quarters

PLEASE NOTE: SNEEZING DURING AN ATTEMPT MAY RESULT IN A HUMAN SLOT MACHINE JACKPOT.

How much is a nose worth? If the nose belongs to Paul Green Jr., the answer is $4.50. Green stuffed eighteen quarters—nine in each nostril—into his schnoz to claim this record. The previous record holder was Robert Stobo, who solicited quarters from passersby at the 2007 Burning Man festival and inserted ten into his nose. Unsurprisingly, no one asked for their money back.

CRITERIA

☐ Must use American quarters.

☐ Quarters must remain in nose unassisted for at least three seconds.

RELATED RECORD

▶ Most Quarters Balanced on Elbow and Caught: 51

RECORD BEGGING TO BE SET

☐ Most Quarters Held in Hand at Once

CAUTION: THIS RECORD IS DANGEROUS. GREEN ADMITTED THE EXPERIENCE WAS "EXTRAORDINARILY PAINFUL."

Largest Nose Hair Collection

RECORD: 584 nose hairs

NAME: Michael Bailey

LOCATION: Springfield, Illinois

DATE: June 19, 2009

TOOLS: Hairy nostrils, high pain tolerance

CRITERIA
☐ Nose hairs must be collected from one nose.

The likes of Eli Broad and Charles Saatchi have spent fortunes on art collecting. Michael Bailey, however, has built a priceless collection of his own without spending a cent. An advocate of the "Grow Your Own" philosophy, Bailey has curated a collection of his personal nose hairs, assiduously plucking—not cutting—the hairs over the last twelve months. Cynics who doubt the validity of Bailey's "harvest" should stop right there. This is a man with values and standards. "I feel strongly that the hairs must be the record setter's own and not donated by friends, which would, you know, be gross."

Tip for Beating This Record

Target the hairiest section of your nostrils for a fast, high-volume harvest, says Bailey. "Your biggest crop comes from inside your nose, closest to the tip."

RELATED RECORDS
▶ Largest Group Eskimo Kiss: 5 people
▶ Longest Nail Fully Inserted into Nostril: 2.625 inches
▶ Largest Nose Flute Orchestra: 109 people

RECORDS BEGGING TO BE SET
☐ Most Sneezes in 30 Seconds
☐ Most Nose Hair Trimmers Given to Someone on Their Birthday

AIM HERE FOR THE CHOICEST LOCKS!

Tallest Nickel Tower

RECORD: 99 nickels

NAME: Teddy Sallen

LOCATION: Detroit, Michigan

DATE: January 22, 2010

TOOLS: Nickels, stacking skills

A pile of nickels won't buy you much these days, but it can secure you a spot in the RecordSetter champion list. Michigander Teddy Sallen stacked ninety-nine of the coins, breaking his own previous records of fifty and seventy-seven. The tower had a cash value of $4.95, but its value as an object of patience and persistence is beyond estimation. As Thomas Jefferson—whose face has graced the nickel since 1938—once said, "It is neither wealth nor splendor, but tranquility and occupation which give you happiness."

CRITERIA

☐ No outside support permitted to keep nickels balanced.

☐ Glue and other adhesives not permitted.

RELATED RECORDS

▶ Tallest Nickel Tower Balanced on Hand: 51 nickels

▶ Tallest Penny Tower: 108 pennies

RECORDS BEGGING TO BE SET

☐ Most Nickels Thrown in a Fountain at Once

☐ Tallest Nickel Tower on Top of a Nickelback CD

SEEING THIS RECORD FILLS ME WITH SHAME.

WHY?

BECAUSE I CRACKED OPEN MY SON'S PIGGY BANK AND SPENT AN ENTIRE SATURDAY TRYING TO BEAT IT.

Cheapest Purchase Made with a Credit Card

RECORD: 1 cent

NAME: David Ross

LOCATION: New York, New York

DATE: July 6, 2010

TOOLS: Credit card, tolerant retail employee

lobal Development Investment Banker David Ross was browsing the screws-and-bolts aisle at Home Depot when the thought came to mind, "What is the cheapest thing that someone can buy with a credit card?" So he decided to find out, splashing out a wimpy seven cents on a Hex nut (6 cents, plus tax) and slapping the whole tab on his credit card. Just over a week later, his home improvement feat was trumped when challenger John Hoyt pumped just 2 cents worth of gas, courtesy of his VISA card. "I was floored," Ross recalled, and it was not long before he stormed into his local post office to purchase a 1-cent stamp. When he handed the confused postal worker his Mastercard, she was flummoxed. But the discomfort was worth it. Stamp: 1 cent. World record: *Priceless.*

CRITERIA
☐ Online purchases not permitted.
☐ Must purchase a new item.
☐ Must submit receipt as evidence.

RELATED RECORD
▶ Longest Time to Balance $100 Bill on Nose: 17.05 seconds

RECORDS BEGGING TO BE SET
☐ Most Expensive Purchase Made with a Credit Card
☐ Most Credit Cards Cut in Half in 30 Seconds

Peter Craig

All-Rounder, Community Builder, Family Man

Australian Web designer Peter Craig is a soft-spoken, community-minded father of four. He also loves to rip freshly set records from the clutches of newly crowned RecordSetter champions. Don't get the wrong idea—he will be very nice about it. He may even throw some words of encouragement your way, or offer pointers on how to improve your technique. But when it comes time to go head-to-head for the glory of a record title, he will not go easy on you. With feats ranging from Fastest Time to Blow Up a Balloon Until It Pops to Longest Headstand on a Soccer Ball, Craig's prolific achievements are motivated by a competitive streak and a desire for self-improvement. "The main thing that drew me in is the challenge of the competition," he says. "Without others to compete with, it kind of misses the point."

After "clicking on a random link" that led him to RecordSetter, Craig browsed the archives and soon found a record he could beat: Most Times Unlocking an iPod Touch in 1 Minute. His sixty-seven unlocks in 60 seconds trounced the three previous attempts and gave him the first of many world record titles. Soon, the quiet achiever was taking on RecordSetter superstars and beating them at their own areas of expertise. Illinois resident Brian Pankey, who holds hundreds of jaw-dropping juggling and balancing records, is a frequent virtual sparring partner. The two trade tips, congratulate each other, and do some occasional trash talking in between beating each other's records. "I'm enjoying sitting back and watching you guys fight it out and ruin your knuckles!" Craig wrote in the comments section of the Most Consecutive Bounces of a Golf Ball on Alternating Sides of the Hand—addressing his comment to Pankey and his other competitor, Nolan Ross—"I'll sneak in later and blitz it."

The sneak-and-blitz method is classic Craig. "I find it difficult coming up with the ideas for setting records," he says. "When I do, they usually involve things that I don't have or can't do. I would love to see someone try an idea that I come up with. Otherwise, when I see records I can beat or that seem pretty simple, I like to at least try them."

The desire to learn new skills is another motivator. "One of the first records I saw was the Fastest Time to Solve a Rubik's Cube on a Unicycle," he says. "That's a record I want to try to beat because I can ride a unicycle, but before RecordSetter, I'd never touched a Rubik's Cube."

Peter is not the only member of the Craig family to get in on the world-beating action. His children, Emma, Madeline, and David, all hold records. Emma set her record, Most Assisted Backflips, with the help of her dad on the same day he set his first record. Peter's wife, Deb, is also a RecordSetter champ, reigning over categories such as Most Cats Drawn on a Hand and Fastest Time to Ball Ten Pairs of Socks.

Involving the whole gang and working on skills such as juggling, skipping, and unicycling allows Craig to get one step closer to a lifelong goal. "It has always been a childhood dream to one day become a professional circus clown or movie stuntman," he says. Being part of his children's records has given him the freedom to play. "It's nice to be sort of a kid again and have no inhibitions—and have fun doing it."

CHAPTER 6

Groups

E *pluribus unum*. Out of many, one. It's a phrase that bestows a sense of gravity wherever it appears, be it on the seal of the United States or at the beginning of our group record chapter. After all, doing the Running Man alone makes as much sound as a tree falling in a forest when no one's around. But executing it in the company of 151 other mover-groovers makes it truly epic. To beat one of the following records requires strength in numbers. So round up your friends, unite your family, mix in a few strangers, put on your awesome hats, and a world record may be yours.

Most People in One Location to Make a Charitable Donation via Text Message

RECORD: 585 people

NAME: Anaheim Angels Fans

LOCATION: Angel Stadium of Anaheim, California

DATE: September 6, 2010

TOOLS: Cell phones, generosity

In the annals of American charity, September 6, 2010, was a great day. Under the watchful eye of RecordSetter cofounder Corey Henderson, Anaheim Angels pitcher Scott Kazmir proved he had a big heart to accompany his strong arm. After the fastballer made a plea from the mound to support the Ovarian Cancer Research Fund (www.ocrf.org), 585 fans responded instantly, sending donations via SMS (Short Message Service). In mere seconds, $2,925 was raised, helping remind us that baseball is about more than just peanuts and Cracker Jacks.

CRITERIA
☐ All money must be donated using mobile phones.
☐ All money must be donated to a registered charity.

RELATED RECORD
▶ Most Frozen Turkeys Fit in a Car and Delivered to a Food Bank: 183

RECORDS BEGGING TO BE SET
☐ Most Money in a Piggy Bank Donated to Charity
　☐ Most Consecutive Days Volunteering at a Soup Kitchen

MORE THAN ANY OTHER FEAT IN THIS BOOK, I'M HOPING THIS RECORD GETS CRUSHED TIME AND TIME AGAIN.

Largest Game of "Never Have I Ever"

RECORD: 82 people

NAME: Alexandra Young

LOCATION: New York, New York

DATE: February 16, 2010

TOOLS: An array of scandalous questions, at least 82 honest and willing participants

CRITERIA

☐ All participants must raise one arm to start game.

☐ When game leader says something participant hasn't done, she/he must drop arm.

☐ Last person with arm raised is the winner.

Yellow Jacket Comment

COREY: That was the night I learned you've peed in a swimming pool.

DAN: Corey, that wasn't supposed to leave the room.

RELATED RECORD

▶ Largest Game of Apples to Apples: 63 people

RECORD BEGGING TO BE SET

☐ Longest Game of Truth or Dare

Alexandra Young was intent on bringing "Never Have I Ever," to a record-breaking level. At a RecordSetter LIVE! event, Young tempted eighty-two audience members to raise their hands and play. She kicked the game off with some relatively tame questions, including "I have never seen an episode of *Friends*" and "I've never vomited in someone's mouth." "It was really exciting to ask total strangers very intimate questions," admits Young. "The girl who won admitted to some revealing stuff, and somehow that made us instant friends." There was more than a little cheating. Not a single participant admitted to joining an online dating site. "About 90 percent of the people I know in New York are signed up for OKCupid," says Young. "I think people were trying to save face."

Largest Group Egg Toss

RECORD: 72 people

NAME: iD Tech Camp at Princeton University

LOCATION: Princeton, New Jersey

DATE: July 19, 2010

TOOLS: Raw eggs, hand-eye coordination

Every summer, fancy universities like Harvard and Princeton open their doors to tech whiz kids for iD camps. Teens and tweens can learn about game design, programming, 3-D modeling, and robotics. They also pick up non-tech skills, such as egg tossing and building an appreciation for terrible puns.

With a shout of "Who's egg-cited?" Princeton's 2010 iD campers beat the record for the largest group egg toss, set at sixty people just 1 month earlier by iD campers at the University of Denver. Not since the battle between Apple and Microsoft has the tech world seen such a fierce tussle for supremacy.

CRITERIA

☐ Pairs must be at least 5 feet apart.

☐ Must use uncooked eggs.

☐ Each participant must make at least one successful catch.

RELATED RECORD

▶ Fastest Rendition of Backwards Alphabet While Balancing Egg on Head and Spoon on Nose: 2.4 seconds

RECORDS BEGGING TO BE SET

☐ Longest Distance to Roll an Egg

☐ Most Egg-Related Puns in 1 Minute

☐ Most Eggs Juggled at Once

Largest Group of Nobel Laureates to Remove a Sword from Someone's Throat

RECORD: 8

NAME: Dan Meyer (sword swallower)

SWORD REMOVERS: Rich Roberts—Nobel Prize in Physiology/Medicine, 1993; Wolfgang Ketterle—Nobel Prize in Physics, 2001; Dudley Herschbach—Nobel Prize in Chemistry, 1986; Paul Krugman—Nobel Prize in Economics, 2008; Roy Glauber—Nobel Prize in Physics, 2005; Frank Wilczek—Nobel Prize in Physics, 2004; Martin Chalfie—Nobel Prize in Chemistry, 2008; William Lipscomb—Nobel Prize in Chemistry, 1976

LOCATION: Boston, Massachusetts

DATE: October 1, 2009

TOOLS: Sword swallower, blade, Nobel Prize winners

CAUTION
SWORD SWALLOWING IS FOR TRAINED PROFESSIONALS ONLY.

Having a sword pulled out of one's throat is impressive, but it rises to a new level if the removal team consists of a gaggle of Nobel Prize winners. Dan Meyer is a professional sword swallower. In 2007, he received the Ig Nobel Prize in Medicine for a research paper he cowrote entitled "Sword Swallowing and Its Side Effects." (The Ig Nobel Prize is an American parody of the Nobel Prize and is awarded for achievements that first make people laugh and then make them think.) The award was presented by a committee of Nobel Laureates, and Meyer seized the opportunity to have them lay their hands on the sword and pull it from his throat. "It was an honor to know that these eminent scientists held my life in their hands," he says.

CRITERIA
☐ Sword swallower must be officially recognized by the Sword Swallowers Association International.
☐ Sword must be a solid steel non-retractable sword at least 15 inches in length.

RELATED RECORD
► Longest Sword Swallowed in Shark-Infested Water: 24 inches

RECORD BEGGING TO BE SET
☐ Longest Sword Fight

Largest Group of People Doing the "Running Man"

RECORD: 152 people

NAME: The Staxx Brothers and their fans

LOCATION: Darrington, Washington

DATE: August 16, 2009

TOOLS: Dancers with knowledge of old-school moves

CRITERIA
☐ Must perform dance for at least 1 minute.

RELATED RECORD
▶ Coldest Temperature in Which to Perform the Centipede While Wearing Boxer Shorts: 13 degrees Fahrenheit

RECORD BEGGING TO BE SET
☐ Longest Distance Moonwalked

Almost anyone can dance the "Running Man." The old-school fad dance that originated in the late '80s is a staple of dancers who just can't dance. When funk rock band The Staxx Brothers prepared to set the world record for Largest Group of People Doing the Running Man at 2009's Summer Meltdown Festival, 149 people joined them. The dance is easy, but the task seemed very difficult at first. Staxx Brother Davin Michael Stedman remembers wondering if they would get even a dozen people. Thankfully, mere seconds into their song "1992," "it looked real good. We had a football field full of hippies high kneeing and doing the dance. It was beautiful."

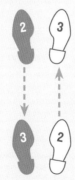
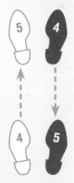
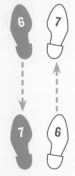

Stand with left foot in front of right.

Step in place with two hopping motions, right coming forward as left hops back.

Repeat, right foot hopping back as left goes forward.

Continue alternating step-hops, adding accompanying arm movements.

Largest Group of People Singing in a Shower

RECORD: 30

NAME: Tyler Gilcrest and 29 friends

LOCATION: Nashville, Tennessee

DATE: February 27, 2010

TOOLS: Large shower cubicle, group of nonclaustrophobic people who don't mind getting wet

Residing in a college dorm, you become accustomed to compromised living conditions: mystery meat, late-night noise, and communal bathrooms. Faced with such indignities, Tyler Gilcrest and twenty-nine of his fellow students decided to put a positive spin on things. The group embarked on a shared showering experience by stripping to their swimwear, cramming themselves into one stall, and belting out the Justin Bieber ditty "One Time" while the water rained down. The resulting video would make an entertaining public service announcement for water conservation.

CRITERIA

☐ Shower must be on while record is set.
☐ Must perform at least one full verse of a song.

Yellow Jacket Comment

DAN: Are you a camp counselor and have thirty-one kids who refuse to shower? Challenge them to beat this record.

RELATED RECORD

▶ Most Consecutive Push-Ups in a Water-Filled Pickup Truck Bed: 7

RECORDS BEGGING TO BE SET

☐ Fastest Time to Use an Entire Bar of Soap
☐ Tallest Shampoo Mohawk

Largest Pajama Party

RECORD: 1,075 people

NAME: Metropolis Fremantle nightclub attendees

LOCATION: Perth, Australia

DATE: December 31, 2009

TOOLS: Discotheque, sea of sleepwear-clad partiers

In the southern hemisphere, New Year's Eve occurs in the middle of summer. Australians are therefore primed to party even harder than their northern neighbors at the end of every December. Taking advantage of this penchant for riotous revelry, Fremantle nightclub manager Ross Madafferi staged a massive pajama party on the last night of 2009, inviting revelers to turn up in their bedtime best and dance the year away. By midnight, RecordSetter officials overseeing the record, including company president Dan Rollman, counted 1,075 people wearing night caps, negligees, bathrobes, and boxers. Metropolis now stages an annual PJ party to ring in each new year, but this sleepy record still stands.

CRITERIA

☐ All participants must wear sleepwear.

RELATED RECORD

▶ Most Consecutive Days Attending Parties: 101

RECORDS BEGGING TO BE SET

☐ Tallest Person Named John to Wear a Pair of Long Johns

☐ Most Pillows Slept on at Once

I ENDED UP STAYING A FEW EXTRA MINUTES AT THE PARTY, SINCE I KNEW I WOULDN'T NEED TO CHANGE INTO SLEEPWEAR WHEN I GOT BACK TO MY HOTEL.

Longest Office Chair Train Pulled by a Motorcycle

RECORD: 19 people

NAME: Wieden+Kennedy's Team Maroon

LOCATION: Portland, Oregon

DATE: April 1, 2010

TOOLS: Motorcycle, office chairs, daredevils

CRITERIA

☐ May use rope to connect participants together.

☐ Must not exceed 10 miles per hour.

☐ Must travel at least 200 feet.

☐ Motorcycle driver must wear helmet and have a valid motorcycle license.

RELATED RECORDS

▶ Most Miles Ridden on a Motorcycle: 1 million

▶ Longest Dryland Waterski Session: 17.34 seconds

RECORDS BEGGING TO BE SET

☐ Longest Office Chair Spin

☐ Most People to Sit on an Office Chair at Once

Wieden+Kennedy's staff are experts at sitting in chairs. This was proven during W+K's annual Founders Day, a party held every year to celebrate the advertising agency's inception. With a motorcycle at the ready and a chain of hardy employees roped together in office chairs, the record attempt took a turn for the surreal when the team spotted NFL quarterback Joey Harrington crossing the street. Harrington agreed to participate in the record attempt, but insisted on popping into a piano store across the street first. He emerged moments later, keyboard in hand, and launched into a spirited playing of the *Chariots of Fire* theme as they headed fearlessly down the road.

Largest Group to Scream and Run at Once

RECORD: 152 people

NAME: Camp Ronald McDonald

LOCATION: Los Angeles, California

DATE: January 20, 2011

TOOLS: Open field, group of people itching to let loose and run wild

When life gets stressful, sometimes the most cathartic thing to do is run into a meadow and yell at the top of your lungs. For many this is just a fantasy, but the kids at Camp Ronald McDonald often play the "run and scream" game. "The object is to run as far as you can while screaming," says Chad Edwards, the Camp's program director. "Everyone gets in a line shoulder to shoulder. When we say 'Go,' you start to scream and run as fast as you can. Whoever runs the farthest is the winner."

It's a rousing display when done in groups of twenty to thirty, but with 152 people, the scene is closer to *Braveheart*.

CRITERIA

☐ All participants must scream and run at once for 10 seconds.

RELATED RECORDS:

▶ Loudest Scream of "It's Christmas!": 105 Decibels

▶ Loudest Horror Actress Scream in a Toyota Prius: 120 Decibels

RECORD BEGGING TO BE SET

☐ Fastest 100-Meter Dash While Wearing a Chicken Costume

Tip for Beating This Record

"Find a ton of hilarious folks who know how to have fun," advises Edwards, who also recommends that participants have big lungs. "The fact we did this in the mountains at around 5,000 feet probably didn't help the lung capacity and screaming ability of everyone!"

Most College Students in an Inflatable Pool Eating Pizza with Snow on the Ground

RECORD: 15

NAME: Michael Smith and 14 fellow Princeton students

LOCATION: Princeton, New Jersey

DATE: February 6, 2010

TOOLS: Inflatable pool, college students, pizza, snowbound location

After piling fourteen of his friends in a pool, and serving them pizza while there was snow on the ground, Michael Smith still had to watch out for campus security: "We had a public safety officer come, and we were sure that he was going to shut us down for some minor reason." Luckily, when the officer arrived at the scene he had just two questions: "Is anyone naked in the swimming pool?" and "Does anyone have a medical condition that could make this dangerous?" The pool-bathing pizza-partiers all replied, "No," and he was on his way. To this day, Smith still calls it "the best interaction with an authority figure, ever."

CRITERIA

☐ Each participant must eat at least one slice of pizza.

☐ Participants must wear bathing suits.

☐ Must be set in below freezing conditions.

RELATED RECORD

▶ Most Consecutive Push-Ups in a Hot Tub: 40

RECORDS BEGGING TO BE SET

☐ Most People Eating Pizza in a Canoe

☐ Most People Dancing the Chicken Dance in a Hot Tub

Loudest Pop Rocks Chorus

RECORD: 72.7 decibels

NAME: Reflections of Christ Student Ministry

LOCATION: Lake City, Florida

DATE: April 3, 2009

TOOLS: Pop Rocks, people with nonticklish tongues, decibel meter

U rban legend has it that if you consume Pop Rocks and soda at the same time, your stomach will explode. It's not true, of course, but the fizzing candy is loud enough to measure 72.7 on a decibel meter. Members of the Reflections of Christ Student Ministry proved this during their Pop Rocks choir experiment, in which they poured the explosive snack on their tongues and stood, gape-mawed, while it snapped and cracked.

In addition to being just plain fun, the record attempt has drawn more people to the ministry. "Our group has grown to over 200 students since we started setting world records," says leader Dustin Busscher. "This has been the most obvious way to prove to teens (who are extremely hard to impress) that they can change the world!"

CRITERIA

☐ Must measure sound level with a decibel meter.

Tip for Beating This Record

Look around the room to see what might interfere with the sound level reading, says Busscher: "We aimed for absolute silence—even AC units were turned off for accuracy's sake."

RELATED RECORD

▶ Most Candy Bars Named in 30 Seconds While Being Tickled: 25

RECORDS BEGGING TO BE SET

☐ Loudest Armpit Fart
☐ Loudest Kazoo Note

DID YOU KNOW?

THE POP ROCKS CRACKLE COMES FROM CARBON DIOXIDE, WHICH CAUSES THE BUBBLES IN FIZZY DRINKS. WHEN THE GASIFIED SUGAR GRANULES GET WET, THEY POP.

POP! POP! POP!

Longest Whisper Chain

RECORD: 59 people

NAME: Jake Bronstein

LOCATION: New York, New York

DATE: July 14, 2009

TOOLS: Soft-spoken people, a life-changing secret message

CRITERIA

☐ Participants must be in same location.

☐ Message must consist of at least five words.

☐ Message must be received verbatim in order to count.

Yellow Jacket Comment

COREY: What would have happened if the wrong message had come through?

DAN: Bite your tongue!

RELATED RECORD

▶ Most Bridesmaids at a Wedding: 103

RECORDS BEGGING TO BE SET

☐ Largest Game of Spin the Bottle

☐ Loudest Wedding Proposal

Jake Bronstein's girlfriend, Kristina Hoge, had been by his side for every one of his world record attempts. She cheered him on when he set a record for sipping from strangers' drinks. She even held the vomit bag ready when he speed-drank a bottle of maple syrup. So when it came time for Bronstein to pop the question to his longtime love, he decided to do it via a new record. At a Manhattan bar, Bronstein began the world's longest whisper chain with a life-changing sentence: "Kristina, will you marry me?" The message passed through fifty-nine strangers, ending, of course, by getting whispered in the ear of a completely stunned Hoge. Following a few moments of confusion and disbelief, she accepted the proposal in front of the captivated crowd.

Most Interviews Conducted on a Ferris Wheel

RECORD: 41

NAME: Nicole Browner

LOCATION: Treasure Island, California

DATE: October 18, 2009

TOOLS: Ferris wheel, investigative journalism skills, interviewees unafflicted by vertigo

Editor Nicole Browner took journalism to new heights at the 2009 Treasure Island Music Festival in California. Browner commandeered a Ferris wheel car on both days of the event, interviewing riders as they enjoyed the view from as high as 60 feet. Browner's questions focused on first concerts, first CD purchases, and guilty-pleasure bands, and responses included "Ace of Base," "Celine Dion," and "Depeche Mode." All this took place inside an open-air car that swung gently back and forth, allowing participants to feel the autumn breeze in their hair as they pondered their answers. Thankfully, none of the interviewees were affected by motion sickness or a case of the "dizzys."

CRITERIA

☐ All interviews must take place within a 48-hour period.

☐ Vomiting during attempt is not permitted.

RELATED RECORD

▶ Most Times Riding a Roller Coaster in 1 Hour: 23

RECORDS BEGGING TO BE SET

☐ Most People Wearing *Star Trek* Costumes on a Ferris Wheel

☐ Most Interviews Conducted on an Escalator

BIRDS OF A FEATHER

RecordSetter LIVE! Events

RecordSetter's live events, held regularly in New York, involve people taking the stage to set or break records in front of a cheering audience. Among the many highlights: group singalongs (in English and in cat meows), a Lady Gaga–themed fashion show, and even a marriage proposal. (She said yes!) A warning for future attendees: If you sit in the front row, there's a chance you'll get covered in water, lobster fragments, or falling Jenga pieces.

I JUST MIGHT HAVE
A PROBLEM THAT
YOU'LL UNDERSTAND
WE ALL NEED
SOMEBODY
TO LEAN ON

Largest Group "Meow" Rendition of "Lean on Me"

RECORD: 117 people

NAME: Kurt Braunohler and audience

LOCATION: New York, New York

DATE: June 29, 2010

Longest Single Breath Beatbox

RECORD: 1 minute, 6.8 seconds

NAME: Chris "Shockwave" Sullivan

LOCATION: New York, New York

DATE: July 27, 2010

Largest Female Accordion Group to Play a Polka Song

RECORD: 6 people

NAME: The Main Squeeze Orchestra

LOCATION: Brooklyn, New York

DATE: January 27, 2011

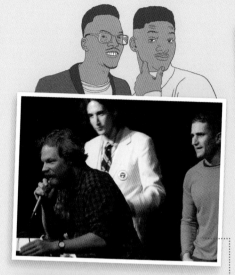

Largest Metamucil Toast

RECORD: 35 people

NAME: Todd Lamb and audience

LOCATION: Brooklyn, New York

DATE: February 24, 2011

Largest Group Singing *The Fresh Prince of Bel-Air* Theme Song in a Round

RECORD: 73 people

NAME: Cory Cavin and audience

LOCATION: Brooklyn, New York

DATE: February 24, 2011

Most Costume Changes While Listening to Lady Gaga's "Bad Romance"

RECORD: 15 costumes

NAME: Brandy Crawford

LOCATION: New York, New York

DATE: September 30, 2010

Most People Simultaneously Flossing with Same Piece of Dental Floss

RECORD: 428

NAME: The Dobson Academy students

LOCATION: Chandler, Arizona

DATE: May 5, 2010

TOOLS: Dental floss, people with enthusiasm for oral hygiene

Flossing is a solitary sport for good reason: bloody gums and pieces of chewed food aren't usually fit for company. But when teacher Brian Stark noticed his canister of Crest Glide Floss contained 328 feet of string, his mind filled with visions of mass flossing. "I wonder how many people could use that at the same time?" he thought. Luckily, he had access to 428 students at the Dobson Academy and, in the name of dental health, all of them lined up holding a single piece of floss and got to work. "Looking down from my observation tower, I saw a second-grade class so scrunched together that their ears were pressed against each other, and their heads had to wobble in unison to keep from breaking the floss."

CRITERIA
☐ May only use one piece of floss (tying pieces together not permitted).

RELATED RECORD
▶ Longest Time Lifting a 151-pound Rice Bag with Teeth: 40.1 seconds

RECORDS BEGGING TO BE SET
☐ Most Strangers' Teeth Brushed in 1 Minute
☐ Fastest Time to Squeeze out an Entire Tube of Toothpaste

Yellow Jacket Comment
COREY: We've been collecting record mementos to display in a RecordSetter museum someday. Fortunately, the 328 feet of used floss did not make the cut.

Most Women Named Wendy to Eat at a Wendy's

RECORD: 23

NAME: Wendy Thomas and twenty-two other Wendys

LOCATION: Columbus, Ohio

DATE: October 1, 2009

TOOLS: Women named Wendy, Wendy's restaurant

CRITERIA
☐ Participants must provide proof of their names.

Yellow Jacket Comment

DAN: Jake bought lunch for all of the Wendys.

COREY: When he discovered that one of them was the real Wendy, he didn't let HER buy?

DAN: Nope. Chivalry at its finest.

RELATED RECORD
▶ Fastest Time for Two People Named Patrick to Name Fifty Famous Patricks on St. Patrick's Day: 45.53 seconds

RECORDS BEGGING TO BE SET
☐ Most Men Named Denny to Eat at a Denny's
☐ Most Men Named Reuben to Share a Reuben Sandwich

Jake Bronstein thinks big. Really big. For this record, his task was to mobilize as many women named Wendy as possible to meet in the parking lot of the Wendy's headquarters in Columbus, Ohio. "It was hard to organize and figure out how to spread the word," he says. "We started a Facebook group, and I started running ads for people named Wendy and looking up Wendys in a phone book."

Though the numbers looked healthy, Bronstein still harbored doubts. He needn't have feared. "We were all standing in this parking lot, and every time a woman would approach we'd go 'Wendy?' And they would say 'Wendy!' We'd all go, 'Wendy!'" This happened twenty-three times, peaking with the arrival of Wendy Thomas, the namesake of the hamburger chain.

Largest Group to Sit on Balloons and Pop Them at Once

Hold balloon to keep it steady.

Apply all your weight in one swift motion.

RECORD: 117 people

NAME: Mason Youth Group at Christ's Church at Mason

LOCATION: Mason, Ohio

DATE: January 22, 2011

TOOLS: Balloons, non-ligyrophobic people (ligyrophobia being a fear of loud noises)

CRITERIA

- ☐ All balloons must be popped within a 10-second time frame.
- ☐ May not wear clothing with sharp points.
- ☐ May only pop one balloon per person.

Tip for Beating This Record

Capan's advice to aspiring record breakers is simple: "Find a store that stocks more than 120 balloons." Buy more than you think you'll need, because there will inevitably be accidental breakages—as well as overly eager people who pop prematurely.

RELATED RECORD

▶ Most People to Pop Bubble Wrap at Once: 1,456

RECORDS BEGGING TO BE SET

- ☐ Most People to Make Balloon Animals at Once
- ☐ Fastest Time to Blow Up and Pop a Balloon Using Nose

The youth group at the Christ's Church of Mason are great believers—in their ability to simultaneously crush balloons with their derrières. In just 10 seconds they destroyed 117 balloons. It's a high number, but the record is most definitely beatable if you get your supplies sorted. In setting up the attempt, the youth group was limited by the number of balloons available for purchase at a Mason, Ohio, store. "We bought every one in stock, but there were only 120," explains Jeremy Capan from Christ's Church. "After a few premature pops, we ended up with 117."

Largest Group Wearing Santa Hats at Once

RECORD: 1,058 people

NAME: Lake Travis Elementary School

LOCATION: Austin, Texas

DATE: December 17, 2010

TOOLS: Santa hats, festive spirit

The sports fields at Lake Travis Elementary School were transformed into a scene resembling Santa's workshop as students, parents, teachers, and staff donned Christmas hats to clinch a holiday-themed world record. Principal Karen Miller-Kopp convinced school bus drivers to join in the fun, as well as getting the mayor to officiate and even bringing in a team of accountants to verify the numbers and tallying method. With the bean counters looking on, the students stood on their sporting field in the shape of a Santa hat, their parents huddling together to form the pom-pom. This is the only time in history that parents have assumed the role of Santa Claus.

CRITERIA
☐ Santa hats may be any color.

RELATED RECORD
▶ Largest Group Wearing Jellyfish Hats at Once: 210

RECORD BEGGING TO BE SET
☐ Most People Sitting on Santa's Lap at Once

Longest Five-Person Tandem Big Wheel Ride

RECORD: 6 minutes, 16.1 seconds

NAME: Rich Dwyer, Greg Obetz, Mike Richwalder, Brice Biruta, and Andrew Hiller

LOCATION: Wilkes-Barre, Pennsylvania

DATE: September 15, 2009

TOOLS: 3 Big Wheel trikes, 5 big kids

CRITERIA
☐ Must ride on a flat surface.
☐ Must stay in motion for duration of attempt.
☐ Touching ground not permitted.

RELATED RECORD
▶ Largest Human Pyramid on a Moving Subway: 6 people

RECORDS BEGGING TO BE SET
☐ Most Big Wheels Donated to Charity
☐ Longest Wheelie on a Big Wheel

Challenged to set a world record for their college business leadership class, Rich Dwyer remembered his collection of Big Wheels left over from childhood. The tricycle, which claims to be the "King of the Sidewalk," is recommended for children aged 3 to 8. Regarding this as a flexible guideline rather than a rule, Rich and four of his friends hauled out the trikes, climbed aboard, and traveled down the sidewalk in pyramid formation. Nobody crashed or fell, but the 6-minute journey was painful nonetheless. Forced to contort themselves into child-sized spaces, the trio of cyclists reported burning calves just 1 minute into the attempt. Mike Richwalder suggests that prospective record breakers spend time rocking some leg curls first. That, or competing in the Tour de France for a few years.

Most Times Slapped in Face in 1 Minute by Multiple People

RECORD: 46

NAME: Lawson Clarke

LOCATION: New York, New York

DATE: April 4, 2009

TOOLS: A face that people want to slap, a willingness to let them do it

Displaying a disturbing inclination for pain, Lawson Clarke invited every female patron of a Manhattan bar—most of whom he had never met—to form an orderly line and slap him in the face, one at a time. But just because he was encouraging them to hit him doesn't mean he wasn't going to take precautions. "I requested the women remove their jewelry on their slapping hands *and* to be only slapped in the meaty portion of my cheeks," he says. Unfortunately, the first woman in line didn't seem to get the message and cuffed him across the ear with a hand full of rings. "Suddenly this record seemed very, very real and very, very stupid," remembers Clarke. In the end, he endured forty-six slaps in 60 seconds, ranging from "manageable, little swats" to "open-hand haymakers that shook my fillings loose."

CRITERIA
- Slappers may not wear jewelry.
- Ear slapping not permitted.

RELATED RECORD
▶ Most Slaps to One's Own Face in 1 Minute: 736

RECORD BEGGING TO BE SET
- Most Buckets of Cold Water Poured on Someone's Head In 1 Minute

199

Alexandra Young

Improviser, Risk Taker, Crowd Pleaser

Alexandra Young sums up her record-setting style in three words: "extreme audience participation." A former comedian with a background in acting and performance studies, Young enjoys performing her feats on stage in front of a live crowd—many of whom find themselves becoming an integral part of the record.

"Being in front of a live audience, you never know what's going to happen," she says, comparing the experience to doing improv in her hometown of San Francisco. "It's exciting, and much more organic than acting with a script."

After setting her first two records—Longest Flute Trill and Longest Scarf Knit in 2 Hours—Young decided to take a big risk for her next one. At a RecordSetter live event in July 2009, she jumped up on stage and announced that she needed someone in the audience to take off their shirt and allow her to write all over their torso with a Sharpie. A few moments of anxiety-inducing silence followed. "I am embarrassed to admit that I never thought about the torso 'quality' when I thought of this idea," she says. "Everyone else's first thought was 'What about hair? What about acne? What if no one wants to take their shirt off?' I got nervous because I didn't think anyone was going to come up," she remembers. But the crowd's initial shyness wore off, and one brave man made his way toward the stage, disrobing as he went. Sixty seconds later, Young and her topless volunteer held a new world record: Most

Autographs Signed on a Stranger's Torso in 1 Minute.

A month later Young returned to the RecordSetter live stage, this time armed with two bags of corn tortillas. Her mission: to Frisbee-toss as many of them as possible into the crowd in 30 seconds. Lest you frown at the wasteful nature of this record, take note that she brought a jar of salsa so that people could catch and enjoy the projectiles.

Young experienced her first—and so far, only—public world-record failure in December 2009, when she attempted to coordinate the longest "Suck-and-Blow" chain. The game, a favorite of middle schoolers nursing crushes on their classmates, involves passing a playing card from your lips to the lips of another person by inhaling and exhaling strategically. Young's target was thirty people. Remove the zero from the number and you're closer to, but still higher than, the actual result. For reasons she is still struggling to understand, the second audience member in the line just couldn't muster the breath control required to pass the playing card along. After a few attempts, and a none-too-subtle reordering of people to move the offender down the line, Young reluctantly declared the record a failure.

Despite the disappointment, Young surged ahead. Having mastered the art of getting audience members to reveal themselves physically during the shirtless signature spectacle, Young stepped it up and began planning a record that would require people to reveal their sordid pasts. Her Largest Game of "Never Have I Ever" record took place at a New York bar and involved eighty-two people confessing intimate details about their lives. The whole game took just over 3 minutes, but provided enough conversation starters for the rest of the night.

Young's ideas continue to flow freely. "I'm thinking about Most Strangers' Hair Braided in One Night. We'd set up a braiding station in the crowd. I'm debating whether I should wear gloves. It might hamper my technique."

CHAPTER 7

Visionaries

Visionaries are those creative, artistic, batty-but-in-a-good-way people who see an opportunity to do something original and run at it as fast as they can. They're the friends you turn to when you need a brilliant costume for a themed party. They're the ones whose ideas make you laugh, shake your head, and wonder, "Why didn't *I* think of that?"

This chapter is stuffed to the gills with record holders who have striven to turn convention on its head. By using wooden spoons, George Foreman Grills, and fire hydrants in ways that the manufacturers never intended, these champs invite us to view the world a little differently.

Largest Lip Balm Collection

RECORD: 415

NAME: Ashlie Munk

LOCATION: Salt Lake City, Utah

DATE: July 13, 2010

TOOLS: Large lip care budget, family of enablers

"Chapstick is my life," admits Ashlie Munk. Her obsession with the mouth goo has not only netted her smooth and colorful lips but also 415 sticks, tubes, and pots of gloss. Though she is proud of her collection, some would prefer she kiss her hobby good-bye. "Everyone in my family thought I was crazy because all I do is buy Chapsticks, which they think are a waste of money," Munk admits. "But once they discovered I set a world record, this changed. Now they have all begun to help by buying me more lip balms." Side benefit: Every member of the Munk family now has soft, moisturized lips.

CRITERIA
☐ Multiples of identical balms not counted.

Yellow Jacket Comment
COREY: What's the difference between lip balm and gloss?

DAN: According to my experience, lip gloss is tastier.

RELATED RECORD
▶ Largest Group to Apply Lip Balm While Wearing Shower Caps and Balancing on One Leg: 371

RECORD BEGGING TO BE SET
☐ Largest Collection of False Eyelashes

Longest "Shh"

RECORD: 1 minute, 44.01 seconds

NAME: Jovah Siegel

LOCATION: Portland, Oregon

DATE: July 26, 2010

TOOLS: Good breath control, contempt for loud noises

Jovah Siegel is an endurance shusher. Taking on the challenge of beating the "Shh" record, which had been broken eight times over 2 years, Siegel applied a "No Pain, No Gain" philosophy. Extensive practice and experimentation took a physical toll. "By the end of the clip my lips looked apneic, which is far from flattering." (Siegel has obviously spent a lot of time reading dictionaries in quiet libraries; a browse through Webster's informs us that "apneic" means "a temporary cessation of breathing.") After regaining his normal pallor, he submitted his record, rendering his competitors speechless with awe. He is now known as Jovah "The Silencer" Siegel.

CRITERIA

☐ "Shh" must be audible for duration of attempt.

RELATED RECORD

▶ Longest Tandem "Shh": 34.55 seconds

RECORDS BEGGING TO BE SET

☐ Most Library Books Checked Out at Once

☐ Quietest Drum Solo

> As an athlete who thinks a lot about lung capacity, I'm envious of Jonah's abilities.

> As a movie buff who hates when people talk in theaters, I'm envious of Jonah's abilities, too.

Longest Time Hopping on One Foot

RECORD: 6 minutes, 13.11 seconds

NAME: Tyler Rolfe

LOCATION: Lake City, Florida

DATE: June 17, 2009

TOOLS: Hopping prowess, stamina, desire to one-up a sibling

Tyler Rolfe's desire to dominate the hopping record—set by Aidan Ludlum at 20.16 seconds—arose out of a casual sibling rivalry. "My brother and I were seeing who could go the longest," he says, "and that's when it turned serious." The two were part of a twenty-person hop-a-thon, each member of the group doing their best to last the longest and claim the new record.

As his friends began to drop out and those around him yelped in pain, Rolfe powered on to an ultimate time of 6 minutes, 13.11 seconds. His monopedal marathon is testament to the power of competition—without a team of rivals to spur him on, Rolfe doubts he would have lasted so long. "It was extremely tough to keep going, knowing I'd already broken the record," he says. "I had to take my mind out of the situation and do as much as my body, or leg in this situation, could do."

CRITERIA

☐ May not switch feet.

☐ Hopping foot must leave ground for each jump.

☐ No external support permitted.

Tip for Beating This Record

Rolfe and his competitors hopped to upbeat music, which can be very helpful for taking your mind off the leg pain and keeping your spirits up. Using a metronome, find the beats-per-minute of your hopping speed and use motivational songs that have a similar beat rate.

RELATED RECORDS

▶ Fewest Toenails on a Foot: 2

▶ Longest Distance to Shoot a Rubber Band Using Feet: 216 inches

RECORD BEGGING TO BE SET

☐ Longest Hopscotch Court

Most Consecutive Push-Ups on Top of the Continental Divide

RECORD: 25

NAME: Chris Sacca

LOCATION: Pagosa Springs, Colorado

DATE: September 28, 2009

TOOLS: Pumped-up pectorals, access to the Continental Divide

Chris Sacca finds room to dream up world records while pedaling his bike. "I have always enjoyed considering the uniqueness of time and place," he says. Unique time: mid-cross-country bike ride. Unique place: 7,275 feet above sea level along America's Continental Divide—the line that separates the stream and rivers flowing east to the Atlantic Ocean from those flowing west to the Pacific. Already two-thirds into that day's 140-mile ride, Sacca claims to have set the bar "low" to "leave room for contenders to bring their A-Games." At least, that will be his excuse when someone beats his record.

Tip for Beating This Record

"Do some research as to the lowest elevations that the Continental Divide passes through," says Sacca. "I took the hard way by setting this record at high altitude."

CRITERIA

- ☐ Body must straddle east and west side anywhere along the Continental Divide.
- ☐ Arms must lock at peak of push-ups and bend 90 degrees at base of push-ups.

RELATED RECORD

▶ Fastest Time for a 5-Year-Old to Complete Fifty Push-Ups: 29.28 seconds

RECORD BEGGING TO BE SET

- ☐ Most Consecutive Jumping Jacks on the Great Wall of China

Most Fire Puffs Blown in 30 Seconds

RECORD: 46

NAME: R. J. Williams

LOCATION: New York, New York

DATE: June 4, 2010

TOOLS: Kerosene, torch, lighter, certification proving you're allowed to do this

R. J. Williams warns off all challengers, labeling his record "a mishap just waiting to happen." Williams, a magician, is a master of Sideshow Arts, a niche that includes sword swallowing, recreational body piercing, lying on a bed of nails, and fire breathing. Even though he is a professional, he still gets nervous about blowing flames.

For this attempt, he swigged from a bottle of kerosene, spraying three spurts per sip at a flaming torch held in his left hand to make it flare. "Aside from nearly melting off my hand and forehead, and singeing some of my facial hair, I came out of it unharmed," he says. Still, that doesn't mean he endorses copycat attempts. "We all know what they say about playing with fire, even those of us who play with it for a living."

CAUTION
FIRE BREATHING IS
EXTREMELY DANGEROUS
AND SHOULD ONLY BE ATTEMPTED BY
TRAINED PROFESSIONALS.

CRITERIA

☐ May use any flammable liquid to blow fire.

☐ May not use any external assistance.

RELATED RECORD

▶ Fastest Time to Blow out 107 Birthday Candles: 4.03 seconds

RECORD BEGGING TO BE SET

☐ Longest Time to Balance Fire Extinguisher on Forehead

R. J. WOULD BE A FUN GUY TO MAKE S'MORES WITH.

Most Times Refusing to Set a World Record in 30 Seconds

RECORD: 32

NAME: Kristen Driggers

LOCATION: Cheraw, South Carolina

DATE: July 1, 2009

TOOLS: Stubbornness, a friend who will happily harangue you

CRITERIA
☐ Count based on each "Do you want to break a world record?"/"No" exchange.
☐ May not overlap questions and answers.

RELATED RECORD
▶ Most RecordSetter World Records Broken in 10 Minutes: 14

RECORD BEGGING TO BE SET
☐ Most Times Refused Entry to a VIP Event in 1 Hour

Kristen Driggers is a paradox with a side of riddle, topped with freshly squeezed contradictions. Her repeated refusal to set a world record resulted in . . . a world record. It all came about when her brother, Chad, set the record for Most Golf Ball Bounces on a Sand Wedge one afternoon. "His desire to rope me into his endeavor was irritating," she remembers. Every time Chad asked, "Do you want to break a world record?" Driggers said no. This gave Chad an idea. He set up a video camera in the backyard and brought out his sister, who was holding her 10-month-old daughter, Londyn, in her arms. There they reenacted the offer-and-refusal routine, scoring Driggers's first world record. Chad was thrilled, Driggers was surprisingly elated, but Londyn was barely moved. According to Driggers, "I am not sure the record-setting experience changed my daughter, but shortly after we set the record, I had to change her."

DO YOU WANT TO BREAK A RECORD?

No...

Most Whoopee Cushions Sat on in 30 Seconds Without Smiling

RECORD: 22

NAME: Jeff Rubin

LOCATION: New York, New York

DATE: November 19, 2009

TOOLS: Whoopee cushions, humorless visage

CRITERIA

☐ Two assistants may be used to place cushions.

☐ Must use standard-sized, fully inflated cushions.

Tip for Beating This Record

To stop yourself from laughing, try doing multiplication tables in your head. (You could also mentally list the names of vegetables, sporting teams, or movies you've seen in the last year.) If you still feel like you're about to lose your composure, gently bite the inside of your cheek.

RELATED RECORD

▶ Largest Armpit Fart Orchestra: 6

RECORD BEGGING TO BE SET

☐ Most People at a Family Reunion to Sit on Whoopee Cushions at Once

The statute of limitations has passed so don't go running to call child services, but as a kid, Jeff Rubin never had a whoopee cushion. This may explain why, as an adult, he finds them so amusing. Jeff is the Executive Editor of CollegeHumor, a site chock-full of frat humor and funny videos.

Rubin took to the stage at a CollegeHumor live show and proceeded to crack up the audience by conjuring a crescendo of fart noises from his cushion collection. Unsurprisingly, Rubin struggled to keep focus. "A heckler screamed, 'Now that time Jeff actually farted,'" he reminisces, "and I almost lost it."

Fastest Time for a Baby to Crawl 10 Feet While Wearing a Fake Mustache

RECORD: 1 minute, 31.5 seconds

NAME: Cooper Lindsay-Abaire

LOCATION: Brooklyn, New York

DATE: April 4, 2009

TOOLS: Speed-crawling baby, false 'stache

Tip for Beating This Record

Lure the baby across the line using something colorful, shiny, or noisy. A basketball did the trick for Lindsay-Abaire, but other items to consider include pinwheels, maracas, and a rainbow xylophone. Avoid anything with a clown motif unless you want to be responsible for a future phobia.

Though his false mustache gives him a mature look, Cooper Lindsay-Abaire is too young to be able to talk about his own record. His mother, however, offers these insights into the infant champion's record preparation. When it came time to don the facial hair, Lindsay-Abaire refused to wear the mustache in the traditional manner, opting instead for the "uni-brow" look inspired by Bert from *Sesame Street*. He began the 10-foot crawl enthusiastically—but lost energy midway through. A bouncing basketball proved enticing enough to get him past the finish line.

CRITERIA
☐ Must crawl unassisted.
☐ Mustache may be worn anywhere on face.

RELATED RECORD
▶ Most Clothes Pins Attached to a Mustache: 10

RECORD BEGGING TO BE SET
☐ Most People Wearing Fake Mustaches in a Swimming Pool at Once

Fastest Time to Direct Twenty Insults at a Fire Hydrant

RECORD: 15.49 seconds

NAME: Sierra Dwyer

LOCATION: Fort Collins, Colorado

DATE: June 1, 2010

TOOLS: Fire hydrant with high self-esteem, arsenal of disparaging witticisms

CRITERIA

☐ Must set record within 5 feet of regulation fire hydrant.

☐ Insults must be longer than one word.

Tip For Beating This Record

Balance wit and brevity, says Dwyer. "Using just shorter insults would most definitely be even faster, but we came up with some pretty funny ones that I wanted to use." To maintain the entertainment factor and still beat the record, challenge yourself to cram the jokes into fewer words. A motor-mouthed delivery will seal the deal.

RELATED RECORD

▶ Most Non-English Curse Words Recited in 30 Seconds: 14

RECORDS BEGGING TO BE SET

☐ Quickest Time to Open a Fire Hydrant

☐ Longest Scream Directed Toward a Stop Sign

YOU'VE NEVER BEEN TO WALMART!

YOU'RE FILTHY!

YOU'VE GOT BUGS ON YOU!

Sierra Dwyer wants to make one thing clear: She does not have an actual beef with the short yellow fire hydrant she chose to hurl twenty insults toward in just over 15 seconds. It's just that when her basketball bounced off the unassuming hydrant, she got "a little worked up." "Your best friend pees on you!" she taunted the mute water source. "You don't have a Facebook page. Firefighters take advantage of you." The hydrant seemed unaffected by the barbs, but it has been placed under observation just in case. Some armchair psychologists suggest that when you tap a hydrant, what gushes forth is not water but repressed anger in liquid form.

Most Empty Boxes Knocked Down with a Broom While Riding a Pallet Jack

RECORD: 44

NAME: Guido Balducci

LOCATION: Sarasota, Florida

DATE: July 22, 2009

TOOLS: Pallet jack, broom, wall of empty boxes, someone or something to break your fall

Ordinarily, a pallet jack is used to lift and transport pallets—those wooden platforms that hold goods when they are delivered to a grocery store. For this record, however, Guido Balducci decided to take his jack for a joyride, creating a wall out of fifty-five stacked empty paper boxes, and then crashing through it aboard his newly repurposed vehicle.

Goodbye wall of boxes, hello world.

CRITERIA
☐ May only pass through wall of boxes once.

RELATED RECORD
▶ Largest Cardboard Fort

RECORDS BEGGING TO BE SET
☐ Most Goals in a Game of Broomball
☐ Tallest Stack of Pallets
☐ Longest Distance Traveled in a Forklift

WHY CALL IT A PALLET "JACK"?

IT LOOKS MORE LIKE A "LARRY" TO ME.

Longest Time to Balance American Flag on Chin While Listening to "God Bless the USA"

RECORD: 58.38 seconds

NAME: Doug McManaman

LOCATION: Amherst, Nova Scotia, Canada

DATE: May 29, 2010

TOOLS: "Stars and Stripes" on a pole, patriotism for the USA regardless of birthplace

CRITERIA

☐ Flag must be at least 5 feet in width.

☐ No adhesives or external support permitted.

☐ May not touch flag or pole during attempt.

☐ Song may be looped repeatedly if needed.

Tip for Beating This Record

"Start with something easy like a broom handle," says McManaman. It will feel weird at first, but don't be discouraged—you'll get used to it. Practice balancing one thing until it becomes very easy before moving on to a larger or more difficult object."

RELATED RECORD

▶ Longest Time to Balance Wheelbarrow on Chin: 51 seconds

RECORD BEGGING TO BE SET

☐ Most American Flags Held at Once

Doug McManaman is a proud Canadian through and through, but when it comes to record setting, this balance king is a global citizen. Inspired by Veteran's Day, the Canuck celebrated the USA by balancing an American flag on his chin while listening to country star Lee Greenwood's "God Bless the USA." Greenwood also recorded a version in honor of the neighbors up north, which McManaman used to set his next record: Longest Time to Balance Canadian Flag on Chin While Listening to Lee Greenwood's "God Bless Canada," at 45.66 seconds.

Most Times Getting a Mattress World Employee to Say "Mattress" on a Phone Call

RECORD: 15

NAME: Jake Bronstein

LOCATION: New York, New York

DATE: April 13, 2010

TOOLS: Telephone, determination, charm

CRITERIA
☐ Employee may not be aware of attempt.

Tip for Beating This Record
Ask for clarifications as often as possible. The key to this successful record was getting the Mattress World employee to repeat the company's website address (www.mattressworldsuperstores.com) a total of five times.

RELATED RECORD
▶ Longest Time to Balance a Queen-Size Box Spring on Chin: 14 seconds

RECORD BEGGING TO BE SET
☐ Longest Distance Tobogganed on a Mattress

"Some of the records I set leave me feeling miserable afterwards," explains Jake Bronstein. This is a likely reference to the time he downed an entire bottle of maple syrup in under 40 seconds. On this occasion, he specifically picked a record he hoped would cheer him up—and keep him from vomiting into a trash can. "I was having a lousy work day, and I thought setting a record would change all of that," he says. It did, but after coaxing an exasperated Mattress World employee to repeat the word "mattress" over the phone fifteen times in just over 3 minutes, perhaps Bronstein was the only one left in good spirits.

Fastest Time to Recite "To Be, or Not to Be" Soliloquy While Balancing on a Rola Bola on a Picnic Table and Juggling Knives

RECORD: 41.21 seconds

NAME: Chad Lunders

LOCATION: Kansas City, Missouri

DATE: October 3, 2009

TOOLS: Good balance, knife-handling skills, ability to channel brooding Danish prince

CRITERIA

☐ Must juggle at least three knives.

☐ Must recite soliloquy from memory.

RELATED RECORD

▶ Fastest Time to Create Ten Different Balloon Animals While Balancing on a Rola Bola: 7 minutes, 57.03 seconds

RECORD BEGGING TO BE SET

☐ Fastest Time to Name All of Shakespeare's Plays While Balancing Quill on Nose

Although Shakespeare is dead and cannot debate this, it is our belief that he always intended for his famous words to be articulated by a performer balanced atop a Rola Bola on a picnic table, while juggling three knives at the same time. Chad Lunders intuitively grasped this, even though he admitted, "There were a lot of things that could have gone wrong; I could have fallen off the picnic table, stabbed myself, or become tongue-tied." Once on the Rola Bola, though, things went smoothly. Rather than suffering the slings and arrows of mistimed knife throws and shuffling off this mortal coil, Lunders sped through his words and lived to tell the tale.

Fastest Time to Recite All Fifty United States in Alphabetical Order While Being Hit in the Head with Wooden Spoons

RECORD: 16.75 seconds

NAME: Stefanie Ward

LOCATION: Pittsburgh, Pennsylvania

DATE: March 1, 2011

TOOLS: Ability to recall all states under adverse conditions, industrial-strength skull, wooden spoons

CRITERIA

☐ Must be hit with spoons for duration of attempt.

☐ May hit self or be hit by someone else.

Tip for Beating This Record

One way to memorize all states of the USA is to put the schoolkid tune "Fifty Nifty United States" on daily rotation. If the earnest young voices are too saccharine for your tastes, pick a song in your preferred genre and replace its lyrics with the A to W of the USA. Heavy metal would be a challenge, but not impossible.

RELATED RECORD

▶ Most Times to Hit a Blindfolded IT Guy with Bouncy Rubber Balls in 30 Seconds: 96

Recalling all fifty U.S. states in alphabetical order is a tough challenge at the best of times, but the task is even harder when both sides of your head are being slapped with wooden spoons. This record category was initiated by radio host Brian Pierce, whose eager cohost Kellie Michaels did the spoon thwacking. Pierce's time of 21.2 seconds was swift, but no match for Stefanie Ward, who got from Alabama to Wyoming in 16.75 seconds. Ward chose to do the record without an assistant, preferring to administer her own head bops. This not only eliminated the surprise factor of not knowing how hard she'd be hit, but it also required greater concentration.

Longest Time to Sit on a Heated George Foreman Grill

RECORD: 29.86 seconds

NAME: Todd DeFazio

LOCATION: Pittsburgh, Pennsylvania

DATE: June 1, 2010

TOOLS: George Foreman Grill, heat-resistant buttocks

George Foreman was a brave man who fought both Joe Frazier and Muhammed Ali. But even he would meet his match in Todd DeFazio, a radio disc jockey who agreed to sit, sans pants, on an open George Foreman grill live on-air. Like Foreman's Rumble in the Jungle, the fight began simply, but the pain came later. "The grill starts out cold and the heat doesn't kick in until about 12 seconds. That's when you really start to feel it and you can eventually smell the skin and hair burning." DeFazio's bottom finished medium-rare, and the grill suddenly lost its communal appeal. "After I used the grill for my bum, no one has dared to put a hamburger on it again."

12 seconds

CRITERIA

☐ Grill must be open and turned on.

☐ Buttocks must touch grill for duration of attempt.

RELATED RECORD

▶ Largest Human Pyramid Dressed In Snuggies Singing "99 Bottles of Beer": 5 people

RECORD BEGGING TO BE SET

☐ Most Snuggies Worn at Once

CAUTION

GRILLS CAN BURN YOUR BUNS.

IF YOU ENJOY SITTING DOWN WITHOUT FEELING PAIN, WE STRONGLY ADVISE AGAINST ATTEMPTING THIS RECORD.

Most Consecutive Arm Wrestling Victories by a Woman in Her Third Trimester of Pregnancy

RECORD: 6

NAME: Emily Wilson

LOCATION: New York, New York

DATE: May 20, 2009

TOOLS: Bun in the oven, brawny biceps

Emily Wilson is a strong woman, but pregnancy turned her into a superhero. With her due date just 1 month away, Wilson won arm wrestles against six people—five women and one man—in under 5 minutes. She succumbed in her seventh bout, but it was for good reason. "I was pretty tired by that time," she remembers. "I didn't want to overdo it and then go into labor." Her son Nigel is now part of the RecordSetter family and seems to be influencing her ideas for future records. "I tried to stack Cheerios on my tongue and sing 'Mary Had a Little Lamb,'" she says. "I think I'll keep practicing that one."

I CAN SAY WITH CERTAINTY THAT I WILL NEVER ATTEMPT THIS RECORD.

CRITERIA

☐ Must be at least 28 weeks pregnant.

☐ Must arm wrestle adults.

☐ Must follow basic arm wrestling precepts: elbows down, opposite hand off the table, winner pins opponent's hand, fingers, or knuckles to table.

RELATED RECORD

▶ Most Peeps Placed on Sleeping Baby in a Stop-Motion Film: 3

RECORD BEGGING TO BE SET

☐ Most People Arm Wrestled in 1 Minute

Most Lit Cigarettes Extinguished in Mouth in I Minute

RECORD: 60

NAME: Richie Magic

LOCATION: New York, New York

DATE: June 29, 2010

TOOLS: Cigarettes, deep hatred of smoking

THE RARE BLACK-TONGUED LIZARD SCARES AWAY PREDATORS.

Richie Magic doesn't mince words when asked how he feels about smoking. "Cigarettes are vile and disgusting," he says. "If you smoke, your mouth will feel, look, smell, and taste like a human ashtray." In order to demonstrate this in a hands-on way, Magic took to the stage at a RecordSetter live event and crammed lit cigarettes into his mouth at the rate of 1 per second, putting them out with a few quick mouth movements and then spitting them into a bowl. After a minute had passed, he stuck out his blackened tongue, causing members of the crowd to cringe. Magic was delighted with the response.

CRITERIA

- ☐ Each cigarette must be fully extinguished on tongue.
- ☐ May extinguish multiple cigarettes at once.
- ☐ May use an assistant to prelight and hand over cigarettes.

RECORD BEGGING TO BE SET

- ☐ Most Cigarettes Put Through a Paper Shredder in 1 Minute

Yellow Jacket Comment

DAN: This record almost got us kicked out of the venue. We neglected to inform the owners that we would be using fire. When the smell of tobacco permeated the room, we were in trouble.

COREY: Fortunately, the chrysanthemums we sent the next day smoothed things over.

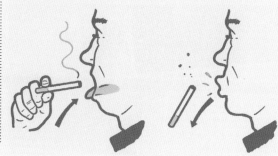

Most Consecutive Bites Taken out of an Apple While Juggling a Flaming Torch, a Bowling Ball, and an Apple

RECORD: 46

NAME: Brian Pankey

LOCATION: Springfield, Illinois

DATE: May 8, 2010

TOOLS: Flaming torch, bowling ball, apple, juggling expertise, speedy nibbling skills

Ever a mascot for multitaskers, Brian Pankey found a way to combine exercise, healthy eating, and manual dexterity into one 30-second performance. By timing his throws just right, he was able to take a bite out of an apple every time it passed his lips in the juggling rotation between flaming torch and bowling ball. That's right: He chewed one of his juggling objects *while* juggling it. By doing the apple trick on a daily basis, Pankey is able to keep the doctor away in the most daredevil manner we've seen.

CRITERIA
☐ Bowling ball must weigh at least 8 pounds.
☐ Must bite apple every time it's caught.

RELATED RECORD
▶ Most Consecutive Bites Taken out of Three Apples in 30 Seconds While Juggling Them: 65

RECORD BEGGING TO BE SET
☐ Most Bites Taken out of a Single Apple

CAUTION BITING INTO THE BOWLING BALL WILL RESULT IN THE OPPOSITE OF KEEPING THE DOCTOR AWAY.

Most Pieces of Chalk Thrown at a Person in a Taco Suit Singing "Space Oddity"

RECORD: 144

NAME: Ella Morton

LOCATION: New York, New York

DATE: May 25, 2010

TOOLS: Taco costume, chalk, appreciation for David Bowie, thrower with good aim

Tip for Beating This Record

"Find a chalk thrower who used to be a varsity softball pitcher," says Morton, who recruited former softballer Emily Casden. "Their arms can handle the fast pace and accurate aim required."

Zack Walsh had a simple goal: to develop a record so complex and obscure it was unbreakable. So he paired a fedora with a taco costume, executed his best David Bowie impression, and got battered by pieces of chalk. But Walsh failed to factor in the tenacity of Ella Morton. Morton was bombarded by 144 pieces of chalk to the sound of a live band at a RecordSetter event, surviving to send some trash talk Walsh's way: "Bet you didn't think anyone would be willing to transform into a warbling Mexican snack despite a glaring lack of singing talent. Well, you thought wrong. Say good-bye to your precious record."

CRITERIA

☐ Must throw pieces of chalk one at a time.

☐ Chalk must hit body to be counted.

☐ Must wear full-body one-piece taco costume.

RELATED RECORD

▸ Tallest Tower of Humans Wearing One Sock Each and Brushing Teeth While Listening to "Thriller": 7

RECORD BEGGING TO BE SET

☐ Most People Wearing Taco Costumes in a Subway Car

BIRDS OF A FEATHER

Cars

The humble automobile provides yet another example of just how creative record setters can get. This collection of achievements provides a wealth of ideas for a drab day. The next time you're bored, try driving around your country, entrapping the nearest 3-year-old in a circle of toys, or testing the patience of other drivers with constant U-turns.

Most Automobile U-Turns in 2 Minutes

RECORD: 11

NAME: Mortimer Blackwell

LOCATION: Yucaipa, California

DATE: December 27, 2009

Fastest Time to Drive to Every Capital City in the U.K. and Ireland

RECORD: 23 hours, 10 minutes

NAME: Matt Piper, Gareth Jones, and Lloyd Jones

LOCATION: London, England

DATE: April 3, 2009

Largest Toy Car Circle Built Around a 3-Year-Old

RECORD: 141 cars

NAME: Cameron Parker

LOCATION: Charfield, England

DATE: June 7, 2010

Slowest Drive Through a Redwood Tree While Listening to Hall & Oates

RECORD: 34.19 seconds

NAME: Dana Cole

LOCATION: Leggett, California

DATE: June 20, 2010

TOOLS: Sequoia tree, Hall & Oates music, lack of traffic

CRITERIA

- ☐ Car must remain in motion for duration of attempt.
- ☐ Timing starts when front bumper enters tree and stops when rear bumper exits tree.
- ☐ May use any Hall & Oates song.

RELATED RECORD

- ▶ Longest Time to Balance a 6-Foot Christmas Tree on Chin While on Knees: 3 minutes, 2.26 seconds

RECORD BEGGING TO BE SET

- ☐ Most Times Singing "Happy Birthday" While Going Through a Car Wash

The United States is home to an array of drive-through experiences: hamburgers, prescriptions, banking, and, in California, trees. In the 1930s, foresters in the hamlet of Leggett cut a 7-foot tunnel through the base of a 315-foot-tall redwood so that a road could pass through its trunk. The tree is now known as the Chandelier Drive-Thru Tree and is the star attraction of Leggett's Drive-Thru Tree Park. Cruising through this idyllic setting, Dana Cole felt the need to enhance the experience with a little bit of '70s soul. With the windows rolled down and friends Gabriel Varney and Mona Brahmbhatt in the backseat of his Honda Accord, Cole took a leisurely 34.19 seconds to drive through the majestic Chandelier tree as "Rich Girl" boomed from the stereo.

Most Straws Fit in Mouth

RECORD: 600

NAME: Dinesh Upadhyaya

LOCATION: Mumbai, India

DATE: January 23, 2011

TOOLS: Drinking straws, elastic lips

Dinesh Upadhyaya is single-handedly—or, rather, single-mouthedly—advancing the art of stuffing masses of household objects in his face. In the same week that his Most Pencils Fit in Mouth record caught the eye of news shows around the world, Upadhyaya proved there's no rest for the loose-lipped, submitting another mouth-stretching world record. The man from Mumbai tied six hundred drinking straws into bunches, then, in the manner of a snake relaxing its jaw to swallow a hippo whole, crammed the lot into his malleable maw. No, he did not follow up by attempting to drink six hundred milkshakes at once.

IF HE EVER WANTED A CAREER CHANGE, DINESH COULD FIND LUCRATIVE WORK AS A FREELANCE STRAW DISPENSER IN FOOD COURTS.

CRITERIA

☐ Straws must have a minimum diameter of 0.25 in.

☐ Straws may be bound with elastic bands to keep them together.

☐ All straws must be held fully within the mouth for them to be counted.

RELATED RECORD

▶ Most Sporks Fit in Open Mouth: 27

RECORDS BEGGING TO BE SET

▶ Farthest Distance to Blow a Straw Wrapper off a Straw

▶ Shortest Straw Used to Drink a Full Can of Soda

Most Times Reciting "Mrs. Smith's Fish Sauce Shop" in 30 Seconds

RECORD: 18

NAME: Stuart Duggan

LOCATION: Sussex, England, U.K.

DATE: March 4, 2010

TOOLS: Agile tongue, calmness under pressure

CRITERIA

☐ Must pronounce all words correctly and distinctly.

Tip for Beating This Record

"I think the adrenaline of doing it live probably helped me," says Duggan. "If you can put yourself into a situation where it would be embarrassing to fail (i.e., on live radio), that could help. Oh, and above all, do not take it too seriously! It is only a bit of fun, after all, eh?"

RELATED RECORD

▶ Most Lies Told About Oneself in 30 Seconds: 34

RECORD BEGGING TO BE SET

☐ Most Shells Sold by the Seashore by Someone Named Sally

Stuart Duggan was working as a journalist and newsreader at Bright FM in Sussex, England, when he was issued his most taxing professional task to date. Chris Bailey, a presenter for the station's morning show, challenged him to beat the RecordSetter world record for most times saying the tongue twister "Mrs. Smith's Fish Sauce Shop" in 30 seconds—live, on air, at a time when most people were still yawning in bed. (Try it, right now. Difficult, isn't it?)

The record stood at seventeen. Never one to back away from a difficult duty, Duggan immediately began to get ready for his moment—though he is quick to assure that he didn't require extensive coaching. "I did a quick run through whilst preparing my news bulletin, but no serious training." he says. When it came time to beat the feat, Duggan executed a calm, near-flawless recitation of eighteen fish sauce shops, to the nail-biting delight of hosts Chris and Anna.

Tallest Pillow Tower Built Inside a Walmart

RECORD: 28 pillows

NAME: Chris Brown and Kevin Weeks

LOCATION: Salem, Virginia

DATE: October 31, 2006

TOOLS: Walmart with a fully stocked pillow section, architectural aspirations

CRITERIA

- ☐ No adhesives or external support permitted.
- ☐ All pillow types acceptable.
- ☐ All pillows must be found inside store.

RELATED RECORD

▶ Tallest Pillow Tower on Which to Perform a Handstand: 10 pillows

RECORDS BEGGING TO BE SET

- ☐ Tallest Human Pyramid in a Starbucks
- ☐ Tallest Cereal Box Tower Built Inside a Target

Chris Brown and Kevin Weeks constructed an impressive pillow tower inside a Walmart as part of a scavenger hunt. Somewhat surprisingly, the megastore could not have been more encouraging during the attempt. "A Walmart employee came over to us and asked what we were doing, and then came back with a ladder!" says Brown. "I think she had visions of us buying them all." After taking a picture to commemorate the feat of bedding architecture, the team quickly deconstructed the pillow skyscraper and left. They got a record. The employee got confused. We imagine she now rests her head on those pillows and wonders if they'll ever return.

FInd a vacant aisle.

Select flat-bottomed pillows for easier stacking.

Keep a lookout for employees while building the tower.

Most Kisses Bestowed on a Person at Once

RECORD: 14

NAME: Paymon Parsia

LOCATION: New York, New York

DATE: April 21, 2010

TOOLS: Kissable person, supple-lipped crowd

What birthday present do you get for the man who has everything? Laura Speier answered that question by gifting best friend Paymon Parsia with a surprise world record for his special day. In the middle of a New York RecordSetter event, a shocked Parsia was called to the stage mid-show. His role as the kissee was relatively simple: sit back, relax, and have fourteen audience members deposit kisses all over his body. Everywhere, that is, apart from his lips. "I was kissed in places I never thought I'd be kissed," he says. "At the time I was a little sad my lips didn't get any action, but retrospectively it worked out well because you can see my big smile and how much fun I'm having, and also how my glasses fogged up."

CRITERIA

☐ All participants' lips must touch record-setter's body or clothing at the same time.

Tip for Beating This Record

"Stand up so you maximize your kissing surface area," says Parsia. "And take off your glasses because it definitely gets a bit heated."

RELATED RECORD

▶ Most Times Kissing a Dog in 30 Seconds While Wearing a Groucho Marx Mask: 77

RECORD BEGGING TO BE SET

☐ Most Layers of Lipstick Applied in 30 Seconds

RECORDSETTER LEGEND

Doug McManaman

The Balance King Who Never Says "I Can't"

"I always figured if you can do something, you might as well do it," says Doug McManaman. It's a sound philosophy, but whereas many people would apply it to, say, pursuing a career in investment banking or taking up gardening, McManaman applies it to balancing lobster traps, a surfboard, or a 40-pound turkey on his chin.

The man now known as The Balance King was born in 1944 in the Nova Scotia town of Amherst—population 9,500. Growing up with five brothers and being involved in Little League, softball, and target shooting, McManaman's competitive instincts were honed at an early age. After serving in the navy in the '60s, he took another physically demanding job, working as a climber who installed steel on tall buildings. "Maybe that's where my sense of balance comes from," he muses.

After a while McManaman missed his favorite pastime as a youngster: perching stacks of objects on his chin. Now he performs at county fairs and parties, customizing his act to fit the audience. "In bars, I balance beer bottles, wine bottles, shot glasses, and challenge the audience to bring something that I can't handle," he says. "If the crowd has kids, I do something fun and easy. I did the Blueberry Festival here and balanced bottles of blueberry juice."

After discovering RecordSetter, McManaman wasted no time in showing the world what the King is capable of. One of his early records, Most Golf Balls Balanced on Chin, featured him perching a custom-made, three-level tower on his face. Each level held around eighteen golf balls, placed precariously in a row, for a total of fifty-six balls balanced.

Over the next 10 months, McManaman submitted eighty-one more records, including Longest Time to Balance a Miniature Guitar on Forehead, Longest Time to Balance Two Eggs on an Ax on Chin, and Longest Time to Balance Suit of Armor on Hand.

As a veteran of the Department of Tourism, McManaman can't help but allow his Canadian pride to filter into some of his records. Hockey pucks, hockey sticks, and snowshoes have enjoyed prime position on his chin, and he often sets his records while wearing the blue-and-green tartan of Nova Scotia. His matching cape features the words "BALANCE KING," spelled out in gold lettering down his spine. In the ultimate show of allegiance, McManaman once balanced the Canadian flag on his chin for 45.66 seconds while listening to "God Bless Canada."

"I come from a small community where there has never been a world record," he says. "A lot of people just can't believe I am making all these records." One exception: his wife, Karen, who has grown accustomed to his determination and drive. "She lets me practice right here in the house—but she doesn't like me practicing with eggs," he says. "Truthfully, she's quite amazed by it. She now claims I can balance anything but my budget."

McManaman, who is 66, hopes his records will allow people of all generations to realize they can stretch beyond their assumed capabilities. "I really hope that young people can see that somebody my age can do these kinds of things and feel inspired to try something themselves," he says. As a veteran leader of the RecordSetter community, who now holds over 200 records, he has found "the opportunity to share with the world what can be accomplished if we try."

CHAPTER 8

Earth and Environment

N o less an expert than Henry David Thoreau remarked that "there is a subtle magnetism in Nature, which, if we unconsciously yield to it, will direct us aright." A philosophy we devoutly adhere to, and which we believe refers to both dog bench-pressing and pretending to be a sea otter. This is a chapter that will appeal to transcendentalists, environmentalists, animal lovers, and even people who just like to get outside and dance.

Most Alternate Paw Handshakes Elicited from a Dog in 30 Seconds

RECORD: 19

NAME: Lyle Bjornson

LOCATION: St. Andrews, Manitoba, Canada

DATE: April 14, 2010

TOOLS: Trained canine with a firm handshake, doggy treats

CRITERIA

☐ Timing starts when paw leaves ground for first time.

☐ Handshakes must alternate between paws.

Yellow Jacket Comment

DAN: That dog would make an excellent politician.

RELATED RECORD

► Most Balloon Dogs Created in 1 Minute: 6

RECORD BEGGING TO BE SET

☐ Most Dogs Walked at Once

Though Lyle Bjornson and his dog hold the current handshaking record, this category was created by Dan Morrison and his pooch Schuma. As part of a record-setting spree (done to secure the world record for the most consecutive days setting world records), Morrison looked around his office for inspiration, his eyes landing on the organization's resident canine companion. Taking advantage of the animal's instincts for diplomacy and obedience, Morrison coaxed Schuma toward sixteen paw shakes in half a minute. Victory was sweet but fleeting—within two weeks, Bjornson and his border collie shook the record loose by three shakes.

Most Bench Presses of a Live Dog in 30 Seconds

RECORD: 30

NAME: Eliot Glazer

LOCATION: New York, New York

DATE: March 18, 2010

TOOLS: A petite and relaxed pup, upper-arm strength

CRITERIA

☐ Dog must be fully supported while being lifted.

☐ Arms must extend for each repetition.

Tip for Beating This Record

Glazer says a puppy from a pet shop just won't cut it: "The key to bench-pressing a live dog is to make sure the dog is a rescue." Not only will this help you break a record, but it will also make you a good person.

RELATED RECORD

▶ Most High Fives from a Dog in 30 Seconds: 15

RECORD BEGGING TO BE SET

☐ Most Bicep Curls of a Turtle in 30 Seconds*

*CAREFULLY, OF COURSE.

I f the Westminster Dog Show had a category for Most Chilled-Out of Breed, Eliot Glazer's pup, Atticus, would be the frontrunner. Atticus is the most docile of dogs, often serving as a 16-pound living barbell when Glazer wants to work on his pecs. The duo performed their bench-pressing record on *Late Night with Jimmy Fallon,* where the audience could barely contain their "ahhs" as they watched Atticus get bounced up and down without so much as blinking. Despite initial concerns that he might be exploiting his dog in order to gain fame, Glazer says, "My bond with Atticus has only grown stronger since he's become a TV star."

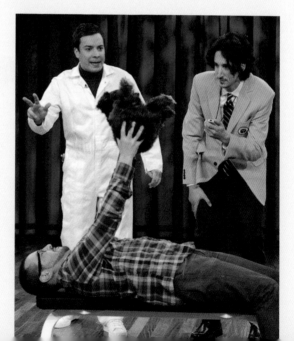

Most Times to Pet a Dog in 30 Seconds

RECORD: 107

NAME: Austin Munn

LOCATION: Indianapolis, Indiana

DATE: January 8, 2011

TOOLS: A dog who loves being stroked, nimble hands, and soft palms

Austin Munn's border collie, Ace, overcame double hip surgery as a young pup before helping his owner become a RecordSetter legend. The patient pooch sat still and silent for half a minute while Munn pet him 107 times—in the opposite direction of his hair growth, no less. Munn and Ace trumped two other human/dog teams in this category: Rob Wilkinson started it all by patting his dog Cassie on the head thirty-seven times while she looked at him adoringly. Then Jordan Drab showed her affection for the family pet, Sawyer, by stroking him sixty-seven times. All three dogs are enamored with their owners, which brings up a good point: If you want to attempt this record, make sure your mutt likes you and finds petting sessions soothing.

CRITERIA

☐ Must take hand off dog between each pet stroke.

☐ Each pet stroke must be in same direction.

Tip for Beating This Record

Use your own pet. It's not a good idea to hand a friend a stopwatch, approach the nearest guard dog, and yell "Go!" as you fervently run your hands down the beast's back.

RELATED RECORD

▶ Most Strangers' Pets' Names Included in an Improvised Song: 20

RECORD BEGGING TO BE SET

☐ Most Pets Petted in a Pet Store

Most "Meows" in a Public Place in 1 Minute

RECORD: 90

NAME: Olli Sulopuisto

LOCATION: Helsinki, Finland

DATE: March 19, 2010

TOOLS: Basic meowing skills, public location, ability to withstand mockery

If you're holidaying in Helsinki and come across a grown man standing in the middle of the sidewalk and meowing, you've probably just met Olli Sulopuisto. The meow man holds the record for the most cat noises made in public in 1 minute, a title he dreamed up after watching multiple videos of cats being ridiculous on YouTube. His forlorn meows were captured on video by his giggling girlfriend. "She's a professional photographer, so I figured this would be an easy task, but no," says Sulopuisto. Due to her laughing at the ridiculousness of the situation, "the first and the second tries were unusable."

CRITERIA
☐ Meows must be audible.
☐ Must be done during the daytime.

Yellow Jacket Comment

COREY: "Meow" in Finnish is actually "miau." It may seem the same, but true animal sound connoisseurs can hear the difference.

Tip for Beating This Record

"Remember to breathe," says Sulopuisto. "You wouldn't want to hyperventilate and pass out when breaking a record." Finding a solemn videographer is also a must. "My advice is to hire someone with no sense of humor, so that the camera will hold still."

RELATED RECORD
▶ Most Different "Meows" in 1 Minute: 20

RECORD BEGGING TO BE SET
☐ Most Different Animal Sounds Made in 10 Seconds

Longest Game of Fetch with a Cat

RECORD: 4 minutes, 11.44 seconds

NAME: Yan Grinshteyn

LOCATION: Queens, New York

DATE: June 16, 2009

TOOLS: A playful cat, something to fetch, catnip for bribery

Cats have a well-earned reputation for being a tad haughty. Unlike man's best friend, your average kitty isn't inclined to jump on you the second you get home or frolic in the grass after fetching a far-flung Frisbee. Yan Grinshteyn's cat, however, is different. Oscar Boxes Slinkybum, as he is known, was born in Mexico and has his own Twitter account, which he uses to post messages such as "You can't keep any secrets from me! Cats' hearing goes up to 65 khz (kilohertz); humans' hearing stops at 20 khz." Oscar also enjoys playing fetch. For this record, Grinshteyn prepared by playing the game with him for up to an hour at a time. But when it came time to officially set the record for Longest Game of Fetch with a Cat, Oscar fetched for just over 4 minutes. Proof that cats are irredeemably snooty? Grinshteyn has another theory: "Maybe Oscar is camera shy."

CRITERIA
☐ Cat must return fetched item each time.
☐ May use any item to play fetch with.

Yellow Jacket Comment

DAN: Yan gets credit for this record, but where is the respect for Oscar Boxes Slinkybum?

COREY: Agreed. Follow Sir Slinkybum on Twitter (@OscarBoxes) and shower him with praise.

RELATED RECORDS
▶ Largest Group "Meow" Rendition of "Lean on Me": 117
▶ Largest Cat Whisker Collection: 1,261

RECORD BEGGING TO BE SET
☐ Longest Staring Contest with a Cow

Oscar Boxes Slinkybum in action.

BIRDS OF A FEATHER

Dogs

Man's best friend features prominently in the annals of RecordSetter history. In some cases, such as Most Times Coaxing a Dog Through a Hoop in 30 Seconds, it's the dog's skills that are on show. More often, however, records display the skills of the human owners, with the pets serving as live props. Judging by the pooch being speed-kissed by a Groucho Marx impersonator, the enjoyment is mutual.

Most Times Kissing a Dog in 30 Seconds While Wearing a Groucho Marx Mask

RECORD: 77

NAME: Caroline Krueger

LOCATION: Lavallette, New Jersey

DATE: August 12, 2009

Most Writing Utensils Fit Inside a Pug's Collar

RECORD: 14

NAME: Nick H

LOCATION: Seabeck, Washington

DATE: March 21, 2009

Most Burps in 10 Seconds While Holding a Dog

RECORD: 43

NAME: Todd P

LOCATION: Winnipeg, Manitoba, Canada

DATE: May 12, 2010

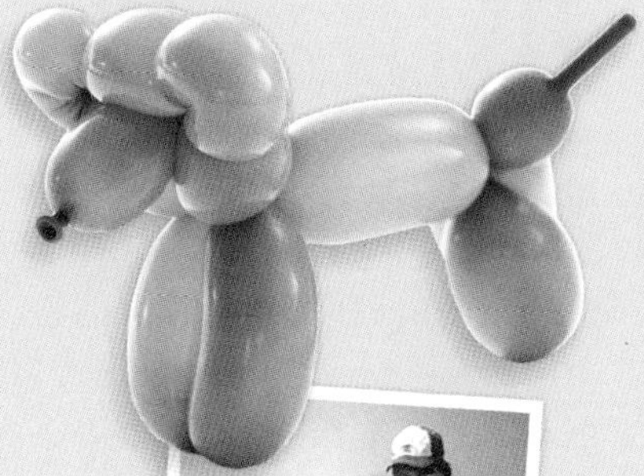

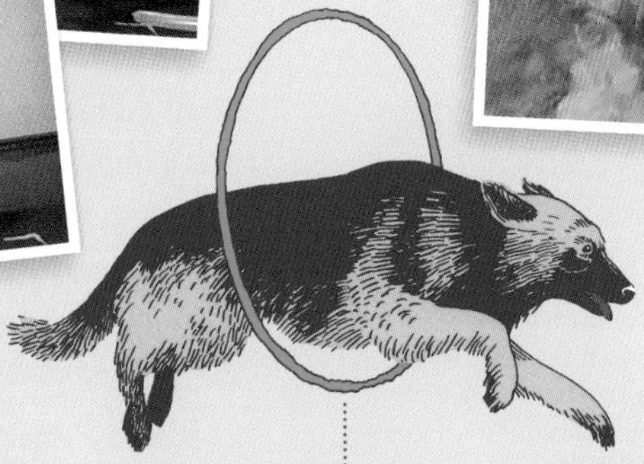

Most Balloon Dogs Created in 1 Minute

RECORD: 6

NAME: Brian Pankey

LOCATION: Springfield, Illinois

DATE: April 24, 2010

Most Times Coaxing a Dog Through a Hoop in 30 Seconds

RECORD: 22

NAME: Sarah Newell

LOCATION: Santa Barbara, California

DATE: August 25, 2009

Most Howls Elicited from a Dog Wearing a Clown Wig in 30 Seconds

RECORD: 22

NAME: Darrow Linder

LOCATION: Brea, California

DATE: August 6, 2009

Most Dog Biscuits Eaten by a Human in 5 Minutes

RECORD: 15

NAME: Mike Squier

LOCATION: Fairfield, Virginia

DATE: October 24, 2009

TOOLS: Dog biscuits (any flavor or shape), iron stomach, in-case-of-emergency, pack of Tums

Tip for Beating This Record

Work on your biscuit-chewing technique, says Squier. "Just eating them the way you would eat a standard cookie was not quick enough. I found that by keeping my jaw and teeth chomping continuously and feeding the biscuits in my mouth from the side mimicked a sawmill cutting wood. When the biscuit was chopped to an even finer texture in my mouth, a swig of water made the biscuit less dense and helped me to swallow it."

Mike Squier was entering a sled dog race and wanted to do a fundraiser for rescued Siberian Huskies. "I didn't want to do the same old fundraisers that people do all the time," says Squier. After hitting upon the idea to chow down on puppy food in front of an audience, Squier's next task was deciding on a biscuit brand. "I looked at a lot of dog biscuit manufacturing companies and decided on a local healthy dog biscuit company," he says. He turbo-chewed his way through fifteen, earning a RecordSetter World Record Holder patch for his efforts. "I sewed the patch onto my dogsled race bag prior to running the race," says Squier. It survived the twenty-two degree conditions and remains on his sled to this day.

CRITERIA

☐ Must eat commercial dog biscuits.

☐ May drink water during attempt.

RELATED RECORD

▸ Greatest Height to Drop a Hot Dog into a Hot Dog Bun: 59 feet, 5 inches

RECORD BEGGING TO BE SET

☐ Most Bags of Dog Food Donated to a Pet Shelter

Largest Group of People Pretending to Be Sea Otters

RECORD: 10

NAME: Piper Kerman and friends

LOCATION: Fire Island, New York

DATE: August 30, 2009

TOOLS: Open beach, friends and/or willing strangers, knowledge of sea otter behavior

CRITERIA

☐ Participants must lie on backs, clap hands, kick feet, and bark like otters.

☐ Record must be attempted on a beach.

Tip for Beating This Record

Consider conditions, and be flexible, says Kerman. "On the day when we actually recruited friends and strangers to help set the record, the ocean was extremely rough; I had envisioned everyone bobbing in the gentle swells on their backs in a 'raft,' barking (though a sea otter really squeals more than barks). However, the surf was just too rough to allow that vision to be realized—instead we lined up on the sand at the surf line, on our backs, to recreate the experience of being beached sea otters."

RELATED RECORDS

▶ Most Celebrity Impressions Performed in 1 Minute: 27

▶ Fewest Pogo Jumps Needed to Circle Around a Sandbox: 28

RECORD BEGGING TO BE SET

☐ Largest Group of People Impersonating Mr. T

Sea otters have always been Piper Kerman's favorite animals. "They are adorable—playful, charming, whiskered, and so smart that they use rocks as tools to crack mollusks open on their bellies," she says. To honor the object of her affection, she was motivated to organize a few friends plus a handful of strangers and line them up along the sand for some sea otter barking and lots of "flipper" waving. Only one "otter" seemed out of place: "We had one naked participant. This was unplanned, but lent an interesting, er, wrinkle to the record."

Most Bunnies Snuggled with in a Hammock

RECORD: 50

NAME: Nathan Morris

LOCATION: Perth, Australia

DATE: July 3, 2009

TOOLS: 50+ bunnies, a hammock big enough for you and those 50+ bunnies, supreme snuggling ability

Lying in a hammock and buried beneath forty-eight bunnies, actress Cameron Diaz first snuggled her way to a world record during a RecordSetter segment on *Late Night with Jimmy Fallon*. Australian radio DJ Nathan Morris witnessed Diaz's achievement and, due to the fact that she was about to appear on his radio show, was inspired to smash the record by snuggling with fifty bunnies. He then broke the news to Diaz live on air. The actress was incensed and had these choice words for her competitor: "Nathan, you have no idea what you've just done to me. I don't think I'll ever be able to forgive you. It is full-on war. It is bunny hammock war." Diaz has yet to reclaim her crown, knowing all too well the perils of success. "This is the problem," she lamented on the show. "This is why you should never hold a world record. It can always be beaten."

CRITERIA

☐ Bunnies must be accompanied by a qualified animal handler.

RELATED RECORD

▶ Most Bunnies Snuggled with in a Bean Bag Chair: 8

RECORD BEGGING TO BE SET

☐ Most Chinchillas Snuggled with in a Sleeping Bag

Smallest Fish Caught Using a Hook

RECORD: 1.06 inches

NAME: Charles Steffes-Clayton

LOCATION: Altoona, Iowa

DATE: August 4, 2009

TOOLS: Fishing tackle, ability to sense tiny nibbles on bait

CRITERIA

☐ Fish must be caught using a standard fishing pole and hook.

☐ Any fish species permitted.

RELATED RECORDS

▶ Most Goldfish Crackers Chicken Pecked Off a Table in 1 Minute: 50

▶ Most Images of Fish Sandwiches Looked at in 1 Minute: 60

RECORD BEGGING TO BE SET

☐ Most Fish Caught in 10 Minutes

Fishing aficionados have a tendency to exaggerate the size of their catches, but Charles Steffes-Clayton is very proud of the 1.06-inch specimen he snared. Angling for a catch at a local bass fishing pond, Steffes-Clayton felt the tiniest of tugs on his rod. At the end of the line was an itty-bitty fish, a baby of the species known as the black crappie. After placing the creature on a penny and taking a happy snap for record-filing purposes, Steffes-Clayton threw it back into the pond to continue its crappie little life. Despite not reeling in a whopper, he was pleased with his session on the shore. "A bad day fishing is still not a bad day," he says. And at least he didn't have to tire himself out: "There's not much struggle with a half-ounce fish."

ACTUAL SIZE!

THE ADULT CRAPPIE IS BETWEEN 6 AND 12 INCHES LONG

Most Times Saying "Galaptasaurus" in 1 Minute

RECORD: 65

NAME: James McGettrick

LOCATION: St. Petersburg, Florida

DATE: May 5, 2009

TOOLS: Superior enunciation skills

This Jurassic lark offers a lesson in the perils of silliness. Record originator Yan Grinshteyn set a low benchmark by reciting "galaptasaurus" four times within 8 seconds, then sitting in silence for the rest of the allocated minute. ("I'm pretty sure I've set the world record by now," he said after his quartet of utterances, "so I'll just wait it out.") A month later California's Danny Puskarcik played along, uttering the word five times in 11 seconds, then staring into his video camera as the clock ticked down. Things got serious with the arrival of James McGettrick, who spurned gimmicks in favor of straight-up speed-talking. His 65 galaptasauruses took up the entire minute, and his record still stands.

The word "galaptasaurus," by the way, was invented by Grinshteyn. He defined it as "a tyrannosaurus that spends way too much time vacationing in the Galapagos." The RecordSetter community: enriching the global lexicon, one fake dinosaur at a time.

CRITERIA

☐ Must clearly enunciate each syllable of the word.

RELATED RECORD

► Fastest Time to Spell "Hippopotomonstrosesquippedaliophobia": 5.40 seconds

RECORD BEGGING TO BE SET

☐ Most (Real) Dinosaurs Named in 15 Seconds

Largest Balloon Arch

RECORD: 1,434 balloons

NAME: Greg Arrigoni

LOCATION: St. Paul, Minnesota

DATE: July 3, 2004

TOOLS: Balloons, helium, structural engineering experience

Six hundred feet wide and 340 feet tall, Greg Arrigoni's red, white, and blue balloon arch was as majestic as the St. Louis iconic Gateway itself. And while it took 2 years to build the Gateway, Arrigoni constructed his marvel in a single day. The certified balloon artist encountered just one problem: no government department would sign off on its construction. "I was bounced between the Coast Guard, Corps of Engineers, the Highway Department, City Risk Management, Homeland Security, the Secret Service, Lightning Protection Co., the FAA (Federal Aviation Administration), and the Aerospace and Engineering Mechanics division at the University of Minnesota," he remembers. The balloon master kept hustling. Once he was greenlit, the arch was woven together with 1,434 Qualtex balloons pumped by sixty-five tanks of helium gas, but his grueling experience makes him eligible for another record: Most Bureaucracies Bounced to for a Single Purpose.

CRITERIA

☐ Must use helium-filled balloons.

RELATED RECORD

▶ Largest Group to Inhale Helium and Sing "Total Eclipse of the Heart": 12

RECORD BEGGING TO BE SET

☐ Largest Group to Sing "99 Red Balloons" at a Karaoke Bar

Tallest Rubber Duck Tower

RECORD: 5 ducks

NAME: David Cole

LOCATION: Boston, Massachusetts

DATE: March 18, 2010

TOOLS: Stockpile of rubber ducks, steady hands

CRITERIA

☐ Must use regular-sized plastic ducks.

☐ Ducks must be balanced on the head of duck below.

☐ Ducks must be positioned upright.

☐ No adhesives or external support permitted.

RELATED RECORDS

▶ Most Chicken Faces Drawn in 1 Minute: 18

▶ Most Names Given to a Plastic Duck in 30 Seconds: 59

RECORD BEGGING TO BE SET

☐ Most Rubber Ducks in a Bathtub

Every year at the company's holiday party, David Cole's boss would distribute a fresh flock of rubber ducks to his staff. "For months they would sit on our shelves, staring back and taunting us," he says. "They knew we were stymied. Without a bath in the office, there was not a lot to do with them, but we dared not throw them out and risk offending our supervisor." A search of the RecordSetter site provided the answer. "We found some joker who stacked up four rubber ducks," remembers Cole. And so the contest for the record was on. Cole's team started to focus their minds on the correct approach, experimenting with size and direction. Their collective creativity paid off as they etched their record in the history books—one that Cole believes will stand the test of time. "The idea of adding a sixth duck is ludicrous," he says. "Five is a perfect number and any attempt to beat it would obviously involve some sort of treachery."

Most TV Shows Named in 1 Minute Replacing One Word in Title with "Horse"

RECORD: 17

NAME: Kumail Nanjiani

LOCATION: New York, New York

DATE: January 19, 2010

TOOLS: Encyclopedic knowledge of TV shows, enthusiasm for equines

Kumail Nanjiani was dissatisfied by the lack of horse-focused shows on television. His solution was to come up with a list of alternative programming featuring equine protagonists in front of a live audience at a sold-out RecordSetter event. The resulting must-see TV included shows like *Touched by a Horse, Deal or No Horse, Who Wants to Be a Horse?,* and *Law and Order: Special Horses Unit.* In the dying seconds, Nanjiani got a bit too clever and tried to sneak *Desperate Horsewives* past the judges. Though entertained, the Yellow Jackets ruled that it violated the record's criteria. Will Nanjiani dispute this denial and take them to *Horse's Court?*

CRITERIA

☐ May not use any show title more than once.

☐ Replacing syllables with "horse" is not permitted.

☐ Must name shows from memory.

Yellow Jacket Comment

DAN: Kumail is amazing. They should feature him on *America's Got Horse.*

RELATED RECORD

▶ Most Monday Night TV Shows Insulted in 45 Seconds While Listening to the Theme Song of a Monday Night TV Show: 16

RECORD BEGGING TO BE SET

☐ Most Times Saying "Horse" in 30 Seconds While Sitting on a Horse

Most Paper Airplanes Constructed and Flown in 1 Minute

RECORD: 7

NAME: Russel Stokely

LOCATION: Austin, Texas

DATE: March 19, 2009

TOOLS: Construction paper, aerogami skills

P aper airplane folding is an activity that's fun, easy, and nonthreatening, unless you happen to be deathly afraid of paper cuts. But Russel Stokely has taken this simple, kid-friendly craft and given it an extreme, edge-of-your-seat twist. Using the basic dart-folding technique familiar to unruly schoolkids everywhere, Stokely constructed seven planes in 60 seconds, sending each model sailing into the air to demonstrate its aerodynamic power.

CRITERIA
☐ Must use basic dart-folding technique.
☐ Planes must be thrown within the time limit.

Tip for Beating This Record
If you draw folding lines on each piece of paper before attempting the record, it will help you speed through the folding process during the attempt.

RELATED RECORDS
▶ Most Paper Airplanes Thrown off a Building in 30 Seconds: 179
▶ Longest Nonstop Karaoke Session Featuring Flight-Related Songs: 240 minutes

RECORD BEGGING TO BE SET
☐ Longest Paper Airplane Flight on an Airplane Flight

Fastest Time to Visit All Eighty-Eight Counties in Ohio

RECORD: 23 hours, 34 minutes, 34 seconds

NAME: Dan Miller

LOCATION: Mason, Ohio

DATE: November 10, 2006

TOOLS: Car, caffeine source, accurate GPS

CRITERIA

☐ Timer begins in the first county and stops when entering the 88th.

☐ No limit to number of drivers involved.

RELATED RECORD

▶ Fastest Time to Write All Fifty U.S. States: 2 minutes, 1 second

RECORD BEGGING TO BE SET

☐ Fastest Time to Visit All 149 Towns in Saskatchewan

D an Miller is an Ohioan born and bred, and so in love with the Buckeye State that he decided to visit every one of its counties in a single day. All went smoothly until MapQuest let him down in the middle of the night, suggesting a road off Route 93 that turned out to be a dirt trail through a dense forest. Miller pressed on through the darkness undeterred, even ensuring through some post-trip analysis that a county border was crossed in the process. The filmmaker's next challenge is to visit every one of the 3,141 counties in the United States. If he pulls that one off in 24 hours, we will write a whole book about him, and probably make a movie too.

MY FAVORITE OHIO COUNTIES ARE LICKING, MUSKINGUM, AND DEFIANCE.

Farthest Distance to Be Carried by Other People

RECORD: 9.4 miles

NAME: Mark Malkoff

LOCATION: New York, New York

DATE: December 18, 2009

TOOLS: Foldable body, winsome personality, warm coat

Mark Malkoff likes to think up tasks that seem impossible and then prove they can be done. In the middle of one winter, the man famous for living in his bathroom for 5 days and visiting all 171 Manhattan Starbucks locations in 24 hours set out to prove that residents of the Big Apple are not as gruff as their reputation suggests. "I want to disprove to the world the myth that New Yorkers are unfriendly," he wrote on his blog, before outlining a bold plan to head to the streets and convince strangers to carry him from the southern tip of Manhattan to the very top.

Beginning at 7:30 A.M. on an 11-degree day, Malkoff chatted up passersby, giving them the option to carry him "like a baby, over their shoulders, or on their backs." While being transported by an assortment of bewildered but amused people, he struck up conversations on topics ranging from relationships to that night's dinner menu, stopped for cider and pretzels from a street vendor, and sang along as a bunch of theater students carried him while belting out hits by Lady Gaga.

The journey hit a snag at 126th Street, when heavy snow and icy winds robbed the roads of people. Malkoff spent a lonely, frostbitten 2 hours at a standstill before being rescued. He made it to 140th Street, but 19 hours after the quest began, he had to abandon plans to go further north due to the unrelenting snow. "While I was touched in some very awkward places by dozens of strange hands, what touched me most was everyone's generosity," he said after ending his expedition. He ain't heavy, he's Mark Malkoff.

CRITERIA

- ☐ May not make forward progress without being carried.
- ☐ Being carried by more than one person at once is permitted.
- ☐ Bathroom and sleep breaks permitted, but attempt must resume in exact location that preceded break.

Tip for Beating This Record

"Seriously consider bringing a helmet in case someone drops you," says Malkoff. Padded clothing would also be beneficial—being carried by people of all sizes and strengths can be jarring on the body. Lastly, do it in mild weather so that passersby are more likely to stop and chat instead of running to warmth and shelter.

RELATED RECORDS

- ► Most People Piggy-Backed at Once: 4
- ► Largest Group Piggy-Back Hug: 32 pairs
- ► Most People Hugged in 1 Minute: 55

RECORD BEGGING TO BE SET

- ☐ Fastest Time to Moonwalk Across Nebraska

Most Countries Visited in 24 Hours

RECORD: 16

NAME: Knut Olav and Astrid Løite

LOCATION: Bad Bentheim, Germany

DATE: June 27, 2009

TOOLS: Car, passport, companion who doesn't have any irritating habits

Fueled by a full tank of gas and a desire to break the existing record (originally set by three Dutch journalists working for car magazine *Autovisie*), Knut Olav and his wife, Astrid Løite, sped their Renault Espace through sixteen countries in just under 24 hours. Meticulous scheduling allowed the couple to charge through Poland, the Czech Republic, Slovakia, Hungary, Austria, Slovenia, Croatia, Italy, San Marino, Switzerland, Liechtenstein, Germany, France, Luxembourg, Belgium, and the Netherlands—with just one 15-minute nap in Italy. "Our critical decision was to perform the attempt on a Sunday as there is almost no commuter traffic, and many countries in Europe have a driving ban for trucks on Sunday," Løite notes.

CRITERIA
☐ Must obey traffic laws.

Yellow Jacket Comment
COREY: Cool record, but if I were friends with Knut and Astrid, I might be annoyed they didn't bring me back souvenirs.

RELATED RECORDS
▶ Most Miles Ridden on a Motorcycle: 1 million
▶ Longest Transcontinental Limousine Journey: 5,959 miles
▶ Fastest Time to Name Every Country in the World (Circa 1998): 1 minute, 44.16 seconds

RECORD BEGGING TO BE SET
☐ Fastest Time to Visit Every Country on Earth

NETHERLANDS
GERMANY
BELGIUM
LUXEMBOURG
FRANCE
LIECHTENSTEIN
SWITZERLAND
ITALY
SAN MARINO
POLAND
CZECH REPUBLIC
SLOVAKIA
AUSTRIA
HUNGARY
SLOVENIA
CROATIA

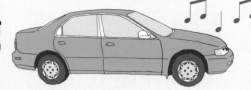

Most People Dancing to a Song Playing from a Car Stereo

RECORD: 208

NAME: Paul Bryan, James Medina, Trevor Johnson, Lee Hanssen, and Tony Lerud

LOCATION: Minneapolis, Minnesota

DATE: December 12, 2009

TOOLS: Automobile with a sweet sound system, bunch of ravers, high-energy song

WANT TO CALL UP SOME FRIENDS AND TRY TO BEAT THIS RECORD?

AS LONG AS I CAN BREAK DANCE ON THE CAR'S ROOF, COUNT ME IN.

Campus police at the University of Minnesota—home of the Golden Gophers—almost shut down this car-side party before Paul, James, Trevor, Lee, Tony, and 203 of their closest friends were able to complete the record. "Lee had to convince the police to let us finish," explains Bryan. Medina, the evening's designated DJ, selected "Cupid Shuffle" by Cupid, as the soundtrack for setting the record. As for finding friends to join the party, Paul had no trouble. "With a quick pitch that they'd be captured on camera for a video being blasted all over the Internet, they were in."

CRITERIA
☐ All people must be dancing at the same time.

RELATED RECORD
▶ Most Dancers Wearing Fake Mustaches in a Can-Can Line: 13

RECORD BEGGING TO BE SET
☐ Most People Dancing to a Band Playing on a Subway Platform

Mortimer Blackwell and Steve Schlacker

Gigglers, Trailblazers, Original Pranksters

When asked how they became RecordSetter legends, Mortimer Blackwell and Steve Schlacker say the secret of their success is a lack of self-consciousness. "We have no shame and do not embarrass easily," says Blackwell. This explains the pair's enthusiasm for doing odd things in public—their records include Most Times Saying "Hey" Loudly in 30 Seconds While Jogging in a Store" and Most U-Turns in 2 Minutes.

The duo began brainstorming stunts soon after Schlacker discovered RecordSetter. "We work really well as a team. One of us will think of something, and the other will elaborate, and that goes back and forth until we have a real humdinger of an idea. Executing them without giggling like a little girl, on the other hand, is the difficult part." Due to his superior ability to remain straight-faced, Blackwell tends to take on the tasks that only require one participant. Schlacker holds the camera, challenging in itself, as his friend runs shouting through the aisles of a drugstore, or in the case of Longest Opening Chess Move Played Against a Snare Drum, spends 5 minutes trying to psychologically manipulate a musical instrument as they face off over a game of chess. "This was one of Morti's ideas," explains Schlacker. "He just pulled it out of thin air. His brain doesn't work the same as most other people's." According to Blackwell, the intimidation of the snare drum was perfectly logical. "Snare drums like to 'bang' out moves, as it were. You can throw them off their game big time by a well-thought-out chess move with a plan behind it."

To celebrate Christmas in 2009, they teamed up to set the record for Most Times for Two People to Be Startled by a Miniature Christmas Tree in 30 Seconds, standing on either side of the tree and gasping a total of 30 times. Though they only needed to keep their composure for half a minute, the sheer silliness of what they were doing made it challenging to get through. "We just couldn't keep it together," says Blackwell. "Now I know how the cast on *Saturday Night Live* feels on an especially caffeine-filled day. It's harder than it looks."

For the quintessential Morti-and-Steve record, look no further than Most Questions Asked During a Single Drive-Through Visit. "We were driving around trying to find a place to set Most U-turns, and it dawned on us how much fun we could have with drive-through people," remembers Schlacker. He drove to the nearest fast-food joint and Blackwell played the part of a charming but dim diner, asking thirty questions about the menu before ordering just one soda. The record has since been beaten by Jacob Rodriguez, who managed to get fifty-three questions answered. But Blackwell is determined to win back the title. "We WILL be taking that record back, and we'll make it damn hard to beat next time," he says. "I'm betting we can double our number successfully, and with no plan. It's a gift, really."

Despite their plans to reclaim lost records, Blackwell and Schlacker both say they get a kick out of the competition. "I love watching people attempt our records and making asshats out of themselves in a style that we created," says Schlacker. Mortimer agrees, "If you do not push your own boundaries and take things too far, you will never know just how far you can go. Steve and I know all too well, and we aren't afraid to blaze new trails."

CHAPTER 9

THE
Human
Body

Scientists widely recognize the theory that humans evolved from ape to man— from stooped and hairy to tall and proud. Yet the transformation did not stop there. Homo sapiens continued to adapt. As we see in the following chapter, the most highly evolved of our species used their proud, erect posture, and flexible limbs to meaningful effect: balancing a shopping cart on their chins, hurling printers, or balancing table tennis balls with their breath. To read onwards is to glimpse a future in which, freed from the shackles of mortality, we will all become superhuman.

Longest Time to Balance a Loveseat on Chin

RECORD: 6.1 seconds

NAME: Brian Pankey

LOCATION: Springfield, Illinois

DATE: May 4, 2010

TOOLS: Loveseat, muscular neck, enough arm strength to lift a sofa up to your chin

With its sweet name and soft cushions, the loveseat seems like an object that can do no harm—unless it's perched on the edge of your face. Brian Pankey tested the limits of love by balancing the couch on his chin for just over 6 seconds. When asked what inspired him to do such a thing, Pankey has a very practical answer. "I always wanted to see the heaviest thing I could balance," he says, "and the loveseat was around 80 pounds." Lifting it high enough to place on his chin was the biggest challenge, but after a few wobbles, Pankey had a face full of furniture—and a sore neck once the couch came crashing down.

CRITERIA

☐ Loveseat must weigh at least 70 pounds.

Tip for Beating This Record

"This is extremely dangerous and can give you pain in your neck and jaw for days afterwards," warns Pankey. "So do neck exercises to build up your neck muscles."

RELATED RECORDS

▸ Most People Sitting on a Loveseat at Once: 19

▸ Longest Time to Juggle Three Beanbag Chairs: 57.1 seconds

▸ Most Barstools Held Aloft at Once: 9

RECORD BEGGING TO BE SET

☐ Longest Kiss on a Loveseat

Longest Time to Balance a Shopping Cart on Chin

RECORD: 17.95 seconds

NAME: Brian Pankey

LOCATION: Springfield, Illinois

DATE: May 3, 2010

TOOLS: Supermarket trolley (emptied of impulse purchases)

Brian Pankey's reputation as a balance master follows him around like a runaway shopping cart with a sticky front wheel. So when he was in the parking lot of a grocery store one day, a friend suggested he pick up one of the stray carts and perch it on his chin—you know, just for fun. "No one was around, so I did it," says Pankey. Emboldened by that experience, he soon bought a cart at a scrap yard so he could continue balancing at home. That's where he set this record, during which he hoisted the 50-pound metal beast, wrangled it so it was vertical, and then rested it on his chin for just under 18 seconds. Attention, shoppers: Do not try this at your local market.

CRITERIA

☐ Shopping cart must weigh at least 50 pounds.

Tip for Beating This Record

Pankey advises taking an incremental approach. "Start small. Try one of those little shopping baskets that hold only a few groceries. Then try a very small cart, working your way up to the standard-size shopping cart."

RELATED RECORDS

▶ Longest Time to Balance Twenty-four Hockey Pucks on Chin: 44.81 seconds

▶ Longest Time to Balance 40-Pound Turkey on Chin: 8.34 seconds

RECORD BEGGING TO BE SET

☐ Most Items Fit in a Shopping Cart

Farthest Distance to Throw a Snowball

RECORD: 223 feet

NAME: Roald Bradstock

LOCATION: Fort Myers, Florida

DATE: January 29, 2010

TOOLS: Snowball, measuring tape

CRITERIA

☐ Distance measured from point of release to location where snowball lands.

☐ Snowball must be made entirely from snow.

Tip for Beating This Record

If you don't live in a snowy area, venture to a colder location and order some snow to go. Bradstock transported a cooler full of snowballs 600 miles by car from Atlanta—site of a recent snowstorm—in order to attempt his feat in Florida.

RELATED RECORDS

▶ Longest Time to Balance Snow Scoop on Head: 59.63 seconds

▶ Longest Time to Balance Snowshoe on Chin: 21.75 seconds

RECORD BEGGING TO BE SET

☐ Most Snowmen Built in 5 Minutes

Roald Bradstock lives to throw. The former Olympic javelin athlete is never happier than when hurling objects into the stratosphere by hand. "There is something so satisfying about the feeling of my entire body focusing on the right way to launch an object," he says. But for Bradstock, throwing is also a mental pursuit. He can't look at an object without assessing its weight, surface area, size, and balance to uncover the perfect way to throw it far, far away. Throwing a javelin is all about the speed of release, angle of attack, flight height, and spin. A snowball is sensitive in flight and must have backspin if it is to gain height and distance. "I think of my throwing as performance art; therefore, it seemed appropriate that I should have some sort of costume," he says, explaining why he set his record while wearing a technicolor bodysuit. "My outfits are hand painted in acrylics by moi." This explains his nickname: The Olympic Picasso.

Farthest Distance to Throw a Banana

RECORD: 150 feet, 10 inches

NAME: Tyler Sytsma

LOCATION: Tempe, Arizona

DATE: June 15, 2010

TOOLS: Aerodynamic banana, pitcher's arm

"I have been told that I have an arm like a rocket," says Tyler Sytsma, "and wanted to put this God-given talent on display by shattering a world record." The obvious choice was to grab a banana from the fruit bowl and hurl it as far as possible. Sytsma and three friends took to the streets under cover of darkness—lest their fruit-flinging activities aroused unwanted attention—and used traffic cones to mark out 50-foot intervals on the road. Then it was tossing time. "The most challenging part about breaking this record was keeping the banana on a straight trajectory," says Sytsma, "and then staying humble afterward."

Whether you're pitching a softball or a banana, always follow through.

CRITERIA

☐ Distance measured from point of release to location where banana lands.

Tip for Beating This Record

Instead of flinging the banana from your arm, use your entire body for a more powerful throw. Step onto the leg opposite your throwing arm, and push off your back leg as you bring the arm over your head in a circular motion around your shoulder. Release the banana. Watch it fly.

RELATED RECORDS

▸ Fastest Time to Peel a Banana: 0.85 seconds

▸ Tallest Banana Tower: 7 bananas

▸ Longest Distance to Throw a Cupcake Wrapped in Saran Wrap: 87.5 feet

RECORD BEGGING TO BE SET

☐ Most Banana Peels Slipped on in 30 Seconds

Fastest Time for Two People to Hug Ten Times

RECORD: 3.36 seconds

NAME: Jason O'Brien and Andrew Chiccini

LOCATION: Sewell, New Jersey

DATE: August 10, 2010

TOOLS: Cuddle buddy, turbo arms

The world would be a better place if there were more men like Jason O'Brien. "I love giving hugs and have been told on plenty of occasions that I give good ones," he says. For his world record attempt, the affectionate O'Brien approached his coworker at Applebees, Andrew Chiccini, a "wild, outgoing individual who was one of the top huggers I knew." The two practiced their technique, then went at it hammer and tongs, embracing each other with near-violent enthusiasm. Pity poor Marc Tatarsky and Matt Wolfson, who unknowingly submitted an attempt in the same category on the same day, only to have their time of 5.36 seconds instantly beaten. At least they know who they can go to if they need hugs to deal with the disappointment.

CRITERIA

☐ Must completely separate between each hug.

☐ Hands must touch each other behind partner's back.

Tip for Beating This Record

O'Brien is precise about prerequisites: "Speed hugging depends on three things: footwork, body position, and willingness to man up and get hugging. Eat right, train hard, and give as many hugs as possible. They are fun to give, and (almost) everyone loves them."

RELATED RECORDS

► Largest Group Piggy-Back Hug: 32 pairs/64 people

► Most People with Same First and Last Name to Hug at Once: 2

► Most People Hugged in 1 Minute: 55

RECORD BEGGING TO BE SET

☐ Most People to Hug One Person at Once

Longest High Five

RECORD: 2.6 miles

NAME: Dave Thompson and Matt Kelly

LOCATION: Brisbane, Australia

DATE: February 26, 2011

TOOLS: Cardiovascular endurance, encouraging support crew

CRITERIA

☐ Both participants must keep "high five" hand raised for duration of feat.

☐ Both participants must run or walk entire distance.

RELATED RECORDS

▶ Loudest High Five: 87.1 decibels

▶ Highest High Five: 9 feet, 6 inches

RECORD BEGGING TO BE SET

☐ Most High Fives with a Mannequin In 30 Seconds

Not since the 2010 Commonwealth Games have relations between Australia and Canada been so tense. The unlikely source of the conflict is the celebratory gesture known as the high five. It all began when Brisbane pair Dave Thompson and Matt Kelly broke the RecordSetter world record for Longest High Five. "Longest" referring to the distance each person runs toward each other before the climactic hand slap takes place. Fifteen months earlier, Toronto duo Sam Stilson and Craig Morrison set the mark at 2.05 miles, or 3.3 kilometers— feel the power of the metric system, America—by jogging from opposite ends of the city, dressed as cowboys, with their right hands raised the whole time. The record lay unchallenged until the Australians donned sparkly spandex pants (Dave) and short-shorts (Matt), rustled up a support crew with oh-so-Oz names like "Tubby" and "Piggy," and ran in approaching directions for 11 minutes, 40 seconds before exchanging their climactic high five. It's gold for Australia and a case of redface for the Canadians. At least, for now.

Tip for Beating This Record

Imagine the agony of two people suffering through a punishing run, thinking of that final, glorious slap of palm on palm—only to miss each other's hands and render the entire attempt a failure. To ensure this doesn't happen, look at the other person's elbow. Your hands will meet and your supporters will applaud.

Longest Hand Coo

RECORD: 31.8 seconds

NAME: Craig Morrison

LOCATION: Toronto, Ontario, Canada

DATE: March 26, 2010

TOOLS: Big lungs, oneness with nature

Dr. Doolittle is not the only human who can talk to the animals. Craig Morrison's ability to commune with nature is rooted in an earlier, simpler age before the invention of cell phones. Morrison and his friends relied on what they referred to as a "loon call" for their primary means of communication. "We all lived in the same neighborhood and would walk out onto our back porches and do the call as loud as possible," he explains. "You usually got one back and then someone would come over." The stamina to loon call like this came from a place of sloth. "The louder and longer you could coo, the lazier you could be and the less you had to move," Morrison remembered.

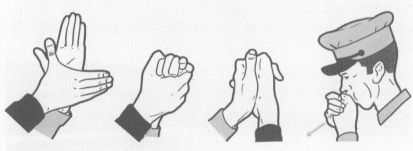

CRITERIA

☐ Must maintain a single note.

☐ No audible pauses permitted.

Yellow Jacket Comment

DAN: I have mixed feelings about this record. On the one hand, it's a tremendously impressive feat. On the other hand, the record was previously held by me. You stole my record, Loon Boy! I'll be back!

RELATED RECORDS

▶ Largest Slide Whistle Orchestra: 9

▶ Most Times Whistling "Happy Birthday" in 1 Minute: 18

RECORD BEGGING TO BE SET

☐ Longest Fake Fart Sound

Longest Time to Hover a Table Tennis Ball Using Breath

RECORD: 3.16 seconds

NAME: Rob Birdsong

LOCATION: Brooklyn, New York

DATE: February 25, 2010

TOOLS: Table tennis ball, ability to create an updraft

CRITERIA

☐ Timing starts when hand lets go of ball.

☐ Timing stops when ball touches mouth or falls below it.

Tip for Beating This Record

"You've got to focus on doing two things right," says Birdsong, "keeping the ball afloat and keeping it in line. Blow too hard and it is tough to keep above your lips. Focus too much on keeping it in line and you lose track of the blowing, and next thing you know, the ball is pinging and ponging all over the kitchen floor. Finding the right balance is critical."

RELATED RECORDS

▶ Longest Party Horn Toot: 12.51 seconds

▶ Most Sharpies Blown Over with a Single Breath: 40

RECORD BEGGING TO BE SET

☐ Fastest Time to Melt an Ice Cube with a Hair Dryer

How do you tame a Ping-Pong ball that has a mind of its own? Rob Birdsong wore down its will with a rigorous regimen of practice, practice, practice. "I trained when I woke up, while waiting for the subway, at work, and before I went to bed," he reminisces. "It is a lot harder than it looks. That little ball is like a piece of fake snow in a snow globe. It wants to fly all over the place."

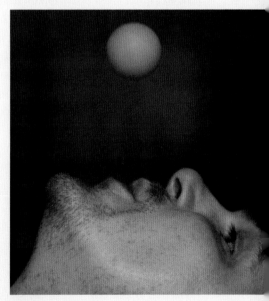

A lot harder than it looks.

263

Fastest Time to Blow Up a Balloon Until It Pops

RECORD: 13.62 seconds

NAME: Peter Craig

LOCATION: Blakeview, Australia

DATE: July 17, 2010

TOOLS: Balloon, penchant for explosive surprises

CRITERIA

☐ Balloon must pop due to pressure from being overinflated.

☐ Must use a standard party balloon that reaches a length of at least 7.87 inches before popping.

Tip for Beating This Record

Craig has some soothing words for apprehensive record setters: "Remember, the balloon's not going to hurt you. Just shut your eyes when it's ready to pop."

RELATED RECORD

► Longest Balloon Squeak: 2 minutes, 27.1 seconds

RECORD BEGGING TO BE SET

☐ Most Dominoes Blown Over in a Single Breath

Inflating a balloon to the point that it bursts in your face is an activity most people would be keen to avoid. But Peter Craig loves the eye-bulging sensation so deeply that he seriously taxes his lung capacity to experience it faster than anyone else in the world. His 13.62-second balloon buster was a marked improvement on category originator Matt Godfrey's time of 19.65 seconds, but Craig still isn't satisfied. "I would love to try and expand upon it," he says, offering Fastest Time to Blow Up a Balloon with Your Nose Until It Pops as a possibility—or maybe even using five balloons. Another potential record that is "much more extreme": blowing up a hot water bottle until it bursts.

Longest Time to Keep a Match Lit

RECORD: 53.31 seconds

NAME: Kyle Lybeck

LOCATION: Kirkland, Washington

DATE: August 21, 2010

TOOLS: Match, fireproof fingers

❝ I've always been a person to play with fire," claims Kyle Lybeck. Literally and figuratively. Lybeck attempted his match-burning record outdoors, tempting fate and the wind to mess with his plans for beating the previous mark of 45.78 seconds. Despite some nail-biting moments in which the fire dwindled to a whisper of blue-flecked flame, Lybeck's technique of gradually tilting the match proved a success.

Tip for Beating This Record:

Use music to motivate yourself and tune out the burning sensation. Some suggested songs:

▸ "Eternal Flame" by The Bangles
▸ "Light My Fire" by The Doors
▸ "Burnin' For You" by The Blue Öyster Cult

CRITERIA

☐ Must use regular-size matchstick.
☐ Must keep match in hand for duration of attempt.

RELATED RECORDS

▸ Most Matches Lit off a Matchbox in 30 Seconds: 14
▸ Longest Time to Hold Flame in Mouth: 9.60 seconds

RECORD BEGGING TO BE SET

☐ Fastest Time to Light Sixteen Candles

IF YOU ATTEMPT TO BEAT THIS RECORD, PLEASE HAVE ADULT SUPERVISION AND AT LEAST ONE BUCKET OF WATER ON HAND.

Most Air Guitar Windmills in 1 Minute

RECORD: 137

NAME: Joseph Gunderson

LOCATION: Chicago, Illinois

DATE: July 19, 2009

TOOLS: Strong rotator cuff, imaginary Fender Stratocaster

Joseph Gunderson describes himself as "the son of an '80s rocker chick." But even though air-guitaring and headbanging are in his blood, becoming a world record holder was still a test of his physical and mental capacity. "About 5 seconds in I felt a pain shoot up my arm," he remembers. "I knew I had to focus and get a rhythm going. My whole arm was practically numb for a couple of days after. I was actually slightly worried but once I had succeeded, the excitement and energy far outweighed all the pain." If you break this record, Joseph will come back at you (once he gets some medical insurance).

CRITERIA

☐ Windmills can be clockwise or counterclockwise, but must rotate wwin same direction for entire attempt.

Tip for Beating This Record

Gunderson has two pointers for taking on the windmill. "Stay limber," he advises. "Start your day by downing a glass of egg yolks followed by extended stretching." His other tip is to rock out on a daily basis. "Your soundtrack should consist of Abe Vigoda [the band, not the actor], Joy Division, The Marked Men, Death from Above 1979, and Wavves."

RELATED RECORDS

▶ Fastest Time to Play Every Note on a Guitar: 3.37 seconds

▶ Most Articles of Clothing Placed on a Guitar: 35

RECORD BEGGING TO BE SET

☐ Fastest Time to Play Guitar Solo from "Smells Like Teen Spirit"

Most Quarters Balanced on Elbow and Caught

RECORD: 51

NAME: Kevin C. Murray

LOCATION: West Hollywood, California

DATE: January 4, 2010

TOOLS: Piggy bank full of quarters, flat forearm

Kevin C. Murray honed his Venus flytrap–caliber reflexes back in college. "We would see how many quarters we could catch off our respective elbows," he says, "but when we reached five dollars, the competition got less friendly. I decided to bow out and save the friendship." His catching skills lay dormant until he took a public speaking class that required an "attention getter" at the beginning of one of his speeches. "I started practicing, and it soon became a competition with my friends Sean and Darren. This time I did not bow out and eventually caught forty-nine quarters, besting my friends and setting my own personal record." Murray is now up to fifty-one quarters.

CRITERIA

☐ Quarters must be balanced in a stack.

☐ Must catch all quarters.

RELATED RECORDS

► Tallest Penny Tower: 108

► Tallest Swedish Kronor Tower: 52

RECORD BEGGING TO BE SET

☐ Most Jelly Beans Balanced on Elbow and Caught

Most Armpit Farts in 30 Seconds

RECORD: 105

NAME: Ryan Loecker

LOCATION: Salina, Kansas

DATE: July 5, 2009

TOOLS: Flatulent armpit, fast arm flapping

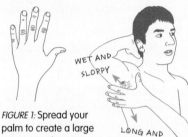

WET AND SLOPPY

LONG AND LOUD

FIGURE 1: Spread your palm to create a large vacuum under your armpit.

FIGURE 2: By shifting your grip you can produce an astounding variety of disgusting noises.

CRITERIA

☐ Each fart must be audible.

Tip for Beating This Record

"The perfect arm fart happens after you get out of the shower or after you finish exercising and your arms are very sweaty and moist," says Loecker.

RELATED RECORDS

▶ Largest Armpit Fart Orchestra: 6

▶ Most Armpits Applied with Same Stick of Old Spice Deodorant in 1 Minute: 32

RECORD BEGGING TO BE SET

☐ Most People to Sit on Whoopee Cushions at Once

Ryan Loecker is *that* guy. The joker in the pack who loves to tell his friends they have something on their shirt and then flick their nose as they make the fatal mistake of glancing downward. But his real mastery is armpit farting, a skill he claims to have perfected before he could walk. Now that he is older, he has realized the practical benefits of this talent. "Arm farting is a popular gag," he claims, "especially with the ladies." Females of the species, if you like what you see, we can put you in touch.

THE ORIGINATOR OF THIS CATEGORY, A BROOKLYN KID BY THE NAME OF SILAS HYDE, DID 10 MINUTES OF JUMPING JACKS BEFORE HIS ATTEMPT IN ORDER TO "HEAT UP HIS ARMPITS."

Most Autographs Signed on a Stranger's Torso in 1 Minute

RECORD: 34

NAME: Alexandra Young

LOCATION: New York, New York

DATE: July 14, 2009

TOOLS: Sharpie, stranger, good penmanship

In a former life, Alexandra Young was a tour manager for such pop music giants as Nick Lachey and New Kids on the Block. In that role she witnessed pop stars signing their names on fan's assorted body parts—chests, hands, and arms—whenever paper was not available. Reminiscing about those days caused a record idea to creep into her head: "What if I had to sign the same person's body over and over again?" The record demanded a high degree of intimacy with a rather hairy stranger, who bravely volunteered after she put out the call in a New York bar. Even as her nose hovered inches from his armpit, Young retained her focus. "He was totally fun and made me feel really comfortable about the whole thing," she says.

CRITERIA

☐ Torso participant must be previously unknown to autograph writer.

RELATED RECORD

▶ Most Autographs on a Shoe: 53 signatures

RECORD BEGGING TO BE SET

☐ Most Portraits of Strangers Drawn in 1 Hour

We don't recommend trying this on strangers at the beach.

Most Stomach Rolls in 30 Seconds

RECORD: 47

NAME: Brian McCarthy

LOCATION: New York, New York

DATE: December 10, 2009

TOOLS: Undulating belly, willingness to show it off in public

Philosophical hippie Brian McCarthy is an accomplished proponent of the weird skill of belly rolling. This hypnotic body isolation involves moving the upper and lower abdominal muscles independently of each other to create a wave effect. Basically, surf's up in his stomach and everyone's invited to check out the swell.

McCarthy jumped up on stage during a RecordSetter event, whipped off his shirt, and let the waves tumble along his toned abdomen. "It was a lot of fun," he says. "I'm usually a poor, unemployed actor, but at least I hold that world record."

CRITERIA

☐ Undulations may not be created by spinal movement.

☐ Body movement must be isolated to torso.

RELATED RECORD

▶ Longest Time Patting Head and Rubbing Stomach Simultaneously: 2 hours

RECORD BEGGING TO BE SET

☐ Most People Doing "The Worm" at Once

Tip for Beating This Record

Get a professional belly dancer to teach you the art of rolling your tummy. You can begin this journey of exploration at www.bellydanceforums.net.

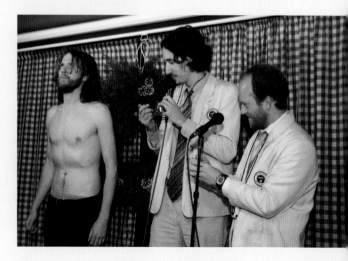

Most Pieces of Tape Taped to Face at Once

RECORD: 615

NAME: Nathan Scarbrough

LOCATION: New Albany, Indiana

DATE: November 8, 2010

TOOLS: Tape, absence of skin allergies related to tape

Within the RecordSetter community, Nathan Scarbrough is known as Tape Face. The man from Indiana demonstrated his devotion to the adhesive arts by defending his record title against a fiercely competitive Mick Cullen. The two became locked in battle when Scarbrough stuck 217 pieces of tape to his head, besting Cullen's effort of 175.

Cullen responded with a video showing him carefully affixing 289 strips to his face. Within 72 hours, Scarbrough had taken the rivalry to extremes, plastering his skin with 615 pieces of Scotch Tape. Unable to speak due to the layers of tape, Scarbrough grabbed a pen and paper, drew a big "X" over the words "Mick Cullen," wrote "Nathan Scarbrough is the winner!" and held it up to the camera.

CRITERIA

☐ Must use Scotch Tape or similar generic competitor.

☐ Once facial skin is covered, may apply pieces of tape over tape.

Yellow Jacket Comment

COREY: If this category explodes and Scotch Tape sales skyrocket, I hope they'll remember us little guys for getting it started.

RELATED RECORDS

▶ Heaviest Ball of Electrical Tape: 340 pounds

▶ Most Times Wrapping Tape Around Hand in 30 Seconds: 51

▶ Most Binder Clips Attached to Face: 34

RECORD BEGGING TO BE SET

☐ Most Red Sticker Dots Attached to Face

Stick with it, young Tape Face.

Most Nipples (Male)

RECORD: 5

NAME: Stephen Detsch

LOCATION: West Lebanon, New Hampshire

DATE: March 2, 2010

TOOLS: A torso full of teats

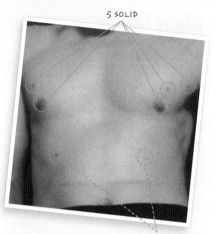

5 SOLID

TWO IN THE MAKING

Proud owner of enough nipples for two and a half people, Stephen Detsch was granted this record by genetics. "These nipples have been confirmed by my primary care physician at Dartmouth Hitchcock Medical Center in New Hampshire," he says. A photo of Detsch's midsection reveals five distinct nipples, some smaller than others, but all equipped with the behaviors of a traditional nipple: hardening when agitated or cold. While Detsch's record may already seem unbeatable for the average dual-nipped gent, Detsch is already hard at work on outdoing himself. A sixth nipple has recently sprouted on the left side of his stomach. "It does not yet have a point unless aroused," he admits, "so I do not feel it would be appropriate to submit as an official nipple—yet."

CRITERIA

☐ Nipples must be confirmed by physician.

RELATED RECORDS

► Most Male Nipples Exposed During a Video Podcast: 19

► Smallest Male Nipple: 0.13 centimeters

RECORD BEGGING TO BE SET

☐ Fastest Time to Make a Slippery Nipple

WE NEED TO INVESTIGATE THIS MAN'S DNA. HE APPEARS TO BE PART CAT.

ACTUALLY, ONE IN EIGHTEEN HUMAN MALES HAVE A SUPERNUMERARY NIPPLE.

Most Ear Wiggles in 30 Seconds

RECORD: 79

NAME: Ross Martin

LOCATION: Monterey, California

DATE: August 29, 2009

TOOLS: Agile ears, wiggle room

WIGGLE IT, JUST A LITTLE BIT.

t is not just Ross Martin's ears that wiggle. It is his whole cranium. The man who became the world's best ear wiggler first discovered his superhuman abilities while sitting in a barber's chair. The hairdresser was having trouble finding the 8-year-old's hairline until he realized the line was in constant motion, as young Martin kept raising and lowering it along with his lobes. The trick became refined through years of bar mitzvah parties and summer camp talent shows. It is now most useful as a way to draw attention during particularly boring work meetings.

CRITERIA
☐ Must wiggle both ears at once.

Tip for Beating This Record

"One trick that can help you learn ear wiggling is to concentrate on lifting your eyebrows in an exaggerated manner, as if someone just said something shockingly inappropriate to you," advises Martin. "After that, it's like a Kegel exercise, but for your head. It's intuitive. Don't think about it, just squeeze your brain."

RELATED RECORDS
▶ Most Coins Magically Pulled from Behind Someone's Ear in 1 Minute: 26
▶ Most Stitches in an Ear: 37

RECORD BEGGING TO BE SET
☐ Most Pairs of Earmuffs Worn at Once

BIRDS OF A FEATHER

Noses

Noses are best known for their ability to smell, breathe, and keep that snazzy pair of sunglasses snug against your head. But they are capable of so much more. A nose can be a comforting cave for your finger. It can wiggle, suction itself shut, and balance a spoon. When was the last time you really got to know your nose and

asked what it can do for you? May these records provide the inspiration to bond with the double-barreled friend in the middle of your face.

Most Nose Wiggles in 1 Minute

RECORD: 117

NAME: Jake Friday

LOCATION: Angwin, California

DATE: July 19, 2009

Most Spoonfuls of Jelly Eaten While Balancing a Spoon on Nose

RECORD: 4

NAME: Madeline Craig

LOCATION: Blakeview, Australia

DATE: November 12, 2010

Deepest Insertion of Finger into One's Own Nose

RECORD: 2.25 inches

NAME: Josh Werner

LOCATION: Avon, Connecticut

DATE: February 18, 2011

Longest Time Sucking Nostrils Closed

RECORD: 25.84 seconds

NAME: Az Fuller

LOCATION: Brooklyn, New York

DATE: April 4, 2009

Longest Time Touching Tongue to Nose

RECORD: 8 minutes, 59.4 seconds

NAME: David McGrath

LOCATION: Weston, Massachusetts

DATE: May 18, 2010

TOOLS: Lizard tongue, a taste for your own nose

David McGrath's nose-tonguing odyssey began on May 6, 2010. That was the fateful day he set a world record by touching the tip of his tongue to his nose for 2 minutes, 29.8 seconds. But he barely had time for a celebratory milkshake before Matt Cairoli, a fellow proponent of the nasolingual arts, swooped in and claimed the record, beating McGrath's effort by almost 5 minutes. Not to be deterred, McGrath regrouped, did some training, and came back 4 days later with a time of 8 minutes, 2.1 seconds. Cairoli snatched it back again within a week, but in a final triumphant display, McGrath battled his way back to the top with a time of 8 minutes, 59.4 seconds. Little-known fact: Victory tastes much sweeter than the tip of your nose.

Tip for Beating This Record

Pick your moment carefully. Good times to attempt this record include while watching TV, sitting in a bath, or during a long-haul flight. Less-than-perfect settings are during a four-course formal dinner, halfway through a job interview, or while browsing the lingerie section at a department store.

CRITERIA

☐ Tongue must touch nose for duration of attempt.

RELATED RECORDS

▶ Most Times Touching Tongue to Nose in 1 Minute: 121

▶ Longest Time Balancing Machete on Tongue: 1 minutes, 19.6 seconds

RECORD BEGGING TO BE SET

☐ Most Noses Pinched in 30 Seconds

Most Tongue Clucks in 10 Seconds

RECORD: 65

NAME: Robbie McAnelly

LOCATION: New Albany, Indiana

DATE: November 5, 2010

TOOLS: Ability to impersonate farm animals, no moral qualms about competing against a 5-year-old girl

CRITERIA

☐ Clucks must be distinct and clearly audible.

RELATED RECORDS

▶ Most Tongue Folds in 30 Seconds: 28

▶ Most Chicken McNuggets Eaten in 10 Minutes with Vuvuzelas on Hands: 4

RECORD BEGGING TO BE SET

☐ Most Verses of "Old MacDonald" Sung in 1 Minute

A long with gum snapping and persistent sniffling, tongue clucks are the sonic scourge of any office or classroom. Not to be confused with a "tsk," a cluck is the hollow sound of tongue going from the roof of the mouth straight down, crashing against the bottom of the mouth, behind lower teeth. The competitors in this category have taken the often-annoying habit and turned it into an athletic feat, speed-clucking their way into the record books. Robbie McAnelly is the current champion, with sixty-five clucks in 10 seconds. He and two other cluckers all bested the effort of category creator Eliot Juvonen, a sweet 5-year-old girl from New York, who managed twenty-eight tongue clucks. It just goes to show that being a talented and adorable child does not safeguard you against having your RecordSetter record snatched away.

FIGURE 1: With your mouth open, put your tongue on the roof of your mouth.

FIGURE 2: Flex your tongue to make it as strong and stiff as possible.

FIGURE 3: Snap your tongue down and forward to emit the cluck.

CLUCK!

Most Alternating Dual Lip Curls in 10 Seconds

RECORD: 39

NAME: Bethany Lee

LOCATION: Cheraw, South Carolina

DATE: July 1, 2009

TOOLS: Limber lips, straight face

"I don't really have any 'record-material' talents," says a modest Bethany Lee, "but I can do this weird thing with my lips." The weird lip thing brought Lee her first RecordSetter world record after a rapid-fire demo of thirty-nine curls in 10 seconds. "I had originally wanted to do the most lip curls in 30 seconds, but I could not be serious for long enough," she says. "Every time, I was good for about 5 seconds, and then I would think about how ridiculous I probably looked. I would burst into laughter, and have to start again!"

Possible second career: Elvis impersonator.

CRITERIA

☐ Lip must curl up and down on each side, always alternating.

Tip for Beating This Record

"I would tell the person trying to break my record to make sure to stretch his or her lips first to keep from getting a lip injury," says Lee. Lip curl exercises include Cheshire Cat smiles, frowning like a frustrated toddler, and dropping one side of the mouth at a time.

RELATED RECORDS

▶ Largest Lip Balm Collection: 415

▶ Most Kisses in 10 Seconds: 51

RECORD BEGGING TO BE SET

☐ Most Times Kissing a Frog in 10 Seconds

Most Vertical Fist Pumps in 30 Seconds

RECORD: 255

NAME: Abraham Collins

LOCATION: Trenton, New Jersey

DATE: April 15, 2009

TOOLS: Fists of fury, love of New Jersey

Fist pumping as a dance move rose to prominence with the arrival of the reality show *Jersey Shore* in 2009, and TV fans in the RecordSetter community were soon raising their hands in the air like they just didn't care. Over four furious weeks, the record was set and broken by three pumped-up competitors, culminating in Abraham Collins's frenzied 255 hand thrusts in 30 seconds. Appropriately enough, Collins resides in the Garden State.

The movement is similar to raising the roof, but with clenched fists.

Keep fingers curled up tight to maintain the "excited gorilla" look.

CRITERIA

☐ Must extend arm fully for each pump.

☐ Must extend fist above head for each pump.

Yellow Jacket Comment

DAN: Fist pumps are an excellent way to punch someone 4 or 5 feet taller than you. For self-defense purposes, obviously.

RELATED RECORDS

▶ Deepest Shoulder Blades: 3.75 inches

▶ Fastest Time to Bring Handcuffed Hands from Back of Body to Front: 2.53 seconds

RECORD BEGGING TO BE SET

☐ Most Punching Bag Punches in 30 Seconds

DID YOU KNOW?

THIS RECORD IS UNOFFICIALLY BROKEN EVERY NIGHT AT CLUBS ALONG THE JERSEY SHORE.

Most Finger Snaps in 1 Minute

RECORD: 172

NAME: Dinesh Upadhyaya

LOCATION: Mumbai, India

DATE: August 28, 2010

TOOLS: Clicky fingers, ability to push far beyond personal pain threshold

Based in Mumbai, the über-prolific record setter Dinesh Upadhyaya challenged himself to aim for 170 snaps. "Initially I was hardly able to reach sixty to seventy snaps per minute," he remembers. "After 3 months of continuous practice (whenever I got free time from my teaching job), I became confident." But there was a difference between practicing alone and setting an official record in front of a video camera. "Many times, in a relaxed mood and without any pressure, I reached 190 to 195 snaps, but at the time of recording the record attempt, I found myself under huge mental pressure," says Upadhyaya. "In my first two attempts, I was unable to cross even 160 snaps. Before my third attempt, I performed some breathing yoga and meditations to release myself from any kind of fear, pain, and pressure. Finally I decided to focus only on my target of 170 plus, and that time I got success."

Tip for Beating This Record

"Those who want to break this record, please mentally prepare to experience tremendous pain," says Upadhyaya, who recalls "the upper part of my forearm felt like it was on fire." Another consideration is the record's audio quality. "You must perform the record attempt in an absolute silent room (acoustics chamber) so each snap is audible."

CRITERIA

☐ Must snap with thumb and either index, middle, or ring finger.

☐ Gloves not permitted.

RELATED RECORDS

▶ Most Triple Finger Snaps in 10 Seconds: 162

▶ Greatest Distance Covered with Stretched Palm: 11 inches

RECORD BEGGING TO BE SET

☐ Largest Group to Do the Jets Versus Sharks Dance from *West Side Story*

Most Phone Books Ripped in Half in 10 Minutes

RECORD: 67

NAME: Michael Martin

LOCATION: San Diego, California

DATE: November 12, 2009

TOOLS: Yellow Pages—a big stack

Got any phone books lying around the house? Hide them now because Samurai Mike is on a rampage. The San Diego resident loves to tear apart the directories, hissing and roaring as he separates Smith from Smyth. The most impressive of his multiple book-breaking records is this 10-minute epic, which features him standing beside a wall of sixty-seven books, channeling his Hulk-like fury into ripping each one. When the time is up, the samurai is seen wading through a pile of tattered pages and torn covers. He looks exhausted, but a glint in his eye suggests this won't be the last time he shows a pile of books who's boss.

CRITERIA

☐ Books must be ripped in half vertically.

☐ Pages must be ripped (ie., may not tear book along spine).

Tip for Beating This Record

"Thicker books are actually easier to rip," says Martin, "because they provide more leverage to your hands when ripping the paper."

NOTE: RECYCLING BOOKS AFTER ATTEMPTING RECORD WILL EARN YOU KARMA POINTS FOR LIFE.

RELATED RECORDS

▶ Most Phone Books Placed on a Couch: 85

▶ Most Imaginary Telephone Conversations Using Non-Telephones in 30 Seconds: 9

RECORD BEGGING TO BE SET

☐ Tallest Tower of Phone Books Sat On

Yellow Jacket Comment

DAN: Please do *not* attempt a record for Most *RecordSetter* Books Ripped in Half in 10 Minutes.

Most Times Slapping Someone in the Face in I Minute

RECORD: 660

NAME: Axel Gage

LOCATION: Västerås, Sweden

DATE: October 9, 2010

TOOLS: Mighty mitts, obedient brother

A xel Gage says he had dual motivations for attempting the face-slapping feat: "breaking a world record and getting a chance to hit my brother a couple hundred times." The brother in question, Petter, was inexplicably game. With his mother giggling away at the back of the room, Gage rained down a torrent of over ten slaps per second, ignoring his aching arms to clinch the record. Both siblings were pleased with the result. "My brother, who was slapped 660 times, said his face was numb for 10 minutes afterwards," says Gage. "So that's a mission well accomplished."

CRITERIA
☐ May use both hands.
☐ Ear slaps not permitted.

CAUTION
TO ENSURE A HARMONIOUS FUTURE RELATIONSHIP —ESPECIALLY IF YOU'RE SIBLINGS—
SLAP GENTLY.

Tip for Beating This Record
"Get a nice rhythm of sixteenths and slap away," advises Gage. In music notation, sixteenths are also known as semiquavers, and are worth one-sixteenth of a full note.

RELATED RECORD
▶ Most Pizza Slice Face Slaps in 15 Seconds: 210

RECORD BEGGING TO BE SET
☐ Most Times Kissing Someone on the Cheek in 1 Minute

Longest Time Balanced on a Closed Folding Ladder

RECORD: 50.94 seconds

NAME: Dominic Pavicic

LOCATION: Perth, Australia

DATE: March 1, 2009

TOOLS: Ladder, fondness for circus performers

CRITERIA

☐ Must have someone on hand to "spot" you.

☐ Ladder must be closed and freestanding.

RELATED RECORDS

▸ Fastest Violin Rendition of "The Star-Spangled Banner" While Balancing Ladder on Chin: 19.75 seconds

▸ Longest Time to Balance 24 Eggs on Chin While Sitting in Chair on Top of 6-Foot Ladder: 14.85 seconds

RECORD BEGGING TO BE SET

☐ Most Snakes on a Ladder

A humble folding ladder became a stairway to record heaven for Dominic Pavicic, who showcased his precision balancing skills as a disbelieving friend looked on. Challenged to cling to a closed ladder for as long as possible, Pavicic slowly and gingerly traveled up the rungs, making it all the way to the fourth step before being hit with a case of the wobbles. He soldiered on a little longer but eventually lost his balance after attempting a one-handed "Ride 'em, cowboy!" move.

IF YOU'RE GOING TO ATTEMPT THIS RECORD, CONSIDER RECRUITING A FRIEND TO SUPERVISE AND 15,000 PILLOWS TO BREAK YOUR FALL.

Most One-Handed Claps in 30 Seconds

RECORD: 181

NAME: Emilie Virgilio

LOCATION: West Chester, Pennsylvania

DATE: June 9, 2010

TOOLS: Elastic hand, Zen outlook

Emilie Virgilio was in ninth grade learning about Buddhism when her teacher posed an age-old philosophical conundrum: What is the sound of one hand clapping? "I guess I took it literally and tried to find the answer," she remembers. An experimental flap of her right hand—slapping her fingers against her palm—changed everything. "That moment was when I realized I could clap with one hand, and other people could not, which led me to believe I have a superhuman skill." Virgilio put this skill to the ultimate test by challenging Justin Kay's RecordSetter record of 174 single-handed claps in 30 seconds. Beating his feat by seven claps cemented her belief that she possesses a unique and socially beneficial talent. "It can be a great conversation starter, especially in fancy restaurants," she says. "I have also realized that I am able to lighten up on hours for community service and extra activities on my college applications because of my skill. I am an anomaly compared to other applicants. How many people do you think one-hand-clap at Yale or Harvard?"

CRITERIA

☐ Contact of fingers against palm must be clearly audible.

Tip For Beating This Record

"The key is in the face," says Virgilio. "The crazier your face is, the louder and faster your clapping will be."

RELATED RECORDS

▶ Most Tandem Knee Slaps in 1 Minute: 592

▶ Most Claps in 30 Seconds While Standing on One Leg: 214

RECORD BEGGING TO BE SET

☐ Longest Standing Ovation

283

Most Unique Adjectives Affixed to a Body

RECORD: 356

NAME: Opus Moreschi

LOCATION: New York, New York

DATE: January 19, 2010

TOOLS: Post-It notes, open body space, unique adjectives

A fixture at New York City RecordSetter LIVE! events, Opus Moreschi's feat was motivated by a desire to bring people together. "I wanted something creative that everybody in the audience could participate in," he says. "And I was strangely interested in a group of strangers laying their hands on me." His request for adjectives on Post-Its yielded such words as "bulbous," "sybaritic," and "Kafka-esque" from the erudite crowd.

CRITERIA

☐ Duplicate adjectives may not be counted.

☐ More than one adjective per Post-It permitted.

☐ All Post-Its must adhere to person at same time.

Tip for Beating This Record

To obtain a wide range of words, seek out people with giant vocabularies. Scrabble players, English Lit professors, and students studying for the SAT Verbal are all good options.

RELATED RECORDS

▶ Most Words Rhymed with "Blue" in 30 Seconds: 22

▶ Most Pounds of Paper Fit in a Car and Driven to a Recycling Station: 1,600 pounds

RECORD BEGGING TO BE SET

☐ Most Scratch-and-Sniff Stickers Affixed to a Body

Longest Continuous Headbang

RECORD: 35 minutes, 53 seconds

NAME: Pat "Metal" Callan

LOCATION: La Crosse, Wisconsin

DATE: January 27, 2007

TOOLS: Heavy metal music, strong neck, EMT (emergency medical technicians) on call

At the Warehouse nightclub in La Crosse, Wisconsin, professional roadie Pat "Metal" Callan headbanged to live heavy metal music for a wickedly awesome 35 minutes, 53 seconds straight. Callan's performance proved that true headbanging is more than a simple nodding acknowledgement of the music. It's a full-body commitment that incorporates circular whipping of requisite long hair with jerky directional changes and petulant plucking of an air guitar that may be imaginary but feels oh-so-real.

Callan's drive to headbang stems from both an insatiable passion for the music and a medical need to combat diabetes: "Banging helps me lower my blood sugars."

CRITERIA

☐ Head must remain in motion throughout attempt.

☐ Head must go all the way up and down.

CAUTION
USE EXTREME CAUTION
IF YOU ATTEMPT THIS
EXTREMELY EXTREME RECORD.

Yellow Jacket Comment

DAN: My headbanging song of choice is Black Sabbath's "Iron Man." Just listen to it and try not to thrash your hair around.

CALLAN HAD EMTS ON THE SCENE TO MONITOR HIS HEALTH AND RECOMMENDS YOU DO LIKEWISE. CONTINUOUS HEADBANGING CAN CAUSE NECK INJURIES.

RELATED RECORDS

▶ Fastest Time to Braid Two People's Hair Together in a Toyota Prius: 28.88 seconds

▶ Longest Hair Twirl: 1 hour, 2 minutes, and 6 seconds

RECORD BEGGING TO BE SET

☐ Most Iron Maiden T-Shirts Worn at Once

RECORDSETTER LEGEND

Dinesh Upadhyaya

Chemisty Teacher, Speed Snapper, International Record Setter

B y day, Dinesh Upadhyaya is an introverted high school chemistry teacher in Mumbai. But when lessons end and the textbooks are put away, Upadhyaya transforms into a determined world champion, following in the footsteps of his idols.

"I have followed world-record breakers since my school days," he says. "At that age they appeared to me like superheroes with great magic powers." His favorite achievers are New Yorker Ashrita "Mr. Versatility" Furman (who has set 333 records including the Fastest Time to Duct Tape Oneself to a Wall), New Zealand's Alastair Galpin (he of the Farthest Champagne Cork Spit), and German Ralf Laue, who once solved three Rubik's Cubes while blindfolded.

"All my Twitter records required extensive research work," he says, referring to feats like Most Chemical Symbols from the Periodic Table of Elements in a Single Tweet and Most Living Celebrities Sharing One's Birthday Named in a Tweet. One in particular needed extra attention: "To set the record of Most Micro-Stories Published on Twitter I worked almost 3 months to summarize Hindu mythological stories into 140 letters without losing their meanings."

After setting a string of Twitter-based records, Upadhyaya grew confident enough to set records in front of a video camera, recruiting his brother Manish, niece Rajshree, and even his students to operate the equipment and serve as official

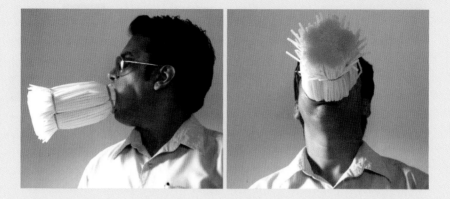

witnesses. His first "performing record," as he calls it, was Most Finger Snaps in 1 Minute. He took on—and surpassed—Ashrita Furman's 170 clicks, logging 172. The record is still one of his favorites. "For the first time in my life it made me tremendously confident that I can beat Mr. Versatility," he says.

Upadhyaya got a taste of fame—as well as wood and graphite—for his next record, Most Pencils Fit in Mouth at Once. After initially packing a bundle of eighty-five pencils into his maw, he added seven more, jamming them in one by one on all sides. The extraordinary sight of his lips stretched into a giant "O" by a tree worth of pencils caught the attention of news channels, websites, and print media around the world.

The most ambitious of his planned accomplishments is the world's largest crossword puzzle, which will measure about 100 square feet and be based on an Indian general knowledge quiz. "I started this project in December 2000," says Upadhyaya. "It covers almost each and every field of India from 5000 B.C. to modern day. Clues are based on history, politics, literature, economics, cinema, art, culture, geography, science, and the personality of India." The questions will be in the form of a book with over one hundred pages.

As a prolific writer of short stories, Upadhyaya also plans to "make and break a number of records in different forms of writing." "There are over fifty records on my hit list," he says. "I am confident that with some practice and efforts, I will set them all."

Most People Wearing Fake Mustaches in a Book

RECORD: 142

TOOLS: Naked upper lip, false mustache, camera to capture the magic

When compiling the book you are now holding, RecordSetter wanted to give as many people as possible the chance to be featured in its pages. But how best to include record setters with wildly varied skills, talents, locations, and ages? The answer: mandatory fake facial hair. We put out the request for people to don their best fake mustaches for a chance to be part of a brand new record: Most People Wearing Fake Mustaches in a Book. Achievers around the globe responded with creativity and verve. Congratulations, champions: Your mustachioed faces are now in print.

CRITERIA

☐ Mustache may be created by any means as long as it is fake.

RELATED RECORD

▸ Fastest Time to Take a Photo of One's Son with an iPhone and Digitally Apply a Mustache to It: 31.05 seconds

PHOTO CREDITS

ILLUSTRATION CREDITS